THE BIRTH OF
THE MIDDLE AGES
395–814

H. St. L. B. MOSS

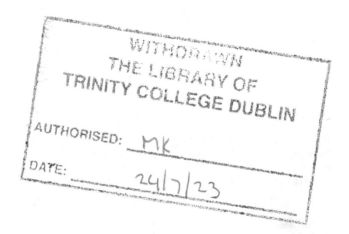

GREENWOOD PRESS, PUBLISHERS
WESTPORT, CONNECTICUT

7790075314

Library of Congress Cataloging in Publication Data

Moss, Henry St. Lawrence Beaufort.
  The birth of the Middle Ages, 395-814.

    Reprint of the 1977 reissue of the 1964 ed.
  published by Oxford University Press, London,
  New York.
    Bibliography: p.
    Includes index.
    1. Europe--History--392-1814. 2. Civilization,
  Medieval. I. Title.
  D121.M6 1980   940.1'2   80-24038
  ISBN 0-313-22708-X (lib. bdg.)

PREFACE

BETWEEN the ancient and the medieval worlds there lies a great gulf, bridged perhaps only, so far as the general reader is concerned, by the magnificent architecture of Gibbon's *Decline and Fall*. Despite the intensive researches of recent years it would be idle to deny that the centuries known as the 'Dark Ages' still remain one of the obscurest stages in European history. Yet progress is undoubtedly being made in the elucidation of many of the principal problems. Certain views have definitely been discarded. The Roman Empire, it is now seen, did not end with the capture of the Western capital or with the deposition of Romulus Augustulus. The catastrophic explanation of the passing of the Roman world yields place, on further analysis, to a more reasoned theory of evolution. Justice is beginning to be done to the greatness of the Byzantine achievement, and to the true character of the civilization which continued the Roman tradition on the shores of the Bosphorus. The Islamic onslaught is no longer viewed through the eyes of medieval opponents, for whom its menace to their religion obscured the common origin of Christian and Mahometan culture. Critical study of the art and literature of this time has in many cases led to a more favourable estimate, and has undoubtedly deepened the sense of continuity between the old order and the new. The great figures of the age stand out more vividly than before, and the findings of archaeology, together with the recent interest in economic conditions, have produced for the imagination a more lively picture of the everyday existence of communities and individuals. In the following pages an attempt is made to present a brief outline of four centuries of European history viewed in the light of these results.

The arbitrary nature of historical periods, which are actually, in certain respects, little more than a superior form of *memoria technica*, is sufficiently obvious to need no emphasis. Organic processes cannot be cleanly bisected with a stroke of the pen, and it is hardly to be expected that all forms of human activity should develop *pari passu*. Various dates have in consequence been given for the beginning of the Middle Ages, ranging from

the third to the eighth century, and each has its justification,
according to the importance attached to a particular aspect of
European civilization. The year 395 has perhaps as good a
claim as any to be regarded in this light, for the death of
Theodosius the Great occurred at a moment of the most critical
importance for Europe. For the last three years, Theodosius
had ruled supreme over Roman territory. Henceforth there is
to be separation of East and West, final in fact though not in
theory. While he lived, Britain, Gaul, and Spain could be
accounted integral parts of the Roman Empire; in less than
a generation all three were in the hands of barbarian conquerors, and Rome itself had fallen a prey to the Visigoths. The
warrior emperor, two of whose immediate predecessors had
fallen in battle on the frontier, is succeeded by a line of puppet
rulers, and the effective control of the Roman State passes for
wellnigh a century into the hands of Masters of the Soldiers.
Internally, less striking changes are observable. The barbarian
inroads, though terrible enough, only accentuated the disorder
and distress from which most of the Western provinces had
suffered ever since the anarchy of the third century. The
momentous reforms of Diocletian and Constantine, which ended
this anarchy, were, to a large extent, only the fulfilment of
tendencies already visible under the earlier Empire, for the close
of the fourth century produced no real break in the system of
Imperial government. They did but expressly recognize the
fact that 'the household of Caesar' had already superseded that
constitutional executive which the Empire had inherited from
the Roman Republic. One change, however, of greater importance than any other for the future of Europe, was introduced
by Constantine, when the Christian Church was admitted to
a share in the government of the State. Here lies the watershed
between two worlds. For the adoption of the new faith altered
the cast of men's minds and determined the policy of their
rulers. Only under Theodosius does the Roman Empire finally
cease to hold the balance between Christian and Pagan, and
thus only at this point do the full consequences of Constantine's
revolutionary action begin to take effect. For this reason, if for
no other, this survey may fitly take as its starting-point the

death of Theodosius the Great, the founder of the Christian State.

It should perhaps be stated that the sketch-maps and pictures included in this volume are intended to serve merely as elucidations of the text. References to some historical atlases and illustrated histories of early medieval art will be found in the bibliography.

I should like to express my gratitude to Prof. N. H. Baynes, for constant help and encouragement in the writing of this book, to Mr. E. L. Woodward, Prof. H. A. R. Gibb, Mr. R. Birley, and Mr. J. N. L. Myres for valuable criticism and suggestions, and to the officers of the Clarendon Press for their courtesy and forbearance.

H. St. L. B. M.

August, 1935.

CONTENTS

DESCRIPTION OF ILLUSTRATIONS

I. 'The Sasanid triumph, assiduously placarded in rock-carving and fresco.' (page 7.)

Relief at Naksh-i-Rustam. Third century A.D. The Emperor Valerian kneeling before Shāpūr I. (Photograph by Professor Dr. Friedrich Sarre) . . . . . . *Facing page* 7

II. *a.* Capitals from the crypt of St. Laurent, Grenoble. Sixth or seventh century. (Photograph, Archives Photo., Paris.)

> The crude workmanship of these is as noticeable as the dependence on Roman and Byzantine models. Cf. R. de Lasteyrie, *L'Architecture religieuse en France à l'époque romane*, p. 101. (Paris, 1912.)

b. Torhalle, Lorsch. Rhineland, eighth or ninth century. (Photograph, Staatliche Bildstelle, Berlin.)

> This building, which appears to have formed the entrance porch to the atrium of the abbey church, has been assigned by most critics to the eighth or early ninth century. The elegant design and the successful assimilation of classical influences indicate the advance made by Frankish architecture at this period. R. de Lasteyrie (op. cit., pp. 167–70) is unable to accept it as being earlier than 1090, but it may reasonably be held that Carolingian work at Aix and elsewhere provides parallels for many of its features.
>
> *Facing page* 68

III. 'Eastern influence . . . with its stylized animal forms, its dark glowing jewels or glass cubes set in gold filigree.' (page 68.)

a. Plaque with animal-ornament in Scythian style from Ordos, N. Asia. Second century B.C.

b. Cloisonné jewellery of Gothic type from Kerch, Crimea. Fourth or fifth century A.D.

c. Cloisonné brooch from Lombardic grave, Belluno, N. Italy. Sixth century A.D.

d. Cloisonné brooch, probably from the Rhineland. Frankish, sixth century A.D.

e. Examples of early Anglo-Saxon animal-ornament from S.E. England. Sixth century A.D.

(All from British Museum.)

> This series is intended to illustrate the 'nomad influence' on the barbarian art of Europe—an influence which is also perceptible among the origins of the Byzantine style (cf. p. 88). The range of the 'animal-ornament' can be traced from the borders of China to the shores of England and Scandinavia, while the cloisonné technique acquired in the Crimean region—a corridor between Europe and Asia—is continued by the Teutonic invaders in their western homes. The sources and cross-currents of these streams of influence are still obscure. For further reference, cf. E. H. Minns, *Scythians and Greeks* (Cambridge, 1925), M. Rostovtzeff, *Iranians and Greeks in South Russia* (Oxford,

1922), G. Borovka, *Scythian Art* (London, 1928), J. Strzygowski, *Altaï-Iran und Völkerwanderungen* (Leipzig, 1917), and B. Salin, *Die altgermanische Thierornamentik* (Stockholm, 1904).

Facing page 69

IV. 'Alexandria, the centre of Hellenistic traditions of modelling, ornament, and ideal presentation of the human form . . . Antioch, representative of the realistic Semitic style.' (page 87.)

a. Adoration of the Magi. Syrian work, sixth century A.D. (British Museum.)

b. Diptych of the Symmachi. Alexandrian school, fourth or fifth century A.D. (Victoria and Albert Museum. Cf. O. M. Dalton, *East Christian Art* (Oxford, 1925), and see Bibliography.)   *Facing page* 87

V. 'Byzantine mosaic. . . . [was] extensively used in the decoration of the Mosques, and there is hardly a feature of structure or ornament which cannot be traced to earlier tradition.' (page 172.)

a. Mosaic from Great Mosque, Damascus. *c.* A.D. 715. (Photograph, de Lorey. For full description, see K. A. C. Creswell, *Early Muslim Architecture*, pp. 239–52. (Oxford, 1932.))

b. Mschatta. Detail of Relief. Eighth century A.D. (Kaiser Friedrich Museum, Berlin.)

The palace of Mschatta lies to the east of the Jordan, on the pilgrim-road between Mecca and Damascus. Dates ranging from the third to the tenth century have been assigned to it Though the question is by no means finally settled, the balance of opinion seems in favour of an eighth-century date. (Cf .Creswell, op. cit., pp. 390 ff., for discussion and tabulation of the various views.) The relief, in any case, shows strikingly the Syrian amalgam of Mesopotamian, Persian, and Hellenistic influences which contributed to form the characteristics of Byzantine and Islamic decoration, and which during these centuries penetrated far into Western Europe (cf. plate facing p. 236).

Facing page 170

VI. 'An interesting example of regional influence is the minaret in its various forms.' (page 172.)

a. Samarra, Mesopotamia. (From F. Sarre and E. E. Herzfeld, *Archäologische Reise im Euphrat- und Tigris-Gebiet*, vol. iii (Dietrich Reimer (E.Vohsen), Berlin).)

b. Kairawan, N. Africa. (Photograph by Sir Alan Cobham.)

c. Mosque of Al-Juyūshī, Cairo. (From M. S. Briggs, *Muhammadan Architecture in Egypt and Palestine* (Clarendon Press).)

d. Arbil, Iraq. (From Sarre and Herzfeld, op. cit., vol. iv.)

e. Mosque of Muhafiz Khan, Ahmedabad, India. (From Burgess, *A. S. Report, Western India*, vol. vii.)

f. St. Sophia, Constantinople.

(For the architectural origin of the minaret, see K. A. C. Creswell, *Burlington Magazine*, xlviii, pp. 139 ff.) .   .   *Facing page* 171

VII. 'Hieratic sculptured scenes, superior in plastic feeling to any contemporary continental work.' (page 236.)

Bewcastle Cross, Cumberland. Detail from E. face (late seventh century). (Photograph, Gibson.)

> For discussion of the date and characteristics of this monument, see A. W. Clapham, *English Romanesque Architecture before the Conquest* (Oxford, 1930), G. Baldwin Brown, *The Arts in Early England*, vol. 5 (London, 1921), J. Brøndsted, *Early English Ornament* (Eng. tr. London, 1924), and W. G. Collingwood, *Northumbrian Crosses of the pre-Norman Age* (London, 1927), who assigns it to the middle of the eighth century.

Facing page 236

VIII. 'The change from ancient to medieval.' (page 252.)

a. Trajanic relief from Forum ('Anaglypha Trajani'). *c.* A.D. 101. (Photograph, Anderson.)

> The scene is probably a proclamation in the Forum by the Emperor Trajan in connexion with measures taken for the relief of poor children. Cf. E. Strong, *Roman Sculpture*, pp. 151–7 (London, 1907).

b. Relief from N. façade, Arch of Constantine, *c.* A.D. 315. (From *The Papers of the British School at Rome*, vol. iv.)

> The Emperor Constantine, standing on the rostra of the Forum, harangues the people. The similarity of subject, and the architectural background used in either case, serve to emphasize the contrast between these two friezes. Cf. E. Strong, op. cit., pp. 332 ff.

Facing page 253

MAPS

PART I

ROMANS AND BARBARIANS

I

THE ROMAN WORLD

THOUGHTS of Imperial Rome conjure up to the mind's eye a picture of war and conquest, of legions marching under the victorious eagle to the subjugation of distant peoples. Yet the real fact which characterizes the first two centuries of the Christian era is the deep peace which descended upon the whole Mediterranean area, and enveloped the greater part of Central and Western Europe. By the time of Augustus the Empire had expanded practically to its fullest extent,[1] and the work of his successors was mainly a work of consolidation. Within the great fortified barriers of Rhine, Danube, and Euphrates, a network of roads covered the vast territories of Rome, from the borders of Scotland to the Arabian deserts. Along these roads passed an ever-increasing traffic, not only of troops and officials, but of traders, merchandise, and even tourists. An interchange of goods between the various provinces rapidly developed, which soon reached a scale unprecedented in previous history, and not repeated until a few centuries ago. Metals mined in the uplands of Western Europe, hides, fleeces, and live-stock from the pastoral districts of Britain, Spain, and the shores of the Black Sea, wine and oil from Provence and Aquitaine, timber, pitch, and wax from South Russia and northern Anatolia, dried fruits from Syria, marble from the Aegean coasts, and—most important of all— grain from the corn-growing districts of North Africa, Egypt, and the Danube valley for the needs of the great cities; all these commodities, under the influence of a highly organized system of transport and marketing, moved freely from one corner of the Empire to the other.

The manufacture of articles for wholesale export received also a great stimulus, and flourishing industries developed in almost

---

[1] With a few important exceptions, e.g. Britain, and the districts north of the Danube and east of the Upper Euphrates.

every province. Commerce and banking had been intensively carried on for centuries in the Hellenistic world, and the eastern end of the Mediterranean was the first to profit by the new order. Broadly speaking, these Eastern provinces were the region of industry and manufacture; the West was the great storehouse of raw materials. Thus from Damascus, Antioch, and Alexandria came blankets, tapestry and rugs, linen, pottery of the finest sort, glass, both cheap and expensive, jewellery, perfumes and cosmetics. During the first two centuries, however, a westward movement of industry can be observed. Fortunes were being made in the corn-lands and ore-producing districts of Gaul, Spain, Italy, and Africa, and to satisfy the demands of a wealthy and luxurious class Greeks, Egyptians, and Syrians crowded to the West to exercise their skill as doctors, artists, teachers, musicians, or silversmiths. The Syrians, in particular, were the supreme traders of this time; as single adventurers or in merchant communities they are found all over Europe, in the cities of Africa and Spain, or thickly clustered along the trade routes of the Po valley and the Rhineland. Even in the fifth century, Jerome bitterly observes them carrying on their gainful traffic amid the ruins of a falling world. The advance of industry is shown in more direct fashion by the appearance in the West of factories of considerable size, pottery and glass centres, for instance, in middle and southern France, in the Rhine valley, or in Britain, where the mass-produced article either killed or else drove into other channels the individual fancy of Celtic design.

Nor was trade limited by the boundaries of the Empire. The frontiers in this respect were not a dividing barrier, but rather a line of outpost settlements, joining the termini of the Roman road system, which furnished markets for the barbarians beyond. Horse-trappings and jewellery, coins and pottery, household ornaments and agricultural implements, bartered against slaves, amber, or hides, passed from the Gallo-Roman workshops over the Rhine and far into central Germany, finding their way into the strongholds of chieftains in Denmark or South Sweden. Roman merchant vessels put in at Irish ports, or roved southwards down the forested coast-line of West Africa. The Eastern traffic held even more romantic possibilities. The Red Sea, connected with Alexandria by a harbour, a canal, and a carefully policed caravan road, equipped with storage depots and water reservoirs, was the terminus of several great shipping routes. One led down past Abyssinia and Somaliland as far as Uganda, south of which the Arab trader retained his monopoly. Ivory, tortoise-shell, and negro slaves from the interior were collected in return for gaily coloured cloths and glass, axes, brass and copper ornaments. The south-west corner of Arabia exported incense and spices to the West, and handled, in addition, the products of India and China, such as cotton, silk, teak, ebony, and sandal-wood, which were unloaded also at the Red Sea ports and the harbours at the head of the Persian Gulf, travelling thence by caravan and arriving finally at Alexandria, or at one of the great Syrian commercial centres, such as Damascus or Antioch. The use of the monsoons, however, had recently been discovered, and direct trade with India, eliminating the Arab middleman, was soon financed on a large scale by Alexandrian and Syrian merchants. At one Red Sea port Strabo was informed that no less than 120 vessels a year sailed for India, and other sources tell of the colonies of foreign merchants settled in the coastal cities of Malabar, of the magnificent harbours of South India and Ceylon, with their lighthouse system and pilot services, their spacious warehouses and wharves, and of the arrival of the Roman argosies,[1] discharging their cargoes of singing-boys and maidens destined for the harems of Indian princes, their silver vessels and bright linens, their Mediterranean wines and their stores of Imperial gold pieces, in payment for the huge sacks of pepper, the heavy cotton-bales, the diamonds, pearls, beryls, drugs, and perfumes which they carried back to the Western world. Gradually the merchants sailed farther eastwards; the Ganges estuary and the Malay Peninsula became known, and about A.D. 160 traders from the Roman Empire established connexion with the Chinese ports. But the great days of Roman commerce were now over; centuries of disorder were in prospect for Europe, and the possibilities of Chinese influence on our civilization were never realized.

Ease of communication and ready exchange of commodities

---

[1] Manned by 'Roman' subjects, in the eyes of their Indian observers, but Syrian or Egyptian, probably, by race.

did much to promote unity, and even uniformity, in the Roman Empire. A common standard of life was shared by the majority of its inhabitants; lamps, drinking-vessels, heating arrangements, interior decoration differed but little in the villas of southern England and those of Algiers. The gold *denarius* commanded equal confidence in the Rhineland, the Crimea, or the Cingalese bazaars. Language became standardized, Latin prevailing in the West, and Greek in the East; in many districts the indigenous speech wholly disappeared. The common institutions under which they lived furnished another bond of union between the peoples of the Empire, for the government of the various provinces, though adaptable to local conditions, was essentially a single system, directed from the centre, a system, moreover, which tended towards increasing uniformity and the elimination of anomalies. Thus in A.D. 212, by a decree of Caracalla, the majority of the Emperor's subjects became Roman citizens, and the inferior status of the 'provincial' disappeared. The administration of Italy herself, though she long retained certain privileges as regards taxation, was eventually assimilated to that of the provinces, and her pride of place in the West, already challenged by Gaul, Africa, and Spain in the fields of literature and commerce, suffered still more from this humiliation. These are but two instances of a far-reaching development. As the dangers to the Empire increased, so her statesmen redoubled their efforts to preserve the tottering edifice by rendering it a homogeneous structure, clamping it together with the iron logic of legal codes and tyrannical enactments, careless of over-rigidity or suppression of living stress and counter-stress, and concerned only to produce the stability of a solid and undifferentiated block of matter.

Vulnerable points in the Imperial system were discovered, not created, by the strains and perils of its later centuries. Modern analogies to the social and economic conditions of the ancient world are often misleading, for they tend to obscure the more primitive aspects of its civilization. Judged by present-day standards, the population of Europe at this time was extremely small; that of the Roman Empire has been estimated at not more than a quarter of the numbers now inhabiting the countries in question. Its distribution was extraordinarily unequal, the Eastern half being preponderant not only in the density of its inhabitants but in its level of wealth and culture. No town in the West, with the exception of Rome and Carthage, could compare with the splendid cities, many of them with a population of over 100,000, which flourished in Asia Minor, Syria, and Egypt. The last-named province, despite its small size, furnished something approaching one-seventh of the whole numbers of the Empire, and the greater part of the revenues was supplied by the countries bordering on the eastern Mediterranean. On the other hand, the total population of the Roman Empire, after three centuries of existence, had become definitely smaller. Italy and Greece, in particular, had suffered, and large tracts of Gaul lay desolate, owing to the ravages of plague and civil war. The cultural influence of Rome was exercised unevenly upon the West. Roman roads, like the modern by-pass or arterial way, left untouched large districts in the interstices of their network, where the language and customs of the natives were barely affected by those of their conquerors. Especially was this so in the regions of the north and west, where tribes of shepherds and primitive agriculturists, thinly scattered amid marsh and forest, did not repay fiscal and commercial exploitation, as did the intensively cultivated Mediterranean area. Further, the Roman influence was diluted in proportion as it approached the confines of the Empire. The frontiers themselves were becoming blurred. German princes beyond the Rhine absorbed Roman culture; masses of barbarians were allowed to settle upon Roman territory in eastern Gaul and the regions south of the Danube. There were even Roman citizens under the later Empire who preferred to dwell at the court of some foreign ruler rather than face the increasing demands of the Imperial tax-collector.

Even in the East, where for three centuries before Rome's arrival the Hellenistic kingdoms which grew out of the conquests of Alexander had been spreading the ideals of Greek city life, national traditions only lay dormant, waiting for the hour of liberation to strike. The Greeks formed only a tiny minority in Syria and Egypt, where their superiority in culture, not in numbers, had given them the advantage. Older civilizations in these lands, though temporarily submerged, retained their vitality, and the growth of Coptic and Syriac literatures, stimulated by the rise of Christian churches, which became a mouthpiece for separatist and local sentiment, fostered a consciousness of alienation from their foreign conquerors, and intensified the bitter opposition to Imperial policy and taxation. The final loss of these provinces was due in great part to such internal causes; Persian and Moslem invaders of the seventh century found support in many disaffected quarters of these regions. In Asia Minor, only the seaboard fringes were truly Hellenized; but the mountainous interior, haunt of brigands and principal recruiting-ground for the later Roman army, possessed no cultural traditions which could serve as a focus of discontent, and Byzantium in consequence retained her grasp upon the whole peninsula until far into medieval times.

The successive shocks which the civilized area of Europe had received since the close of the first century revealed the insecurity of the Imperial structure. The reign of Marcus Aurelius (161–80) witnessed the turning of the tide of Roman prosperity, and the end of the Antonine house was followed by a century of disorder in which the central power wavered, passing rapidly from one short-lived emperor to another, made and unmade by their capricious or covetous legions. Military absolutism appeared, effacing the last vestiges of the fictitious 'diarchy' of Augustus. The influence of the armies increased as the need for them became greater. The frontiers were threatened unceasingly; Germanic tribes from the Low Countries to the Danube mouth pressed against the restraining barriers, and Saxon pirates in the Channel had their counterpart in the Gothic sea-raiders of the Black Sea and northern Aegean coasts. A fresh peril arose in the East when the Parthian rulers of Persia were replaced by the aggressive Sasanid house (227). The Euphrates line now demanded constant reinforcements, and the Roman Empire, with its insufficient troops, was henceforth condemned to struggle with the problem of a double front. After a lapse of nearly six centuries Persia renewed her attempts, crushed by the victorious advance of Alexander the Great, to regain the sovereignty of western Asia. The Great King .1e days of Marathon appeared once more, claiming equality

THE EMPEROR VALERIAN KNEELING BEFORE SHĀPŪR I

of status with the other world-ruler at Rome. More than once during the third century the Persian horsemen swept through Syria almost to the Aegean, threatening the commerce of one of the richest provinces. A climax was reached in the disastrous campaign of 260, when Valerian, a Roman Emperor, was taken prisoner by the Persian monarch. It is probable that Rome's prestige in the Near East never recovered from this blow. The Sasanid triumph, assiduously placarded in rock-sculpture and fresco,[1] must have spread like wildfire through the cities of that great caravan-world, stretching from the eastern Mediterranean to the Persian Gulf, whose strange mixture of cosmopolitan luxury and desert squalor, commercial interests, brigandage, and fiery fanaticism shaped, a few centuries later, the career of Mahomet and the progress of Islam. The mighty power of Rome, which had paved with stone blocks the desert-routes, garrisoned the oasis fortresses, and extended its sphere of influence ever farther along the traffic-lines of camel-borne merchandise from India and the Far East, was now fighting on equal terms with the Iranian forces, and maintaining with increased difficulty its traditional frontier.[2] Significant of Rome's weakness was the sudden rise of the short-lived empire of Palmyra, based on the caravan trade, which maintained a brief but glorious independence until its queen, Zenobia, was overthrown by Aurelian. A similar phenomenon was taking place in the West, where the Gallic provinces, which had revolted from the central power, offered a successful resistance for over ten years. Even Italy herself was in danger of barbarian invasion; Aurelian's great walls, which still encircle Rome, indicate, like those of other Italian towns rebuilt at this time, the coming transformation of the open cities of the ancient world into the moated and turreted strongholds of the Middle Ages.[3]

The economic crisis of the Empire reached its height during

[1] Cf. *Excavations at Dura-Europos*, 4th season (Newhaven, 1933), pp. 182–99, and the reliefs still visible at Naksh-i-Rustam. See Plate I.

[2] For the subsequent history of the Euphrates frontier, see below, pp. 118 ff.

[3] Walled towns were, of course, no novelty; but the security given by the *Pax Romana* and the development of communications under the early Empire minimized the need for fortification and encouraged the spread of suburbs along the main roads. The contrast in appearance between the ancient and medieval cities of Western Europe must have been very striking.

these years, and the need for precious metal to provide donatives for the legions, on whose purchased loyalty the power of the Emperor depended, coincided with a disastrous shortage of gold and silver ore, and a precipitous fall in the revenues obtained from taxation. The balance of trade during the first two centuries A.D. had probably been in favour of the exporting countries of Asia, and indications exist, though exact assessment is not possible, of an eastward drain of specie from the Roman Empire. More serious, perhaps, was the falling-off in the production of the European mines. A marked deterioration of the currency is noticeable at this time. Gold vanished from circulation, and the silver of earlier days became little more than a thinly washed copper coin. Despite the debasement, prices retained a certain stability, apart from a considerable rise due to the decreased bullion-value of the *denarius*, until the reign of Gallienus (253–68). A period of extreme inflation now set in. Under Aurelian the price of wheat in Egypt soared to dizzy heights, followed at some distance by the rate of wages. Banks closed, and were commanded to reopen; speculation in currency was rife. Trade with the East, which had been based on a gold coinage of full weight and purity, was seriously affected, and showed no real revival until the days of Justinian, though the Mediterranean traffic still continued with much of its former intensity.

One of the first tasks, in Diocletian's great reorganization of the Empire, was the restoration of a gold and silver coinage, which was carried out more successfully than his subsequent attempts to control by edict the market-price of foodstuffs. How far he can be said to have checked the transition from the 'money' economy of the early Empire to the 'natural' economy of the Middle Ages[1] is a question probably impossible to answer. The army and civil service, both meagrely paid, had always maintained themselves largely from other sources—the provision of quarters and rations, transport and other services was exacted by the soldiers, and fees, *douceurs*, travelling facilities and free lodging by the officials. To what extent these were estimated in currency values it is difficult to determine, but the system remained in force under Diocletian and Constantine, and the finan-

[1] See Appendix B.

cial machinery which they created was, in essence, merely a legalization of such semi-regular practices.

It is no derogation of the magnificent services of these two men, whose work saved the Empire from imminent dissolution, to hold that their reorganization was in fact a realist acceptance of the actual situation, rather than the creation of a new model of government. Changes in the army had already been made by former rulers; the sharp distinction of the frontier troops, which had steadily deteriorated into a militia of settled farmers, from the field army of picked fighting men is only a recognition of the needs of the time. A mobile striking force, capable of being thrown at short notice into any outlying province, would at least serve to expel barbarian raiders whose entry the frontier garrisons had been unable to prevent. The weakness of the central power is acknowledged by the decentralization of provincial government, smaller units being created in the interests of efficiency, while the position of the emperor himself, degraded of late by dependence on legionary caprice, is raised high above all sectional interests by the accentuation of his semi-divine status, already foreshadowed by former emperors, and its expression in elaborate court ceremonial, influenced, perhaps, by Persian example. Even the foundation of Constantinople, which marks, indeed, the beginning of a new era, may, in another aspect, be regarded simply as a full confession of the fact that the city of Rome was no longer the centre of the Empire.

One startling innovation, however, was destined to alter the whole basis of the Roman state—the transformation of Christianity, by Constantine's action, from the position of a proscribed religion to that of the honoured faith of the Imperial house. Three centuries of development, in dogma, administration, and geographical extension, lay behind it by this time. It numbered several millions of adherents, far the greater part of whom belonged to the eastern provinces, though the activities, noted above, of Greeks and Syrians in Western Europe had carried the new teaching into the commercial centres of these regions. The first primitive communities had long been replaced by the beginnings of an ecclesiastical hierarchy, for which the civil machinery of Roman provincial government provided the model, while the

political and economic importance of the metropolitan cities
determined, to some extent, the authority enjoyed by the bishops
of Rome, Carthage, Antioch, Ephesus, and Alexandria. Christianity had begun among the lowliest classes of society, and its
membership was still largely confined to the uneducated, though
Christians were to be found in every rank of life and even in Court
circles. Three centuries of contact, however, with the world of
the early Roman Empire had profoundly modified the terms in
which it expressed itself, and the fourth century, with its altered
conditions, accelerated the results of such interaction. Inadequate
though it must be, some account must nevertheless be given of the
atmosphere which prevailed at the time of Theodosius the Great.

During these centuries the character of paganism had been
completely transformed. Genuine allegiance to the old city-state
deities of Greece and Rome had long ceased among the thinking
members of society, but their thrones did not remain unoccupied.
Scepticism, though prominent in literature, was steadily giving
place to a different conception of religion, based on the desire for
personal communion with the divine. In many shapes and combinations the mystery-cults of Thrace, Egypt, Syria, Asia Minor,
and Persia were adopted by the Roman world, and Hellenic
myths, if not discarded, were woven in stylized form into the
patterned texture of these composite faiths. Political conditions
favoured the fusion of localized worships into a larger whole.
Even at the far-off beginnings of the city-state in mainland
Greece, many a village god had faded into an adjective of Zeus or
Athena; a similar process can be seen at Rome, though the unifying tendency here was offset by her readiness to receive foreign
deities into her crowded pantheon. The rise of the Hellenistic
monarchies, which ended the vivid community-life of the city-
state, turned the minds of men inwards, each one seeking a path
to individual salvation, while the absolutism of the new kingdoms,
modelled on Asiatic example, accustomed the Greek-speaking
world to the idea of ruler-worship, which, as a powerful instrument of state, was carefully fostered by the reigning dynasties.
Rome reaped the results of this when she introduced her Imperial
cult, and the Stoic doctrine of an all-seeing, beneficent Provi-
dence may well have assisted the humble provincial in his concep-

tion of the omnipotent Emperor, whose justice determined the lives and welfare of vast populations.

The development of philosophic thought was no longer antagonistic to popular beliefs, but aided powerfully the henotheistic currents of religious feeling. Old myths were first rationalized, then symbolized, and the common features of various cults, recognized as approaches to a single divine power, were mingled eventually in a nebulous mass, out of which the noble mind of Plotinus, applying the canons of Hellenic reasoning to matter unsusceptible of such treatment, strove to create an ordered system. Neoplatonism, however, in his hands was less a doctrine than a way of life. A contemplative attitude had replaced the practical Stoic outlook, with its emphasis on conduct, and although the rationalizing element in Plotinus, the Greek presupposition of an intelligible universe, whose phases are logical consequences one of another, must not be overlooked, the essence of his thought is a mystical, almost sensual apprehension of reality, an immediate awareness, without the interposition of the reasoning faculty. This is made possible by the internal affinities existing among all persons and objects in the universe, which lie hidden under the surface of appearance, and phenomena such as telepathy, omens, and astrological combinations can readily be explained by the same theory. Thaumaturgy, ritual purification and divination, however, form only a small part of the system of Plotinus. It remained for his successors, in their attempt to gather together all the forces of paganism against the common enemy, to enlist such magical aids to capture the emotions of the multitude, while to close the ranks of the intellectuals a blending of almost every doctrine of the ancient world, from Plato and Aristotle to the Stoics and Cynics, was ingeniously accomplished. The mystic cosmology of Neoplatonism and its scheme of redemption, as developed by Iamblichus, was thus the final shape assumed by organized Paganism in its struggle with Christianity,[1]

[1] This applies principally to the East, where the term 'Hellenism', applied by Christians to their opponents, reveals the conscious, though unsuccessful, attempt to muster the traditions of classical culture in defence of the old religion. 'Paganism', its Latin counterpart in the West, points to the sporadic survival of primitive village rites. Only at Rome, with her historical memories, a political and aristocratic cult of the old deities still held its own.

and the contest must be viewed not as a battle between faith and scepticism, but as a rivalry between two competing mystery-religions, both speaking the language of their time.[1] Dogma apart, there is hardly an aspect which is not found equally in pagan and Christian—asceticism, fasts, vigils, puritanism, ritual, saints, angels, demons, and the reliance on visions and *sortes*. Pagan and Christian art use the same symbolism, and are often indistinguishable, save where exclusively Christian motives are employed; modern criticism, moreover, has tended to lessen the number of these.[2] Christians, by the fourth century, had accepted and absorbed the pagan learning, and the issues of the great Councils turn on Platonic and Aristotelian concepts, which conditioned men's thinking in this age much as the evolutionary and psychological standpoints govern it to-day. It is significant that Julian, in his efforts to restore pagan worship, aimed at establishing a kind of Church, similar in many respects to the Christian organization; a fixed dogma, a regular hierarchy, a system of hospitals, almshouses, and poor-relief were established, and even, for the clergy, an Index Expurgatorius.[3]

The strength of the Christian position was convincingly shown by Julian's failure to accomplish his purpose in face of public opinion. Rationalized myths and synthetic deities lacked the popular appeal of the Gospel stories, so much closer in time and spirit to the world of the fourth century. The esoteric subtleties of Neoplatonism and the fluid, accommodating character of pagan syncretism were equally deficient in compelling power. In its exclusive monotheism Christianity shared with Judaism, in contrast with other ancient religions, an immense source of stability. There was no place in it for other deities, save in the guise of malevolent demons. A hard core of doctrine was steadily forming, reinforced by the possession of an authoritative scripture. Here, too, a need of the times was met, for an increased reliance on authority is characteristic of the later stages of Graeco-Roman thought. The original, inventive genius of Greece had long since

---

[1] Julian, the pagan champion, attacks far more bitterly the rationalizing Cynics who deride the classical myths than the upholders of Christianity. Cf. J. Bidez, *La Vie de l'Empereur Julien*, (Paris, 1930) pp. 248 ff.

[2] e.g. the fish symbol. Cf. F. X. J. Dölger, 'ΙΧΘΥΣ (Münster, 1910–32).

[3] Cf. Bidez, op. cit., p. 269.

disappeared, and the Roman triumphs in literature, art, architecture, engineering, and even law were, in the main, the result of a brilliant application of principles already discovered.[1] Men were aware that the Golden Age lay behind them; nostalgia for the past and consciousness of present inferiority are themes familiar in the writings of this period. The Emperor Constantius, visiting Rome for the first time towards the end of his career, reserved his highest admiration for the Forum of Trajan; but he considered it far beyond mortal resources to rival so great a work, and declared himself competent only to imitate the horse of Trajan's equestrian statue.[2]

The fourth century is, above all, an age dominated by the Unseen. Mysterious threads linked every object in the Universe in bands of sympathy or antipathy. Sun and moon exercised their influence on the creatures belonging to their kingdoms. Cockcrow at morning, flowers turning to the sunshine had their mystical significance.[3] Man himself, born under an astral combination, accompanied through life by a guardian spirit, was placed in a world where even inanimate substances possessed magical qualities, and the least action or incident might prove ominous or disastrous. Never was the divine voice heard more frequently or more plainly. Visions and their interpretation became ever more prominent, and the world of dreams steadily encroached upon men's waking hours. A strongly subjective tinge colours the thought of this time; the internal conflict and emotional experience of the individual take on a heightened value, beside which the outer world fades into unreality. Even the great work of Augustine, whose influence on the Middle Ages can hardly be over-estimated, is characterized by this dream-like quality. The sharpened points of his magnificent, though often contradictory, rhetoric furnished a whole armoury of weapons for medieval controversialists of varied and even opposite schools, and the claims of Papacy and Empire, in a Western Europe

[1] Cf. Bury's trenchant verdict: 'The Romans of the Empire originated nothing. It is not too much to say that, from Augustus to Augustulus, poverty of ideas, incapacity for hard thinking, and excessive deference to authority characterized the Roman world.'

[2] Ammian, XVI. X. 15.

[3] Memories of much of this late paganism can be divined in the magical practices of the Middle Ages.

which Augustine never imagined, were debated in terms of his dialectic. But Augustine of the fourth century must be distinguished from the superstructure reared on his foundations by the systematizing energy of subsequent centuries. Augustine stands in the midst of the ancient world, bounded by the limits of the Roman Empire, and still in possession of the full resources of Western culture. He stands at the same time apart from this world, enclosed in his dream of a heavenly city, whose denizens are but strangers and pilgrims on the earth. Both these aspects —the unity of pagan and Christian civilization, on the one hand, and the deep cleft between them on the other—were equally alien to the Middle Ages, when its former subjection to the Roman Emperors had become no more than a memory in the west of Europe,[1] and the full stream of classical learning had dwindled to a few runlets, carefully guided into ecclesiastical channels. Viewed from the standpoint of his age, the *Civitas Dei* of Augustine is less a 'philosophy of history' than a passionate assertion of Divine intervention in human affairs; less a prophetical formulation of the future limits of Church and State than the ecstatic vision of a philosopher-mystic, transcending the mournful realities of his time in the description of an ideal society, founded on the principle of true justice, whose gaze is fixed, not on the world of sense, but on the battlements of an eternal city not made with hands.

At the death of Theodosius, the Roman Empire was divided between his two sons, Arcadius, aged 18, inheriting the eastern part, and Honorius, aged 11, the western. This division was not a new thing. There had always been certain differences between the Western provinces, whose culture and city-life were largely the creation of Rome, and the Eastern districts which still retained the Hellenistic tradition. The reorganization of the Empire under Diocletian and Constantine, which provided for the joint rule of two emperors, had established itself as the normal arrangement, persisting through the disturbances of the fourth century.[2]

---

[1] The profound influence of that memory is well known: but it was an influence exercised in the realm of ideas, not of facts.

[2] See below, p. 23. From 480 onwards the Empire was once more subject to a single ruler.

Thus the first action of Valentinian (364), on being proclaimed Emperor, was to appoint Valens as his colleague. From now on, the two halves fall rapidly apart. Occasions of united action become few and far between; perhaps the last one was the great naval expedition in 468 against Gaiseric, the Vandal conqueror of Africa, whose piracies were threatening all commerce in the Mediterranean; and this attempt at co-operation was an utter failure.

Yet it is important to remember that in the eyes of contemporaries, the Empire was still one and indivisible. It is false to the ideas of this time to speak of 'the Eastern and the Western Empires'; the two halves of the Empire were thought of as 'the Eastern, or Western parts' (*partes orientis vel occidentis*). It is commonly said that 'the Western Empire' fell in 476 when Romulus Augustulus was deposed by Odoacer, but this is a double mistake. Romulus was a usurper; the legitimate Emperor of 'the Western parts', who had taken refuge in Dalmatia some years before, died in 480. His death meant that, constitutionally speaking, Zeno now ruled from Byzantium over the undivided Roman Empire. This principle of the continuity of the Empire was recognized by the barbarians themselves, and some of their leaders genuinely supported it.[1] Long after 476, the years were still dated by the names of the two consuls, one in Rome, the other in Constantinople; and imperial constitutions were still promulgated in the name of both Emperors, though after 450 the Western codes are not published in the East. It was, in theory, a single *respublica* with which the barbarians made treaties, although actually we find the *foederati*, or barbarian mercenaries, of the East fighting against those of the West. Stilicho, the general of Honorius, was once proclaimed a 'public enemy' at Constantinople because he tried to detach the prefecture of Illyricum from the East and add it to his master's share. The Emperor Zeno did not hesitate to inflict war upon Italy, when by sending Theoderic to attack Odoacer

[1] e.g. Alaric, Ataulf, Theoderic. Cf. pp. 46, 69. It is a striking fact that throughout the Dark Ages the claim of the rulers of Byzantium to exercise sovereignty over Rome's former dominions in Western Europe is constantly asserted; and the position of Charlemagne cannot be understood without reference to it. Even in the eighth century a Byzantine chronicler can speak of France as a diocese of the Roman Empire.

he could relieve Thrace of the presence of his Goths, and the Byzantine treasury of large expenditure on subsidies for them.

Ever since Constantine, in 330, had inaugurated his new capital, Constantinople had been growing at the expense of Rome. Commercially, it was far more important; the centre of the world's trade had passed to the eastern Mediterranean, and a serious rival to Antioch and Alexandria was already apparent. The eminence of bishops corresponded largely to that of their cities; and so the see of Constantinople, at first subordinate to Heraclea, was coveted by metropolitans, and finally declared higher in rank than Alexandria and Antioch, and second only to the see of Peter: 'for Constantinople is New Rome'. Politically, the city was the head-quarters of a great military and administrative system. It had even a Senate of its own, and to it came the corn from Egypt which it had once been Rome's privilege to receive.

During the last 100 years only three emperors, the poet Claudian laments, had entered Rome. She had become a provincial town. Milan, which lay within easy reach of the Italian frontier, was the Imperial residence until Honorius, in fear of Alaric, retired to the marshes of Ravenna, which was to be the seat of government for over a century. The absence of its Emperor left Rome in the hands of the Popes, who now began gradually to develop their medieval powers. Unlike the Patriarchs of Constantinople, who lived under the shadow of the Palace, they could on occasion challenge the Emperor, negotiate with the barbarians, and more than hold their own against the remnants of the Roman aristocracy led by the City Prefect, head of their order. When Rome fell, the civilized world, from Augustine at Hippo to Jerome at Bethlehem, was profoundly shaken. But the shock was one of sentiment (though none the less real for that). Rome was the Sacred City, which enshrined alike the ancient order and the new faith, the hut of Romulus and the tomb of Peter. But she had long ceased to be the actual centre of the Empire.

In 395 the north-western provinces of the Empire were on the eve of important changes. In Britain the defence of the 'Saxon

shore', the seaboard, that is, exposed to the attacks of the Saxons
on the North Sea and both sides of the English Channel, had been
the chief care of Rome during the fourth century; towards the
end of it, the system of forts seems to have been extended northward along the Yorkshire coast. But in 402 troops were withdrawn for the defence of Italy; in 407 a would-be Emperor,
called Constantine, crossed to Gaul with most of the Roman forces
and was finally defeated and killed by Honorius' generals. The
troops did not return, and for the next hundred years little is
known of Britain. Archaeological evidence, and especially the
coin finds, indicate the abandonment of Roman stations and
the burning of towns. Scots from Ireland harried the west
coast; on one of their raids Patrick was carried off, probably
from the Severn estuary. Teutonic tribes pushed up river
valleys and Roman roads on east and south. Henceforward
only rumours and legends about Britain came through to the
Roman world. Procopius, in the next century, regards it as a
land half filled with serpents, a shadowy Island of the Dead to
which souls are ferried across from Brittany.

The Rhine frontier was also on the brink of a collapse. Julian
had restored order in 357 in a series of brilliant campaigns against
the invading Franks and Alamans; Valentinian had continued
the struggle and set the newly come Burgundians to fight the
Alamans; and Stilicho, about 395, had secured the defences of
Gaul, as of Britain, for another ten years. But the eastern districts
were heavily Germanized. There were settlements of Teutonic
folk on both sides of the Rhine, and its defence consisted largely
of *foederati*, barbarian tribes who were ready at one moment to
fight against their kinsfolk or rivals in return for Roman pay or
lands, and at the next to join their late enemies in extorting
plunder or better terms from the Empire. When most of the
regular frontier-guards were called away to defend Italy from
Alaric, whole tribes could cross the Rhine on a dark night when
the river was frozen, and enter Roman territory with impunity.
Thus a mixed horde of Vandals, Sueves, and Alans passed the
Rhine about 406, defeating Frankish resistance, and wandered
about Gaul for some time, sacking most of the towns and causing
disorder and famine, until in 408 they finally managed to cross

the Pyrenees, and settled in Spain with similar but more lasting results. It is plain that the Imperial hold on the provinces beyond the Alps was becoming precarious. If further evidence is needed, it may be found in the fact that Constantine, the usurper from Britain, was able to call himself master of Gaul for four years by dint of avoiding the wandering barbarians. The campaigns of Constantine and other 'Roman' leaders against the generals of Honorius assume an air of unreality when we realize that, apart from Provence and the north-east corner of Spain, these provinces were already in fact, if not in name, passing into the hands of the barbarians.

This, however, was not apparent in 395;[1] the main pressure area seemed then to be the Danube region. In 376 the Goths, driven forward by Hun invasion, streamed over the frontier, ravaged Macedonia, and at the disastrous battle of Adrianople in 378 defeated a Roman army and killed an Emperor. On that occasion they had marched to the very walls of Constantinople, and though Theodosius had come to terms with them, they still menaced the capital. Large numbers of them were in the Roman army, others were *foederati*, settled within the Empire as national units demanding large subsidies.

But Constantinople was to survive. For one thing, as we shall see, the Goths were diverted to the West; for another, the Eastern frontier was quiet during the whole of the fifth century. Armenia, which had been a buffer state between Rome and Persia since the time of Augustus, was partitioned in 387, and the long struggle to gain 'spheres of influence' came to an end. Farther south, the line of the Euphrates was untroubled, since Persia was menaced by other foes in the Oxus district; and the chain of Roman fortresses sufficed to check the wandering bands of Arabs in that region.

In Africa, too, the desert frontier was maintained, though with lessening efficiency, against raiding nomads; Synesius, bishop of Cyrene, found the regular forces more cowardly than the local troops of neighbours which he raised and led. In the West, the

[1] Claudian, a contemporary poet, sings confidently of the overwhelming victories of Stilicho and the Roman armies in Britain and Gaul, comparing them to Marius' defeat of the Cimbri and Teutones. But it is true that he was a Court poet and a clever propagandist.

Moorish and Punic population was taking advantage of religious and social disturbances[1] to throw off Roman influence.

The state of the army about A.D. 400 is a mirror of general conditions in the Empire. Officially, the main structure of the reforms of Diocletian and Constantine still existed. The purpose of these had been, first, to promote efficiency by separating military from civil commands, and secondly, to secure the frontiers by permanent lines of camps, while the flower of the army (apart from various regiments of household troops) formed a mobile force which could be moved to any point threatened by invasion.[2] During the fourth century the difference in quality between the field army (*comitatenses*) and the frontier troops (*limitanei*) had increased; the latter, distributed in permanent camps or small settlements with land attached, had become practically a militia of farmers; and owing to inter-marriage and constant infiltration along the border marches, were often of semi-barbarian descent, and differed little from the wholly barbarian settlements of *laeti* or *gentiles* which had been allowed to settle inside the Empire at various points, in return for a certain amount of military service. They were regarded as second-class troops at best, and contrasted unfavourably with the regulars.

The army-list shows a great increase in the number of legions; but we gather from other sources that many of these existed only on paper or were simply detachments of the same legion. In fact, the usual strength of an effective unit was now 1,000 not 6,000. It was commanded no longer by a prefect, but by a tribune. Smaller units of various kinds (*numeri*), consisting of about 500 men, were frequently employed. The actual numbers of the Roman field forces during the fifth century seem to have been surprisingly small, and they were usually increased by hiring barbarian allies, often unreliable and always expensive.

The Roman soldier at this time would hardly have been recognized as such by the legionary of the early Empire. The cuirass was worn only by cavalry and a few of the infantry. The old rectangular shield had been replaced by a round, hollow buckler which often bore the regimental badge. The short stabbing sword

[1] Cf. p. 27.   [2] See Appendix A.

(*gladius*) was still used, but the long *spatha*, a barbarian weapon, was replacing it. The traditional *pilum*, or heavy throwing spear, was seldom carried except by barbarian troops. The long medieval pikes were coming in, and the cavalry in the next century all carried the lance. The bow had been borrowed from the Parthians, and was soon to be the weapon of horse and foot soldiers alike. During the fourth century there had been a real improvement in cavalry: the disaster of Adrianople had proved its importance, and the armoured horsemen of the Middle Ages make their appearance in the *cataphractarii*, or mailed cavalry, which is henceforward the deciding force. Many German words and customs had crept in. We hear of the *drungus*, a globe-shaped formation of troops; while the *barritus*, a warcry that swelled from a murmur to a terrible roar, had now spread from the German *auxilia* to the whole army.

A striking detail of the un-Roman appearance of the Imperial forces at this period is the standard of the new legions, taken over, probably, from the cohorts of the old full legion, to which they corresponded roughly in size. It consisted of a Dragon (*draco*)—an emblem perhaps borrowed from the Dacians—a huge creature of barbaric aspect, inflated with air and fastened to the top of a spear.

These signs of barbarism are only symptoms of a deeper change. The Roman soldier now fought on level terms with the barbarian. In old days he had often been physically as well as numerically inferior; but by perfect drill and organization, as well as by superior weapons and transport methods he had conquered. Now all this was gone. Complicated tactics were no longer possible; even the great camps which the legionary built each night, and so increased his morale and his mobility, had ceased to be customary. Many of the barbarians were better armed, and had even served in the Roman forces at some time. The Imperial machine was breaking up. Commissariat and pay were precarious; disorder was rife.

One result of this was the growth of personal retainers; big landowners took the law into their own hands, and paid, armed, and fed their followers. The practice grew, influenced probably by the widespread German institution of the *comitatus*, which Tacitus describes.[1] It was officially recognized by Justinian's time, when all the generals and even civil officials and private people were followed by *buccellarii*.[2] Belisarius, for example, had as many as 7,000, but this was exceptional. Narses had only 400.

The Roman legions had originally been composed of Italians; the provincials had later to be called upon, and finally the least civilized parts of the Empire—Gaul, Illyria, Isauria—became the main recruiting grounds. Compulsory levies still existed within the Empire—landowners were forced to supply a certain number of men; but since they either sent the most useless, or else compounded by paying money, the practice had almost ceased. Barbarian prisoners, tribes who had submitted on terms, peoples settled on or near the frontiers, or free *foederati*—such was the material of the army. The more barbarian, the better soldier. At the end of the fourth century a turning-point was reached. Theodosius let in an overwhelming number of Goths, and it was no longer possible to infuse even a smattering of Roman methods by distributing them among various units.

Of the higher command, since Julian's time at least half had been German, and many of the rest were of barbarian extraction. Popular speech had, as always, been adapted to the realities of the situation. The military treasury was known as the *fiscus barbaricus*. And it is significant that an Egyptian mother, in an appeal for the release of her son, states that he has 'gone off with the barbarians'. She means that he has enlisted in the Roman legions.

The position of the Emperor at this time was, in a sense, the logical result of the work of Augustus. The so-called 'diarchy', or sharing of the sovereign power between Princeps and Senate, had from the first been largely a fiction, and it had been abandoned before Diocletian. Henceforth the Emperor was supreme in all spheres, and the government of the Empire, down to its fall in 1453, may be styled an autocracy. It was, however, in

---

[1] Cf. pp. 41–2.
[2] *Buccellarii* seems to be derived from *buccella*, a biscuit; perhaps because they received better food than the ordinary coarse meal of the common soldier.

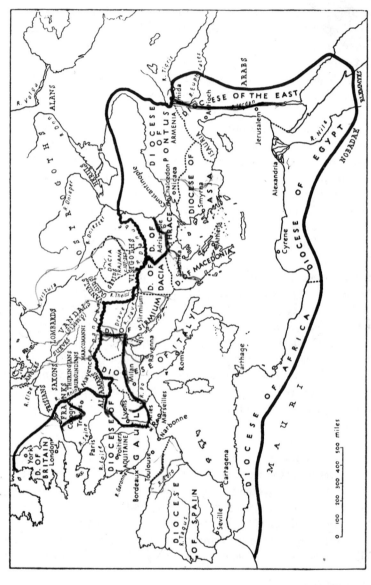

ROMAN EMPIRE IN 4TH CENTURY

Mommsen's phrase 'an autocracy tempered by the legal right of revolution'. The Emperor had always to fear the possibility of a rival. According to the original theory of Augustus an Emperor was elected to office by Senate and people. This had in practice been modified into acclamation by Senate and army, though the original principle survived at Byzantium in a ceremony in the Hippodrome before all the world. And if a rival could cause himself to be proclaimed Emperor by part of the army, he had 'a presumptive constitutional status, which the event might either confirm or annul' (Bury). If he failed in his *coup d'état* he was a rebel. If he succeeded, he was the legitimate ruler.

This was not, however, the usual procedure at the death of an Emperor. Most rulers had a younger colleague when they died, and in that case there was no election. This dynastic principle, which was apparent in Augustus's policy, had become a recognized custom: the Emperor had 'the right of devolving the Imperial dignity upon others'. His colleague or colleagues would be subordinate to him, for there was only one supreme ruler of the Empire. (In this respect the period from Diocletian to Julius Nepos (d. 480) is exceptional.)[1] Thus elective succession remained in the background, and in exceptional cases the Senate played an important part in this.

There were other checks on the Imperial power. Although the Emperor was, in theory, above the law, yet there was an unwritten obligation upon him to maintain the Roman laws and institutions. He must be an orthodox Christian: an undertaking to this effect was exacted at his accession from Anastasius (491), who was known to have heretical views, and at a later period a regular coronation oath became customary. But there was no permanent claim by the Church to exercise supremacy over the State, as in the Holy Roman Empire. Byzantium had no need of a Dante or an Occam to elaborate theories on this point. The Church was a department of the State; the Emperor was head of the Church, the Patriarch his Minister for Religion. The ruler received his power directly from God; and although he was not worshipped, as in Pagan times, his palace and his chamber were called sacred in official titles. Persian influence may perhaps be

[1] See p. 14.

seen in this; it is certainly apparent in other ceremonial details. The Diadem, a white band set with pearls, had become the chief of the insignia; purple boots were also a part of the Imperial dress. Eunuchs and women dominated the Courts of Arcadius and Honorius; one of the four most important officials, the *Praepositus Sacri Cubiculi*, or Grand Chamberlain, was a eunuch. The Emperor was hedged round with a barrier of etiquette (which required an enormous army of courtiers and servants for its expression) and fenced off from contact with reality.

It is a curious paradox that at the same time administrative centralization had reached its highest point. The Emperor held all the threads of government; he was the sole source of law, and his jurists interpreted it; his council consisted of the heads of the great departments of state; the revenues of the Empire were no longer distinguishable from his private resources. He employed a large body of special agents (*curiosi* or *agentes in rebus*) who were commissioned to inquire into every point in the administration, and report directly to him. The Theodosian Code, to which we owe so much of our information at this time, is full of Imperial rescripts intended to remedy injustice and abuses. Yet their very repetition indicates failure. And in fact the vast bulk and complexity of the machinery of government overpowered the activities of any individual; it was impossible to alter the movement of even the smallest of the interlocking wheels. The machine itself was threatened by yet larger forces; to stem the barbarian onrush became the first consideration. The *magistri militum* in this century were the real power, and an unwarlike emperor took inevitably a secondary place.

The Senate of Rome had dwindled into a municipal council, with the Urban Prefect at its head, controlling the *aerarium*, which had long ceased to be the State treasury, and now provided for the city aqueducts and food-supplies. Its degradation was apparent after the Court had moved first to Milan and finally to Ravenna. The body which had once directed the Empire now concerned itself with the University and archives of the capital. Yet in theory it retained its ancient powers, and in moments of crisis might prove a decisive factor. At Byzantium, owing to more centralized conditions, the Senate became indistinguishable from the *consistorium* or council of the Emperor. The old offices of consul and praetor still survived, and formed the highest ambition of the nobility of the capitals or provinces. But their duties were chiefly to supply games or shows for the populace.

The *senatus*, or senate proper, formed a very small proportion of the *ordo senatorius*, the large class of rich landowners which exercised enormous, though largely unofficial, influence and authority throughout the Empire. Unless he belonged to it by birth, a man entered the order either by special permission of Emperor or Senate, or on becoming *illustris*, *spectabilis*, or *clarissimus*—a member, that is, of the three highest ranks of nobility. Every important official post in the Empire had some title attached to it, or obtainable on retirement. These titles were constantly changing and increasing in number during the fourth and fifth centuries. They were not merely honorary, but conferred various forms of immunity from taxation, and were prized accordingly. Whole classes of functionaries passed automatically in this way into the senatorial order. It is not possible to describe in detail the official hierarchy. Below the three ranks already mentioned were the *perfectissimi*, a class consisting of minor officials and the heads of certain corporations; it was often a stepping-stone to the senatorial order. Below this class again the population was organized, as we shall see, in occupational divisions.

After the disastrous chaos of the third century, stability was the main object, and this was secured by a resolute fixing and simplifying of all the elements of administration. The cost of foodstuffs had soared; Diocletian sought to regulate it by enforcing a universal scale of maximum prices. This led to many prosecutions but did not meet with any appreciable success. The coinage was debased and silver and gold had become scarce; Constantine introduced a gold *solidus*, which for centuries remained the standard coin, though the real unit of value was the pound weight of gold. Taxation in the early Empire had been based on the customs prevailing in various districts; it was a highly complicated system, and most of the revenue was derived from indirect taxes and from the produce of Imperial estates. The heaviest burdens were the irregular exactions in money and in kind, for provisions and transport of Roman armies and travelling officials. These requisitions increased enormously during the troubles of the third century when almost every province created an emperor or pretender, and regular trade was made almost impossible. But instead of going back to the earlier system, Diocletian decided to perpetuate these practices in the *annona*, and to substitute for the old system of assessment a simpler and rougher method of calculation (*iugatio*) which took less account of local peculiarities.[1] The Empire must be saved at the expense of its people. In face of declining revenue, trade, population, and initiative, this was to be achieved only by turning the whole organism into a standardized machine for producing money and the necessities of life.

The peasants were the basis of the State. They must therefore be coerced and yet protected. Most small farmers (*coloni*) were no longer freeholders; they had become, partly by contract or legislation, but more by economic necessity, tenants on the estates of big landowners. Their personal freedom was now curtailed. They and their sons were bound to the soil; if they contemplated flight, they were to be put in fetters. But their *patronus* must not rack-rent; and he might not transfer *coloni* to another place when he sold the land on which they worked. The landowners were finally made responsible for the collection of the taxes paid by their tenants; and this completed the subjection of the *coloni*. They now formed a class of half-free persons, intermediate between free citizens and slaves.

The desperate state of agrarian depression and its significance for the Empire are shown by the various expedients of the government to prevent land falling into disuse. A nominal rent was exacted in return for hereditary tenure of waste land which the occupier engaged himself to plant with olives and vines (*emphyteusis*). Or it was made a duty for possessors of estates to take over and be taxed for a certain amount of uncultivated land (*epibolé*). Numbers of papyri recently discovered in Egypt put vividly before us the hardships of this system, which went on into Byzantine times. Any one showing signs of prosperity was saddled with waste plots. Constant requisitions of camels, arms, boats, slaves,

[1] See Appendix A.

and other means of transport rendered trade impossible. Fugitives became brigands, and left their fellows with increased taxes to pay. The sands of the Sahara were already closing in upon cornfields and vineyards left desolate by their owners.

There were peasant risings in various parts. In Gaul and Spain the *Bagaudae*, bands of rebels, waged intermittent war during the fourth and fifth centuries, and on several occasions gave help to the barbarians. Salvian, a priest in southern Gaul who describes them, tells also of men who fled to the barbarians to escape the tax-collector. Slaves in some districts rose against their masters; and Priscus, in mid-fifth century, who went on an embassy to Attila, north of the Danube, found a Greek merchant living among the Huns, who gave him detailed reasons for preferring barbarism to civilization. In Africa, peasant disaffection, strengthened by Punic and Moorish racial feeling, was fanned into a flame by the Donatist schism, and the *circumcelliones* (bands of flagellants and other fanatics) produced disturbances which paved the way for the Vandal invaders. The sudden efflorescence of Celtic art in Britain, of Coptic and Syriac literature in Egypt and Syria, shows that suppressed cultures elsewhere were only awaiting the weakening of Roman rule to renew their forces.

But such movements were exceptional. Apathy was the characteristic mood of the peasant, for whom no prospect of better conditions was visible, and whose only object was to avert starvation for the coming year.

Trade and industry had likewise to undergo State control. Even in Hellenistic times Egypt had known corporations of shipowners and merchants in the service of the State. By the time of Claudius the practice had spread to the similar associations (*collegia*) of *navicularii* and *mercatores* in the Italian ports; and from Aurelian onwards the *collegia* of all trades came to be recognized, protected, and controlled by the government. Except perhaps in the Syrian caravan trade, they bore no resemblance to modern joint-stock companies, but merely provided a convenient 'legal personality' in dealings with the State. Industry was, throughout the period, mainly an affair of individual enterprise.

The *collegia* of the *navicularii* are perhaps the best known, through numerous inscriptions, and may serve as an example.

Diocletian required them to transport the food supplies, not only for the population of the capitals, but also for the armies. Their own property was responsible for the safe arrival of the cargoes. They were bound to proceed by the shortest route, and not to stop anywhere without absolute necessity. Their service was hereditary. Bakers, pork-merchants, suppliers of wood for bath-furnaces and other crafts and trades both in the capitals and the smaller towns were organized on the same lines, in *collegia* from which no escape was permitted. Munitions for the army were produced in State factories by the sweated labour of slaves.

Local administration and tax-collection were likewise made an integral part of the great machine, and the *curiales*, who were responsible for them, were perhaps more wretched than any other class of the population. The early Empire had been (in one aspect) an aggregation of municipalities which retained a large measure of independence. By Trajan's time this was becoming curtailed; Imperial agents (*correctores, curatores*) were sent to regulate the finances of some of the cities of Greece and Asia Minor. With the growth of this practice municipal patriotism declined, public benefactions became exceptional; and the rise of Christianity, which demolished the temples of the *polis*-deities, the foci for so many centuries of communal loyalty and worship, helped to put an end to the forces which had kept the old city-state in being. But the need for local government persisted; and it was therefore necessary to compel the *curiales*, the well-to-do townsmen or landowners who were eligible for the city senates or for executive offices, to continue to undertake the charges (*munera*) of petty justice, deputations, inspection of buildings, postal and transport service, collection of rates, &c., none of which carried a salary. A distinction had formerly been drawn between *munera* and *honores*, the latter term being used of offices which were a coveted prize. It is significant of the state of public feeling that this difference was no longer maintained.

The most onerous duty was that of assessing or collecting the Imperial taxes. The *curiales* were personally liable for these, and the demands of the Imperial Exchequer were continually increasing. All manner of obstacles were put in their way. The big landowners refused to give information, and even armed their retainers to drive out the tax-collector. A bad harvest or an invading army might ruin the whole *curia*, for the deficit had to be made out of their own pockets. The ill feeling between town and country was heightened by the corruption and extortion to which the *curiales* were driven.

In the enactments stretching from Constantine to Majorian which are included in the code of Justinian, we can trace, through 150 years and 192 edicts, the slow destruction of the middle classes. Their desperate efforts to reach the senatorial order, with its prestige and immunities, are checked with increasing severity. The army, the church, the civil service are closed to them. Membership of the curial class becomes hereditary; it is glorified by high-sounding titles; it is the 'lesser Senate', the 'splendid dignity'; but the *curiales* are forbidden to travel abroad or even to reside in the country, for 'they are to remain in the bosom of their native place, as it were dedicated with sacred fillets, and guarding the eternal mystery which they cannot abandon without impiety'. This is a good example both of the rhetoric of the Code and of its complete denial of personal freedom. Other edicts show further restrictions, and stop various attempts to escape. In Egypt and the East the *curiales* fled to the desert hermitages; elsewhere, they sought to join more humble *collegia*, or placed themselves under the patronage of some powerful landowner; many small proprietors parted secretly with their estates under pressure of debt, and joined the ranks of the *coloni*.

In complete contrast to these miserable conditions stands the luxurious life of the upper classes. Their revenues had in many cases increased, while that of the Imperial Exchequer dwindled. Secure in their country fastnesses, they defied the tax-gatherer, and formed a vast freemasonry of governors and officials, connected by ties of blood and class, to defeat the ends of justice and nullify any reforming edicts. They present a curious mixture of ancient and medieval characteristics. There is a distinctly feudal flavour about the great families of the period—the Anicii, for instance, at Rome, the Apion house in Egypt, the inter-related aristocracy of southern France with their huge domains like little kingdoms, their seignorial justice and bands of mounted retainers. Mosaics from the floors of African villas show us something like a castle or fortified manor; the serfs render services or payments in kind; a self-contained 'house-economy' is practised, and all the needs of life are met by local industry.[1] The lord and his companions are seen riding out to the hunt or entertaining men, of learning. Ausonius and others give a similar picture of conditions in southern France. The days of city life are passing. The old spacious towns of classical form, unwalled, with baths, temples, porticoes, and approaches lined with villas and tombs, are soon to become huddled, and enclosed by walls and bastions, often hastily put together from grave-stones or blocks from the cornice of some public building. Luxury departs to the country as commerce declines. Roads are infested by brigands, and the great inter-provincial trade-routes no longer bring pottery and metal-ware to the home of the peasant or artisan. Village life grows up round the manor: many French hamlets to-day take their name from the original Roman landowner who lived on his estate at this time, only coming into the town, it might be, for Easter or an important lawsuit. But it is the next century that sees the full development of this process. At the close of the fourth century sea-borne trade was still considerable. Many parts of the Empire still prospered; the brilliant city-life of towns like Antioch and Alexandria continued, and though agriculture had long been depressed in Greece and Italy, there was no general fall in the productivity of the soil. Syria, Egypt, North Africa, Spain, and Southern Gaul still produced teeming harvests: and it must be remembered that the basic industry of the Roman Empire had always been the cultivation of the soil. Further, the feudal life we have described is only one aspect. On the social side, at first glance, we might fancy ourselves back in the world of Juvenal, Martial, or the Younger Pliny. The satire of Ammian and Jerome plays round the extravagant dresses and dinners of the Roman nobles, the courtesans, parasites, clients, and slaves. In the East, Chrysostom thunders against silk and jewels, gold-

---

[1] The fourth century villa at Chedworth in the Cotswolds, with its interesting dyeing establishment, may be compared. It is probable, to judge by its size, that it was designed to serve the needs of the district.

and silver-plated furniture and chariots, and describes the customary procession, in military formation, of slaves, eunuchs, and mule-drawn cars (which Ammian notes also at Rome), when the noble leaves Constantinople or Antioch for his country seat, elaborately furnished and provisioned for a few days sojourn. The scene recalls that of the coaches of Le Grand Monarque setting out from Versailles on the road to Marly, but the general atmosphere is not essentially different from that of the age of Tacitus, or even Horace.

A principal cause of this conservatism of manners lies in the social importance given to a form of education which tended to perpetuate old standards. The study of grammar and rhetoric was necessary as a preparation not only for the civil service— and most members of the upper classes were or had been Imperial officials—but also for polite intercourse. A cultured man was well acquainted with his classical models in verse or prose, and appreciated fully their technical perfection; antiquarian or grammatical points were often subjects of table talk or leisurely correspondence. But this insistence on form rather than on matter is the symptom of two great defects in the thought and literature of the time. In the first place they were unreal, archaic, academic: the written word bore small relation to common speech, which by now had gone far down the slope towards the 'Low Latin' of medieval times. The letters of Symmachus are conscious exercises in elegant expression rather than spontaneous utterance; and Ausonius, who can sketch a given scene—cattle watering, an angler, sunset on the river—with all the delicate precision of a Proust, and in a few adjectives presents a whole gallery of provincial portraits, Bordeaux professors, country gentlemen, maiden aunts worthy of Cambray, too often lets in a flood of irrelevant mythology or classical epithets. A vineyard seen on the Garonne inevitably provokes a mention of Rhodope and Pangaeus; a country house irresistibly recalls all the buildings constructed by famous architects from Daedalus onwards.

The second and more serious defect is the overwhelming influence of Rhetoric. All other considerations—rhythm, vocabulary, emphasis—are subordinate to one sole purpose, dialectic victory. It is the vicious principle personified by the

Ἄδικος Λόγος of Aristophanes' *Clouds*, and its results are seen in
Christian and Pagan writers alike, in garish tinsel ornament,
systematic exaggeration, deliberate unfairness to opponents and
general loss of integrity. It pervades equally the diatribes of
Jerome and the periods of Libanius, and is seen at its worst in
the multitude of ecclesiastical controversialists. Even Augustine
does not wholly escape it, though a feverish sincerity glows
through the *Confessions*; and the magnificent organ-notes of
Claudian are music of the mind, not the heart. The mystery and
symbolism of the Christian belief called for new means of expression. The stately hymns of Hilary and Ambrose and the magical
lyrics of Prudentius, greatest of Roman Christian poets, fuse the
strangely evocative Hebrew imagery of the Septuagint with the
sonorous incomprehensibilities of Christian dogma. The medieval mind, whose orderly universe with its scheme of salvation,
its antithetical virtues and vices, its recurrent cycles of seasons
and festivals—a refuge built foursquare against the demon-
haunted terrors of outer chaos—may be seen graven upon the
portals of Chartres, is already apparent in the *Psychomachia* and
the *Cathemerinon Liber*.[1]

It is useless to outline in mechanical abstractions the tendencies
of this transitional age in art, literature, religion, philosophy, and
science. The interaction of Christianity and Paganism, the confluence of Roman, Greek, and Oriental streams of culture, can
be depicted, if at all, only by copious and detailed illustration.
Yet from the writers of the fourth and fifth centuries certain
characteristics of the educated classes may be drawn; an elegant
pedantry, a vague liberalism, a watery humanity, a fluid panthe-
ism, and above all, a vast superstition, creeping up from the lower
classes as rationalism decayed. It is not among the extremists
that we must look for the authentic expression of this period.
Symmachus, adept of innumerable cults, and Flavianus, 'last of
the pagans', who directed the final revival of the old religion at
Rome on the eve of Theodosius' Christian victory,[2] look back
to an earlier time. Augustine, Simeon Stylites, and Ambrose

---

[1] Cf. F. J. E. Raby, *A History of Christian-Latin Poetry* (Oxford, 1927), ch. ii on
Prudentius.

[2] At the battle of the Frigidus (394), near Aquileia, Theodosius I utterly defeated
the Western army under Arbogast the Frank and Eugenius his puppet-emperor.

herald the schoolmen, hermits, and dominating prelates of the Middle Ages. But the great mass of educated opinion is neither Christian nor pagan. It is significant that the religion of so many of the chief writers of this time—Ausonius, Claudian, Nonnus, to name no others—is still a subject of controversy.

The reign of Theodosius marks a stage in the relations of Church and State. Both externally and internally there was a brief space of comparative calm. During the fourth century the churches had been divided by heresy and schism, which were aggravated, if not engendered, by the resurgence of racial feeling or local patriotism. Antioch, Alexandria, Constantinople contended for the primacy of the East. Donatists in Africa, Priscillianists in Spain, wandering ascetic bands in Egypt and the Near East with pronounced views on diet, marriage, property, and clothing, all received support from the populace in their war against authority. And this authority itself, in the person of the Emperors, had, since the death of Constantine, been mainly Arian or semi-Arian. In conformity with Imperial policy there had been depositions of prelates in many sees; and when this was contrary to popular feeling, two or more rival bishops or metropolitans, each with an excitable following, divided the loyalties of the big cities. In Rome the Papal party of Damasus, anticipating the tumults of medieval times, stormed the church of Ursinus, the anti-Pope, killing over a hundred of his supporters on one day (Oct. 26, 366).

Since the Council of Nicaea (325) there had been repeated efforts to formulate dogma, and a series of creeds was produced, representing various shades of doctrine, often concluding with anathemas pronounced upon opponents. The constant regrouping of different parties was bound to produce disturbance, especially when complicated by political, personal, or patriotic interests. But for the moment affairs wore a more settled aspect. The Emperor was Catholic: severe measures were passed against different heresies: the anti-pagan edicts took a stronger form. Within the Church, Rome and the Eastern sees were once more in communion—Constantinople, Alexandria, and Antioch reconciled for the nonce. Arianism was a lost cause inside the Empire, though growing rapidly among the barbarians along its borders. Monophysitism had not yet appeared. The organization of the Church was becoming more regular and its relation to the State ever closer. Privileges, such as freedom from the *curia* or from military service, and testamentary and property-holding rights, were established or enlarged. Bishops received civil jurisdiction, while secular control of ecclesiastical elections was exercised, with varying success, in the interests of public order and the unity of the Empire.

In the fourth century, doctrinal controversy centred round the relation of the Son to the Father; in the fifth century, round the nature of the Son. The two problems were not unconnected. Arianism, by subordinating the Son to the Father, was considered by the Athanasians to deny the full divinity of the Son. Sabellianism, at the other extreme, by insufficient differentiation denied, the Arians thought, his full humanity. Constantine had summoned the Council of Nicaea, at which the Imperial will had triumphed, and Arius had been condemned. Various councils during the fourth century sought to establish creeds of a semi-Arian or non-committal nature. Finally, Theodosius convoked the Council of Constantinople (381), which reaffirmed the creed of Nicaea, and Arianism was henceforth sternly suppressed.

In the next century disputes arose over the relation of human and divine in the nature and personality of the Son. Their importance for the general historian lies largely in the political issues involved. Perhaps the chief of these was the rivalry between Constantinople and Alexandria, and the workings of this rivalry illustrate many aspects of the religious controversies of the age. The Church had, from early times, adopted the divisions of the State in its organization. Cities became the seats of bishops, who met in synod in the provincial capitals. The bishops of these capitals became metropolitans, controlling the election of subordinate bishops.[1] Finally, the over-metropolitan, or patriarch, appears in the great apostolic sees of Rome, Antioch, Alexandria, Ephesus, and he in turn controls the election of metropolitans. A new and disturbing factor was introduced when Constantine

[1] These developments were still unfamiliar in the West during the fourth century.

founded his city, which from 330 grew rapidly in importance. The bishop of Byzantium had in theory been subject to the metropolitan of Heraclea. This soon became absurd in view of his political status, and in 381 the Council of Constantinople declared him second in honour only to the bishop of Rome 'because the city of which he is bishop is New Rome'. The principle was clear, and so was the threat to Alexandria.

From 395, when Theodosius died, to 450, when Marcian succeeded Theodosius II, the star of Egypt was in the ascendant, for the throne was occupied by weaklings, and the see of Alexandria was ruled by what amounted to a dynasty of strong and unscrupulous prelates, with a traditional technique which included bribery, anathemas, exploitation of national animosity, and the terrorizing of councils by the use of armed sailors from the ports of Alexandria and monks from the Thebaid. Egyptian policy was directed by a series of commanding personalities and able theologians. There are four stages in the contest; the first two end with a decisive victory for Alexandria, the third with bare success, and the fourth with her downfall.

First Stage. 398. Theophilus, bishop of Alexandria, fails to prevent the election of Chrysostom to the see of Constantinople owing to the support of Eutropius, the eunuch chamberlain of Arcadius.

403. Theophilus, by making use of the Empress Eudoxia, whom Chrysostom had offended, and of opposing groups in Asia, secures the deposition of Chrysostom at the *Synod of the Oak*. Chrysostom is finally sent into exile.

Second Stage. 431. *Council of Ephesus.* Cyril, bishop of Alexandria, by similar methods deposes and excommunicates Nestorius, patriarch of Constantinople, on the accusation that he has divided too trenchantly the personality of Christ.

Third Stage. 449. *Second Council (or 'Latrocinium') of Ephesus.* Dioscorus, bishop of Alexandria, succeeds in deposing Flavian, bishop of Constantinople, and restoring Eutyches, a monk who had, when attacking Nestorius, maintained not only the single personality but also the single nature of Christ. This success was gained not only by bribery of the eunuch chamberlain Chrysaphius and other courtiers, but also by armed force employed at the council. Rome, which had supported Alexandria in 431, was now hostile, and Antioch wavering.

Fourth Stage. 450. Theodosius II dies. Pulcheria, his sister, overthrows Chrysaphius, causes Marcian to be elected Emperor, and the *Council of Chalcedon* (451) to be summoned. Eutyches is condemned, Dioscorus banished, and the domination of Alexandria finally ended.

Even more important than the downfall of Alexandria were the other effects of Chalcedon. The doctrine of the two natures of Christ, which Leo of Rome had formulated, was accepted. The Alexandrian party resisted this, and ultimately in both Egypt and Syria the Monophysite heresy prevailed, which proclaimed one nature only. Henceforth the emperors at Constantinople had to choose between communion with orthodox Rome and peace with two very important provinces. Zeno, in 482, by issuing his *Henoticon*,[1] chose the latter, and Anastasius followed him. Justinian successively chose both. Not till Syria and Egypt fell into Mahometan hands was the problem at an end.

Egypt had been the centre of these conflicts; she was also the original home of monasticism. There had been and continued to be, in all parts of the Empire, numbers of men and women (*confessors* and *virgins*) who practised continence and were assiduous in attending church services. But Antony (*c.* 270) became the leader of a portentous movement when he forsook not only the world but the organized church by going into the desert as a hermit. His example was widely followed; there were soon over five thousand settlers round the salt lakes of the Wadi Natrūn and in the desert of Skêtê, which contained 'the most celebrated virtuosi of asceticism' (Duchesne). Their feats of endurance caught the imagination of the East, as did those of the pillar-saints later on. A more fruitful system was introduced by Pachomius during the fourth century. Groups of monasteries were formed, each with a common rule and subject to a single authority. They were visited by pilgrims from Rome, Gaul, and

---

[1] The Henoticon, or Scheme of Union, was an attempt to prohibit further controversy, by declaring the sufficiency of the faith as defined at Nicaea and Constantinople, and at the same time to conciliate the Egyptian Church by virtually leaving the decision of Chalcedon an open question. It was wrecked mainly by the opposition of Rome.

Spain, who introduced their practices to the West. The Sinai district, as well as Palestine and Syria, were soon filled with monks, isolated or in communities. In Asia Minor, Basil was responsible for a code of rules which improved on those of Pachomius in moderation and discipline, and which from that day to this has governed all the monasteries of the Greek and Slavonic world. The monks came sometimes into conflict with the authorities both of Church and State; armed with clubs, they broke up councils or demolished the shrines of pagans or heretics. The growing nationalism which is heralded by the appearance of popular Coptic and Syriac literature found its champions in figures like Shenūti, who from the bastions of his white hill-top monastery led hundreds of followers against the heathen, wrongdoers, unjust judges, and landowners of Egypt.

But the political influence of the monks was local and intermittent. More significant was the increasing secular power of the Church as a huge corporation with an army of dependants, owning lands, wealth, and charitable institutions, and controlled by bishops who in many provincial cities had become the most important personage. Acacius at Amida, Synesius at Cyrene, Sidonius in Auvergne, and others like them, are the natural leaders of the community; they head embassies to the barbarians, protect their flock from famine and outrage, and even organize armed resistance to the enemy.

II

THE BARBARIAN WORLD

A GLANCE at the map is enough to show the dangerous position of the Empire in 395. On the Rhine, the places of those scattered tribes whom Caesar and Tacitus had known were taken by a formidable line of peoples who had travelled slowly westward from the Baltic region, gaining in cohesion and military value by their approach to the Roman confines. The two Frankish groups were the most powerful of these peoples; but the Alamans who had found their way into the re-entrant angle between Rhine and Danube were an equal menace, owing to their strategic position. The other re-entrant, formed by the southward and eastward turns of the Danube near Budapest and Belgrade, had been largely filled up when the province of Dacia (Transylvania and Rumania) was created; but this was abandoned to the barbarians after 257: the Asding Vandals now held the north-west, the Visigoths, since 364, had been pressing southward against the Danube, and shut in behind these two were the Gepids. The Ostrogoths still wandered in the great plains of South Russia and had not yet, save for a few roving bands, come into immediate contact with the Empire. Still farther east, on Don and Volga, were the Alans, an Iranian people. Behind this first line were other restless tribes, preparing to play their part— Saxons on the Weser, Angles in Schleswig-Holstein; Sueves on the Elbe, Lombards in Silesia, Heruls in the Crimea, and Slavs beyond the Pripet marshes.

Each section of the long frontier had at one time or another been threatened or even broken through; but the Romans possessed interior lines of communication, and troops were hurried to the spot. Now this was of no avail. A new force had appeared from the Asian steppes, under whose impact were set in motion the barbarian attacks, incessant and ubiquitous, which in little more than a generation finally broke up the Empire in the West. This force was the Huns. Soon after 355 they reached the Volga, overpowered the Alans and hurled back the Ostrogoths behind the Dniester (c. 370); the impact drove the Visigoths over the

Danube, and the great battle of Adrianople is the beginning of Rome's disasters. Checked for a few years by Theodosius, at his death the Visigoths ravage Greece (396) and install themselves in Epirus (399), threatening both peninsulas; held for a time by Stilicho, they finally capture Rome (410), then pass over into Aquitaine (416) where their Tolosan kingdom is eventually founded. Meanwhile the Alans, fleeing westward, are joined by the Asding Vandals (401) who had become too populous for the Theiss valley, and go to swell the numbers of their kinsfolk in Silesia. They are reinforced by Sueves, and the four peoples force the Rhine frontier (406), wander through Gaul, cross the Pyrenees (409) and ravage Spain for twenty years, before the Vandals finally take possession of their African kingdom. Fifty years later Ostrogoths are in Italy, Franks and Burgundians dividing the rest of Gaul, Angles and Saxons well launched on their conquest of Britain; and by the end of the century all the Western provinces are in barbarian hands.

The early history of Germany is dim and mist-shrouded like the forests and swamps which covered the greater part of the country. On the Baltic shores, between Elbe and Oder, were the primitive German settlements, groups of huts in a clearing in the woods, or on high ground, occupied by hunting and pastoral tribes. As population increases or game becomes scarce they move westwards, driving before them the Celtic peoples, earlier inhabitants of western and southern Germany. By about 200 B.C. they have reached the Rhine and a century later Bavaria has ceased to be Celtic. Caesar's Gallic conquests established the Rhine frontier; faced by this barrier, the West Germans can expand no further. They are forced into more intensive methods of food-production. Agriculture develops; institutions crystallize, and Roman traders bring new wares and foreign manners. Tacitus, writing a hundred and fifty years later, describes a considerably more advanced type of culture than that noticed by Caesar.

Meanwhile other German tribes had, from the sixth to the third centuries B.C., been crossing from Scandinavia to the Baltic shore between Oder and Vistula. These East Germans took a different path; during the following centuries they found their way across Europe in a southerly direction, up the Vistula to the Carpathians or through Poland and the Pripet marshes to the great plains which lie north of the Black Sea. Continually moving to fresh pastures, they retained, unlike the West Germans, their primitive ways of life. The composite picture which can be drawn from Caesar, Tacitus and other travellers or *savants* who set down the curiosities of the German folk must, therefore, be applied with some qualification, considering the different stages of development (of which we know little) among the various tribes. And it has always been difficult for civilized observers to avoid attributing too great rigidity and regularity to the vague concepts and changing customs of more simple races. A fundamental difference, moreover, existed between the Germans and the peoples of the Mediterranean city-state culture. For centuries past, the individual in these cities had been subordinated to the state; apart from it, he was an outcast: he was incompletely human. The German, living in isolation or in a small family settlement, was above all things an individual, resenting any interference, and recognizing no obligation except that of loyalty to his plighted word when given to another individual. Hence a constant centrifugal tendency; all through his early constitutional development, the ties of family, clan and state are continually broken. Misunderstanding was inevitable. German perfidy becomes a byword among the Romans owing to breaking of treaties and treacherous warfare. And the personal loyalty, which is perhaps the true explanation of Stilicho's baffling character, may account for the hatred felt by his opponents for that which they could not comprehend.

Each tribe, when it was, for the time being, stationary, had a district bounded by natural obstacles, such as marshes, forests, or rivers. It was divided into *gaus*, communities of varying size which furnished 1,000 to 1,500 warriors for the host. Each *gau* was further divided into *hundreds*, personal bands of 100 to 120 freemen, for war or judicial purposes. The hundred is connected with the clan, a group of 10 to 20 families which persists through all changes and forms the basis of the final constitutional forms. (Here, as elsewhere, a symmetry and precision are observable which must not be applied too literally.)

Sovereignty rested in the folk-moot ('thing' or *mallus*), the gathering of all free warriors, which elected the rulers, and decided treaties, war and peace, and adoption of new members of the community. It was summoned and presided over by the king, or by a *gau*-chief (in non-monarchical tribes), and a high-priest offered sacrifices and punished violations of the assembly-truce. The chief of the *gau* led his contingent in war, gave justice in his court with the help of the hundred-chiefs, and assigned lands to the various families. The king, in early times, had very restricted powers; some tribes had two kings, some none; some elected a leader merely for a campaign, or a *gau*-chief to preside at the moot; in others kingship gave way to priestly rule. Offending monarchs could be deposed at will; and though the kings were chosen usually from the same family, any member of it might be elected. A strong personality could make a kingship a real force, especially in war-time; and contact with Roman absolutism generally increased the power of the king, especially when the tribe settled actually within the Empire.

The army, which coincided as in the early history of Greece and Rome with the whole body of freemen, was organized by thousands, hundreds, and clans. The regular battle formation was the *cuneus* or wedge. Cavalry was as a rule the more important arm, but the Franks fought mainly on foot. Metal was scarce. Leather caps, round shields of wood or wicker covered with hide, lances (the chief weapon), clubs, bows, battle-axes, and swords were used in battle. Circular hill-top ramparts or lines of locked waggons were their fortifications. Boat-making, among the maritime tribes, evolved from dug-outs, holding up to thirty men, into the plank-built galleys on Viking lines, which held over a hundred, and the pirate Saxon ships, with their leather sails, which became the terror of the Channel ports.

Apart from a few household servants, mostly captured in war, the lowest class consisted of subject populations who worked on the land; their numbers increased as agriculture developed (for the free German scorned to handle the plough), until raids came to be made largely for the purpose of acquiring them. The second class, the freemen, formed the bulk of the population. The nobles were the families of kings and *gau*-chiefs. Each king or chief had the right to a *comitatus*, a band of free retainers who fed at his table in time of peace, and formed his bodyguard in battle.

The preceding account applies more to the settled West Germans than to those primitive tribes whose wanderings we are about to trace.[1] Cattle were the chief source of food when on the march, and this must largely explain the astonishing mobility of the migrating hordes. Their beasts needed no means of transport; while their waggons were actually drawn by oxen. It is difficult to estimate the numbers of the invading peoples; probably the larger ones varied from 80,000 to 120,000, and the smaller from 25,000 to 50,000. About one-fifth of the whole people can be reckoned as fighting men; so that in the great battles between Imperial troops and their German enemies only about 20,000 were engaged on either side. The Roman Empire cannot be said to have fallen to the attack of overwhelming numbers.

It is not easy for us to see these people 'in their habit as they lived'. The Romans took an anthropological interest in these tall, fair-haired children, decked out in gold armlets and chains, drowsing for weeks before the fire, drinking for whole nights and days together, or stirred to sudden grief or passion, bursting into tears or striking a slave dead; brawling with their neighbours, raiding cattle, applauding their leaders in council with beating of spear upon shield, or following them to the death in battle. To us they appear all alike; to the eye as skin-clad barbarians, to the mind as hungry masses driven onward by economic forces. Hardly can nations be distinguished. The Lombards carry the long battle-axe (*barda*), the Franks the deadly *francisca*, the Saxons a short sword (*sah*). Burgundians, Sidonius writes in the late fifth century, are seven feet high, grease their hair with rancid butter, have enormous appetites and speak in stentorian tones. The Frank is grey-eyed, clean-shaven, has yellow hair and a close-fitting tunic. Still less do personalities emerge. Marbod and Ermanaric, overlords of scattered empires, are scarcely more than names. The times of wandering were a Heroic Age for the

[1] The habit of mind which produced this culture, however, was common to all the Teutonic peoples, and institutions existing only in primitive form during the migratory period developed speedily when once the wanderings were over. The conflict of these institutions with the Roman civilization will constitute the background of the next chapter.

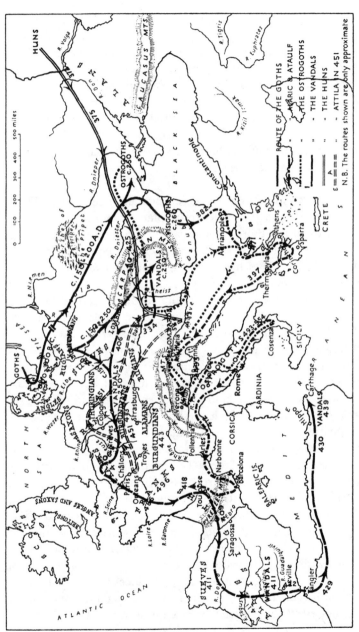

BARBARIAN INVASIONS

German peoples, and the figures and incidents which struck their imagination we see only through a glass darkly, in fragments of folk-tales or great epic cycles, distorted by later centuries. The legend of the hind that guided the Huns through the Crimean marshes to surprise the Alans still holds something of the terror of that time. The mighty figure of Theoderic and his long siege of the secret city of Ravenna are reflected in the saga cycle of *Dietrich von Bern*[1] and the *Rabenschlacht*. And in the *Nibelungenlied* we catch a faint glimmer of the doomed splendour of Gunderic's Burgundian palace on the Rhine.

Ostrogoths and Visigoths were originally one people. From their legends and the evidence of place-names they appear to have crossed the Baltic, from Scandinavia to the mouth of the Vistula, well before the fourth century B.C. About A.D. 150 some of the Gothic tribes began a long south-eastward movement, which led them up the Vistula through the Pripet marshes, and finally to the lower Dnieper and the northern coast of the Black Sea. There they split into two stems, whose names were, in view of later events, taken to mean 'East' and 'West' Goths. The Ostrogoth tribes soon spread over South Russia, while the Visigoths turned westwards, continually harrying the Roman province of Dacia, and even Macedonia and Greece. At last Rome could no longer hold Dacia; her traders and officials re-crossed the Danube, which, freshly fortified, again became the frontier as in the time before Trajan.

Great changes were now imminent. Arian Christianity was introduced, producing internal faction. Its heretical form was destined to play a great part, here as in other German peoples, in sharpening the hostility between Roman and barbarian. More important still were the results of the Hun invasion. The Visigoths, seized by panic, obtained permission from the Emperor to cross the Danube into lower Moesia (Bulgaria), and they finally settled within the Empire as a national unit. This is a foretaste of the manner in which the Western provinces were shortly to be dismembered. But the settlement was only temporary; and it was not effected till after four years of warfare, due to the mis-

---

[1] i.e. Theoderic of Verona.

handling of the refugees by Roman officials, and culminating in the great disaster of 378.[1] The battle of Adrianople has a twofold significance. It is one of Rome's most signal defeats at German hands, to be classed with the tragedy of Varus in A.D. 9, and the death of the Emperor Decius in 251. And it is the real beginning of medieval warfare; the heavy cavalry which rode down the Imperial legions was henceforth to be the decider of battles until Swiss pikemen and English archers in the fourteenth century challenged its supremacy.[2]

Perhaps the most momentous event of all was the election of Alaric by the Visigoths to be their king, which took place soon after the death of Theodosius. Like so many other able Germans he had to some extent broken away from the ties of blood, and entered on a career in the Roman federate troops. He hoped probably to rise to an important position in the Empire, as Arbogast, Stilicho, and others had done. His strange manoeuvres during the next fifteen years may perhaps be explained by this assumption that his interests were not wholly Visigothic (those of his people were limited to subsidies and land), but were concerned with achieving a definite place in the government of the Empire. He began by ravaging the whole of Greece, including the Peloponnese. The Roman troops were led by Stilicho, who for various reasons[3] offered no effective resistance. Alaric was next made Master of Soldiers in Illyricum, which satisfied him for four years. But his expectation of further promotion from Constantinople was probably ended by the anti-German crisis which had convulsed that city,[4] and he turned his eyes to the West. No better fortune, however, awaited him there. If he had hopes of coming to an arrangement with Stilicho, they were dashed to the ground when a similar anti-German reaction on western soil was followed by Stilicho's murder and the subsequent massacre of barbarians throughout Italy. Neither of Alaric's demands, permanent lands for his people and high office for himself in the Western part of the Empire, seemed likely to be granted. He marched into central Italy. The Roman government was by turns obstinate and

---

[1] See p. 39.

[2] It is true, however, that the importance of cavalry is noticeable early in the fourth century; and especially at the battle of Mursa in 351.

[3] See pp. 40, 58.

[4] See pp. 60 ff.

yielding. Angered by suspicion of treachery, Alaric finally invested Rome, which had bought him off on a previous occasion, and on August 24, 410, the Imperial City fell. The houses of the nobles were plundered and burnt, but few lives were lost. Churches were spared (Alaric was an Arian Christian) and no great damage was done to the ancient monuments. But the news of the disaster re-echoed through the civilized world; to many it seemed that the end of the world had come.[1]

Alaric now proposed to cross to Africa, either to settle his people permanently in that rich province, or to control Italy by holding her granary. But his transport ships were wrecked by a sudden storm, and Alaric himself died before the end of the year. It is important to remember that his invasion was not a hostile attack upon the Empire. Like other Germans, he regarded it as a necessary institution in which he and his people had a natural right to a place. This idea is found in a more remarkable form in Ataulf, his brother and successor. He had been heard to say that he aspired to 'turn Romania into Gothia', and make himself a Gothic Emperor. Later, becoming convinced that the Goths were too lawless and intractable to succeed the Romans, he resolved to use his people in the service of the Empire, and to earn the name of restorer of the Roman world (*restitutor orbis Romani*). This change of view may already have taken place when he passed into Gaul, fought there in the Imperial interests, and at Narbonne married Galla Placidia, sister of the Emperor, who had been taken captive from Rome. This last act, however, offended Honorius; the Goths were cut off from their food supplies by a Roman fleet, and Ataulf led them into Spain, where he died in the following year. After a brief anti-Roman reaction, during which Galla Placidia was subjected to various indignities, Wallia, the next king, came to an agreement with Rome: in return for corn supplies Galla Placidia was to be sent back, and the Visigoths were to clear Spain of the invading Vandals, Sueves, and Alans. Having exterminated the Siling Vandals and most

---

[1] Augustine's greatest work, the *De Civitate Dei*, was written in response to the need felt by Christians for some philosophy of history which should explain this calamity, and account for the disturbing fact that the City, which had survived its pagan emperors, should have fallen at last when its rulers had embraced the Christian religion.

of the Alans, the Visigoths received a permanent home, but in France, not Spain, where they had proved themselves too powerful. Henceforth, as *foederati*, they held what is now Aquitaine, the region between Loire and Garonne. This district, which included Poitiers, Bordeaux, and Toulouse, still remained in the Empire, and its Roman inhabitants, though they had to surrender two-thirds of their lands to the new-comers, remained outside the authority of the Visigoths, and subject to the Imperial administration.

Meanwhile the Burgundians, an East German people who had passed into Silesia about A.D. 150 and thence a hundred years later to the valley of the Main, had forced their way through the Alamans to the Rhine, which they reached at the end of the fourth century. Under their Gibichung dynasty (the name rouses Wagnerian echoes) who ruled at Worms, they were allowed lands on either side of the river in order to protect the frontier against Alamannic raids. Farther north, the two groups of peoples known as the Salian and Ripuarian Franks had for nearly two centuries been a continual danger, taking advantage of any crisis in the Empire to cross the river on plundering expeditions. The Emperor Julian had restored order (357–60) and the Salians were allowed to remain in Belgium as subjects of the Empire. The Ripuarians were for a time driven back over the Rhine; but the pressure, especially in the region of Cologne, grew ever more insistent, and in spite of repeated fortification, the great city was doomed. The administrative capital of Gaul was removed from Trèves to Arles early in the fourth century, and twenty years later Trèves had already been stormed three times. Honorius, however, had renewed the treaty with the Franks, and in 416 officially Gaul was at peace. For a moment it may have seemed to Rome that the solution of her problem had been found, and that the invading masses were to be assimilated peacefully in the Western provinces. Three barbarian peoples were now settled in France (Salian Franks, Burgundians, and Visigoths), and two in Spain (Vandals and Sueves). We have next to trace the wanderings of the Vandals up to and beyond their Spanish settlement.

The Vandals were an East German folk, who left the Baltic coast earlier than the Goths, and by the first century A.D. are found in Silesia and Bohemia. Owing to the disturbances caused by the Marcoman War, about A.D. 166 a general dispersion of peoples took place, and the Asding Vandals, whose name was probably derived from that of their royal house, moved south-ward to Hungary. The Siling Vandals remained in Silesia, which appears to be a Slavonic form of the earlier 'Silingia'; about a century later a number of them migrated to the middle Main. The Asdings were for some time weakened by conflicts with the Goths, but about 400 they found their territory on the Theiss too small to support them, and under its king Godigisel a large part of the population left its lands and joining the Alans (who had fled westward under the Hun onset) crossed the upper Danube. Here they were checked, and for five years dwelt inside the Empire as *foederati*. But in 406, to meet the danger from Alaric and his Visigoths, the Rhine frontier was denuded of troops. The chance was immediately taken. Asding Vandals and Alans, their numbers swollen by Sueves and by Siling Van-dals, streamed across the frozen river on the last night of the year. Their scattered bands of horsemen ravaged for two years the greater part of France, meeting with no organized opposition, though Toulouse, ably defended by its bishop, resisted all attacks. In contemporary poems we find graphic pictures of the invasion. Strong cities are given up to fire and sword: castles perched on precipitous rocks, lonely hermitages in the woods, churches guarded by relics of saints and martyrs fall to the barbarians. 'Gaul smoked to heaven in one continuous pyre'.[1]

But the storm was passing. In the spring of 408 the Vandals and their allies crossed the Pyrenees and descended on Spain, where for another two years they continued their ravages. Rome now intervened, and a temporary settlement took place (410). The Asdings and Sueves were placed in Galicia, the Silings in Andalusia, while the Alans settled in Portugal and north-east Spain. However, Rome's old policy, 'divide and conquer', was not forgotten; one of the best-tried methods of dealing with her enemies was brought into play in 416 when Wallia, the Visigoth king, was commissioned to attack the barbarians in Spain. It was hoped that in this way the numbers on both sides would be

---

[1] *Uno fumavit Gallia tota rogo.*

reduced. Wallia performed his task with such success that the Silings were practically wiped out, and the remnant of the Alans forced to amalgamate with the Asding Vandals. Roman policy now followed its usual course. The Visigoths were recalled from Spain, where they had become too strong, and granted settlements in Aquitaine. Support was given to the Sueves against the augmented power of Vandals and Alans, who were consequently defeated and driven into southern Spain. Here, however, they rallied, beating back the Roman troops, and under assaults from sea and land the strongly fortified coast-towns fell successively into their hands. That Rome had seen clearly the danger of barbarian sea-power is shown by her efforts to retain the southern shores of France and Spain; it is significant that about this time a law was passed at Constantinople which punished with death any person who should instruct the barbarians in ship-building. But she was powerless to avert the peril. Seville and Cartagena were taken and plundered, and now a greater enterprise was in sight.

In 428 Gaiseric became king of the Vandals. One of the most remarkable figures of this period, he is more definitely a statesman than any other barbarian except Theoderic and Clovis, besides being a fearless and successful fighter. The invasion of Africa was directed by him, and it is probable that he weighed the consequences. On the one hand the country was in an unsettled state; the Moorish population was in revolt, and the Donatist schism had increased the disorder. Count Boniface, the Roman general, had insufficient troops, and in fact was not able to repel the invaders. On the other hand, the master of Africa held the key to Italy. This had long been recognized, and the possession of those provinces formed an essential part of the strategy of Vespasian, and later of Severus. The loss of tribute which Rome suffered as a result of Gaiseric's conquest was considerable, but far more serious was the fact that her corn-supplies were now at the mercy of the barbarian. With the growth of Vandal sea-power, not only was Africa inaccessible to Imperial troops, but all the seaports, all the commerce of the western Mediterranean were exposed to the depredations of pirates, while Vandal forces might without warning be landed at any point in Italy or Sicily.

In the year 429 Gaiseric led his people, numbering in all about 80,000, across the Straits of Gibraltar. The rich plains were soon overrun, but Carthage and other strongholds could not be stormed. The Roman troops were reinforced, and after heavy defeats Gaiseric entered into a treaty by which the Vandals were settled as *foederati*. This was clearly a calculated move. Four years later he suddenly seized Carthage. To prevent Roman counter-attacks, a powerful fleet was dispatched to ravage Sicily and Sardinia (which now formed the main source of Rome's food supplies), and in 442, as the price of peace, Rome was forced to recognize Gaiseric as the *independent* ruler of the greater part of the African provinces. His position was thus totally different from that of the Gothic and Burgundian kings, who still remained subjects of the Roman Empire.

From time to time in European history a window is flung open and we look out on an unknown country of vast steppes, gravel or sandy deserts, gleaming black rocks, and high mountain pastures. Small groups of riders move over its surface, driving before them numbers of sheep and horses. In the summer they are found far to the north on the great plains which stretch up to the Siberian pine forests. At the approach of autumn tents are packed and the camps, consisting of five or six families, travel southward, traversing in succession the great loam-steppes, salt-steppes, gravel deserts, and wastes of drifting sand until they reach the basins of the Caspian and Ural Seas. Some of these tribes range between 10° of latitude every year, a thousand miles each way. The journey is necessary, for in winter the northern plain is deep in snow; in summer the heat shrivels up all the southern pastures. Centuries of these conditions have produced the nomad culture. To cover rapidly vast distances of desert land, a race of horses has been bred which will gallop for twenty miles at a stretch, and cover well over a hundred miles a day. The men spend their lives on horseback. Their feet are turned outwards, their calves little developed. They are of Mongol type: squat, big-headed, wheat-coloured, with slit eyes, large mouth, stiff black hair. Oxen cannot be used—they would die in the deserts, moreover they are too slow. Agriculture is equally impossible for the real nomad. His staple food is the milk of mares and sheep prepared in various ways. His appetite is huge; but on occasion he can go without water for days and without food for weeks. This corresponds to his conditions of life, semi-starvation in winter, boundless plenty in summer. The camp is his social unit: grazing-grounds and wells will not accommodate larger numbers. But the camp forms part of the clan, the clan of the tribe, the tribe of the folk; sometimes a great *khan* or chief sweeps the folks into a horde: if the horde is weaker than its neighbouring hordes, it is pushed out of the steppe zone and descends upon Persia, Armenia, South Russia, or Hungary. The horde may break up on the death of the Khan; or its component peoples may for centuries oppress the conquered race, returning in winter to demand their food supplies and their women. Culture in those regions becomes debased, the inhabitants treacherous and subservient. The conquerors themselves gradually form a mixed race and to some extent lose their Mongol characteristics. This has been the case with the Scythians whom the ancients knew and with the Magyars in our own time.

It is clear that the invasions of these Altaic peoples are totally different from the German migrations. Teuton and Roman alike regarded the Huns with superstitious horror and physical disgust. Owing to their extraordinary mobility, magical powers were attributed to them, and their numbers were greatly exaggerated. Actually the greater part of the Hun forces consisted of conquered tribes, especially Gepids, with Alans, Goths, Slavs and others, whom they had dragged in their train as they advanced from South Russia into Central Europe.[1] Their head-quarters were in Hungary; Attila, who had succeeded to the rule in 433, together with his brother Bleda, whom he seems eventually to have set aside, exercised a loose but effective sway over the Ostrogoths and Slavs in South Russia, and the various German tribes on the Danube. From his central position he threatened equally both halves of the Empire, continually demanding the return of fugitives, and exacting an enormous tribute in gold. For the first six years, occupied with Slav conquests, he refrained from open attacks on the West, even lending Hun mercenaries to the Romans

[1] See p. 38.

to fight for them against Burgundians and Visigoths; at the same time a humiliating treaty was imposed upon Constantinople. After 440 relations became more hostile; the Danube frontier was attacked and broken and northern Greece terribly ravaged. When peace was made in 447, huge indemnities were demanded and the boundary was fixed at Nish, considerably south of the Danube.

In 450 came a change. Marcian was now Emperor in the East and further tribute to the Huns was refused. The West soon followed his example. Attila at this point seems to have determined on definite conquest. At Easter, 451, he forced the lower Rhine, and advanced on Orleans. He had hoped that the Visigoths in Aquitaine would remain neutral; but they decided to fight for Rome, and this turned the scale of the battle. On the Mauriac Plain, near Troyes, the issue was joined. The Visigoth king was killed, but after heavy losses on both sides Attila was finally driven to his camp, and the legend of Hun invincibility was at an end. Aëtius, the Roman general, however, saw more danger for the moment in Visigoths than in Huns, and the latter were allowed to escape.

The fight has often been regarded as one of the decisive battles of history; but it is probable that the Hun army was in any case doomed to speedy dissolution on the death of its ruler. The geography of Europe, rather than any political or military factors, saved it, here as in other struggles with the nomad culture, from sharing the fate of Asia, which remains sunk in barbarism to this day. 'Had Germany or France possessed steppes like Hungary, where the nomads could also have maintained themselves and thence completed their work of destruction, in all probability the light of West European civilization would long ago have been extinguished, the entire Old World would have been barbarized, and at the head of civilization to-day would be stagnant China' (Peisker).

Attila now retired to Hungary, and in the following year invaded North Italy, when Aquileia and most of the other fortresses (but not Ravenna, safe in its marshes) fell before his assaults. His march on Rome, however, was not carried out. Famine, disease, and the arrival of Imperial reinforcements from the East added strength to the arguments which the embassy of Romans, impressively headed by Pope Leo I, laid before him in his camp on the Mincio. He returned home, to prepare war against Constantinople; but by the next year he was dead.

His sons divided the inheritance; but the Danube peoples had seen their chance, and fell like wolves upon their hated overlords. Led by the Gepids, the various tribes of Goths, Rugii, Sueves, and Heruls inflicted a crushing defeat upon the Huns at the River Nedao (453) and drove them back into the Russian plains, only a few scattered bands remaining in Hungary. For the next hundred years the Danube region was a maelstrom of struggling peoples; strife was encouraged by East Roman diplomacy, pursuing its traditional tactics against the barbarians. The Gepids, an East German folk, dominated Hungary and Rumania, contesting with the Ostrogoths, now settled to the west of them, the possession of Sirmium (not far from Belgrade) which commanded the great Roman road from West to East. At the death of Theoderic the Great (526), the Gepids seemed to have obtained their object; but a new claimant, in the shape of the Lombards, had by this time appeared, altering the whole Danube situation. An alliance between Gepids and Lombards was formed, but conflicting interests proved too strong. Bitter and prolonged warfare ended in 567 with the utter defeat of the Gepids, who play no further part in history.

The lands north of the Black Sea between the Dniester on the west and the Don on the east (between, that is, the settlements of Visigoths and Alans) were occupied about 350 by the powerful Ostrogoths, under their King Ermanaric, who exercised a loose hegemony over the Slav tribes to the north of them. The Hun invasion broke up this empire, and drove the Goths westward, in fugitive bands, to the Balkans. Many of the Ostrogoths, after an unsuccessful stand on the Dniester, joined their Visigothic kinsfolk in crossing the Danube,[1] and took part in the fight at Adrianople. In 380 they entered into a pact with Theodosius I, and were given settlements in Lower Hungary. Although still dominated by the Huns, who had extended their rule into

[1] See p. 44.

Hungary, they were now united under one king, and later under his three sons, except for scattered bodies which entered Roman service, or those who joined the mixed forces of Radagaisus, which made a sudden and dangerous inroad into Italy in 404–5 and were annihilated by Stilicho on the heights of Fiesole. As subject-allies they fought for Attila at the Mauriac Plain, but took a prominent part in the coalition of peoples which overthrew the Huns after Attila's death, while more than holding their own in the struggles of Danube tribes which followed. In 471 Theoderic, afterwards called the Great, became one of their chieftains. He had spent ten years of his boyhood as a hostage at Constantinople, and like Alaric (whose career resembles his in many ways) must have learnt a good deal about the organization of a civilized state, though to the end of his days he was unable to write, and in order to sign his name had to make use of a gold stencil.

Having exhausted the resources of Pannonia, his people moved about this time to the neighbourhood of Salonika, whence they exercised continual pressure on the capital. The next ten years saw a triangular contest between the Emperor Zeno, Theoderic and another Theoderic surnamed Strabo (also an Ostrogoth) who commanded a contingent of his countrymen in the Roman service. The Emperor's policy was to play off one Theoderic against the other; but on the death of Theoderic Strabo in 481, some other means had to be found of relieving Constantinople from the disastrous subsidies. Odoacer[1] had ruled Italy since 476, but Zeno had given him only formal recognition, and was waiting his chance to regain control over the West. It is doubtful whether, after his experience of him, he expected Theoderic to prove a more amenable vice-regent than Odoacer; but the first consideration was to rid Illyria of a crushing incubus; and if Odoacer and Theoderic destroyed each other, only good could come of it.

Theoderic accepted the mission, and set out for Italy in 488, leading, as Imperial *magister militum*, a mixed body of Ostrogoth and other adventurers. The decisive battle of the campaign was fought on the Adda in August 490, and Odoacer, utterly defeated, hastened to take refuge in impregnable Ravenna. The Roman

[1] See p. 60.

Senate at this point decided to support Theoderic, and he was acknowledged ruler of Italy. Several towns still held out for Odoacer, and Theoderic successfully incited the Roman population to a general massacre of these barbarian garrisons. The Vandals also were ravaging Sicily; after hard fighting they were forced to give up their claims to the island. Odoacer, finally, was still to be reckoned with; Theoderic entered upon the last stage of his conquest when he began the three years siege of Ravenna.

The imagination of the Germans was haunted by this strange city, for it is celebrated in the cycle of saga which surrounds the name of Theoderic. Till yesterday it was a silent and ruinous town, a cluster of bell-towers in a steamy plain of malarial swamps and maize fields, traversed by sluggish streams half choked with reeds and water-lilies. Something of its former glory still remains. San Vitale, its most magnificent church, glowing with jewelled mosaics and translucent marble, belongs to the time of Justinian, when Ravenna reached the summit of its beauty. During four centuries, however, it had been famous as the head-quarters of a Roman fleet. Washed by the Adriatic, its temples and storehouses stood upon islands rising from canals as Venice does to-day. The sea had gradually receded, but still at this period the city was connected with the mainland only by a long causeway through the marshes which, continuing through the town, conducted the traveller to the battlements and lighthouse of the seaport Classis. For nearly a century it had been the residence of the Emperor and his court. Honorius and Valentinian III, those shadowy figures, lived out their quiet lives here among the intrigues of women and eunuchs, priests and courtiers, far from the dust and clamour of a changing world, where Stilicho and Aëtius led the last Roman legions against the invaders.

Here in a small cruciform building, whose walls and ceiling glitter with gold stars, spangled on a deep azure background, lies the massive sarcophagus of Galla Placidia. This Roman princess, whose life mirrors the history of her times, was daughter of Theodosius the Great, and sister of Arcadius and Honorius, Emperors in East and West; she was taken prisoner at the sack of Rome, became the wife of Ataulf, king of the Visigoths, and went with him into France and Spain. Later she married

Constantius, the famous Roman general, and after his death and that of Honorius she was for twenty-five years virtual ruler of the West during the minority and the weak reign of her effeminate son, Valentinian III. Her celebrated beauty, and the turn of her fortunes, curiously entangled with those of Western Europe, combine to make her the most romantic figure of the century. But she has still another aspect, no less characteristic of the times. Under her influence the atmosphere of the Court became yet more heavily charged with the incense-clouds of mystical religion. Perhaps it is not upon the battle-fields of the frontier but in the twilight of the Mausoleum of Galla Placidia that we should interrogate the dim ghosts of this obscure period. Their motives are for ever hidden; but some glimmer of understanding may strike our eyes when they are met by the mysterious symbols and hieratic figures of doves and deer, sheep and fountains, flowers and interlacing vines, Evangelists and Saints, which shine out of the darkness, presaging an unearthly happiness.

Then, as now, Ravenna kept her secrets. Theoderic, unable to penetrate the defences, came to terms with Odoacer. Both were to exercise equal rule over Italy. Treachery seems to have been intended from the first. Ten days after his entry Theoderic invited Odoacer to a feast. As they sat at table, two men knelt before Odoacer with a petition and clasped his hands. Theoderic's hidden soldiers rushed out, but hesitated to strike down the old man. Theoderic himself stepped forward and raised his sword. 'Where is God?' cried Odoacer. 'Thus didst thou to my friends,' said Theoderic, and clave him from the collar-bone to the loin. Surprised at his own stroke, he exclaimed, 'The wretch can have no bones in his body.' Orders had already been given for a massacre of the hostile mercenaries, and Theoderic met with no further resistance to his claims to the lordship of Italy.

III

THE CLASH OF CULTURES

THE preceding chapters have dealt with the Roman and Barbarian worlds of A.D. 395. It has been necessary to anticipate
events by tracing, so far as possible in isolation, the wanderings
of the principal Barbarian peoples. What was the result of the
impact of the two cultures, as exhibited in the confused and
troubled history of the fifth century? The process should perhaps
rather be called the acceleration of a gradual development; for
it must be remembered that the population of large portions of
the Empire was already barbarian, that the army had long been
predominantly German, and that no leader of the invaders, with
the possible exception of Gaiseric, desired the downfall of the
Roman Empire.

It is impossible to explain psychologically the actions of the
chief Roman figures in this period; access has been forbidden to
the Courts of Ravenna and Constantinople, where, like jewelled
Eastern potentates in sacred chambers guarded jealously from
the outside world, sat the two sons of Theodosius the warrior
Emperor. It is true that these *pauvres jeunes princes, pâles fleurs du
gynécée*, as Duchesne calls them, were merely the centre of the
multifarious intrigues of the palace; but of these intrigues our
knowledge is scarcely greater. Nearest to the Emperor stood the
Grand Chamberlain, a eunuch, who controlled the Imperial
Household, and by enlarging the scope of his department sought
to increase the personal government of the sovereign at the
expense of the great State offices. In the West the feudal landowners of France and Italy proved too strong for the central
power. In the East the heads of the civil service, being mainly of
humble origin, showed less resistance to the absolutism of the
Byzantine monarchy, and the all-powerful Chamberlain was
free, like Eutropius, to choose the Emperor a wife or intrigue with
disloyal generals. The courtiers and officials, however, in both
palaces were a strong faction, calling loudly on occasion for anti-
German measures. The women of the household played a great

part—though perhaps not so great as romance-scenting Byzantine historians would have us believe—often controlling the feebler emperors as they themselves were, for the most part, controlled by their spiritual advisers. The atmosphere is thick with suspicion and self-seeking. Spies are everywhere, favourites rise and fall, no moral principles of action are observable, no friendship is safe.

Against this background stands a series of great figures, the *magistri militum* of the fifth century. In their hands is the real power, for upon the army, which they control, depend the fortunes of the Empire. Being for the most part barbarians, they cannot, as the generals of the third century had done, depose the emperor and assume the purple. Hated and feared by the anti-German party and the Emperor, they are nevertheless indispensable and omnipotent. Sometimes this hate overpowers all other considerations. Honorius executes Stilicho (408); Valentinian III strikes down Aëtius (454) and soon afterwards meets with a similar fate. In the next stage it is the *magister militum*, Ricimer (d. 472), who sets up puppet emperors, killing or deposing them if they prove too independent. Finally, Odoacer (476) dispenses with the Emperor and rules Italy in person as nominal vice-regent of the power at Constantinople.

The ascendency of Stilicho lasted from 395 to his death in 408. He was constantly accused of treachery; it is not difficult to see the reason for these charges. He had repeatedly allowed Alaric to retire, both in Greece (397) and in Italy (403) when he could almost certainly have destroyed his forces, and thus prevented the fall of Rome in 410. Further, he had not saved Gaul from the terrible invasion of 406 which delivered two provinces to the ravages of the Vandals and their allies. His policy appears to have been governed by three principles. He had been the right-hand man of Theodosius, and was made guardian of his young sons in 395. Personal loyalty was a German characteristic, and Stilicho never wavered in his loyalty to the Theodosian House. All means might be used to gain ascendency over Arcadius, but the Emperor's person was never in danger. And it is a notable fact that Stilicho allowed no resistance to be made when Honorius gave the order for his execution. His second principle, which may have been adopted later when the anti-German reaction at Constantinople destroyed his hopes in that quarter, is the determination to secure the Illyrian prefecture[1]—an invaluable recruiting-ground—for the Western half of the Empire. To this end he employed the forces of Alaric; on account of his attempts on it he was declared a public enemy by Arcadius's government; for its sake he sacrificed Gaul to the barbarian onset which it was his duty to stem. The third principle was imposed upon him by the fact that he was a barbarian. The rapid growth of German influence in high quarters naturally met with his approval; German and Roman had an equal right to a place within the Empire. This may account for his view of Alaric as a useful ally rather than a public enemy; it certainly accounts for his support of Gaïnas and the German party in Constantinople; and it amply explains the hostility of the Roman conservatives, which brought him finally to his death.

The next period (408–23) saw the establishment of barbarian federate settlements in Gaul and Spain, and the skilful direction of these movements[2] was due to Constantius, Roman *magister militum*, who married Galla Placidia in 417, and became the father of Valentinian III. His work in Gaul is of the first importance. That France to-day can boast herself a Latin country must be ascribed partly to the fact that he made it possible for the barbarians to settle comparatively peacefully in Roman territory, absorbing the laws and institutions of the inhabitants. New military arrangements were made in north-west Gaul, and a focus of Roman influence was provided by the Council of the Seven Provinces, held annually at Arles, and attended by representatives from both Roman and Visigothic territory.

Constantius died in 421, and the Emperor Honorius in 423. Over the next thirty years (423–53) falls the mighty shadow of Aëtius, 'the last of the Romans'. Applied to his character and exploits, the title may be justified. But he was in constant opposition to the 'Roman party' at Ravenna; and he maintained himself against Galla Placidia and the rival generals, Felix and Boniface, only by the help of his Hunnish mercenaries. His chief care was Gaul; the Visigoths, seeking to expand into Provence, were

---

[1] See Appendix A. [2] Cf. pp. 46–7.

thrown back; the Burgundian kingdom of Worms, which had been plundering its neighbours, was practically wiped out (436) by means of Hun *foederati* (the *Nibelungenlied* has taken this as the work of Attila—unless 'Etzel' be a conflation of the names Attila and Aëtius), and the remnant settled in Savoy. Ironically enough, it was Aëtius who met the invasion of Attila in 451, and with Visigoth help turned it back upon the Mauriac Plain. Three years later he was stabbed by Valentinian III in the Council-chamber; and the murder of Valentinian himself in the following year extinguished the Theodosian House.

The final stage is now reached. In twenty years no less than nine puppet-emperors appear, made and unmade by the *magistri militum*, Ricimer and his successors. The Vandals attack Italy with impunity, and Rome herself is taken and plundered. The semblance of Roman authority fades out in Gaul and Spain, after the assassination of Majorian, who had proved too capable an Emperor to suit his creator Ricimer. Odoacer, a leader of the German *foederati* in Italy, granted their demand to receive settlements on Italian soil, as other barbarians had done in Gaul and Spain, and was acclaimed their king (476). He set aside the boy-emperor Romulus Augustulus, created by his predecessor (the legitimate ruler, Nepos, whom the East acknowledged, had fled two years previously to Dalmatia), and until the coming of Theoderic ruled Italy just as Ricimer had done, save that after the death of Nepos (480) the constitutional sovereign was no longer a puppet at Rome or Ravenna, but the emperor at Constantinople, for whom, in theory, Odoacer acted as vice-regent.

The history of the Eastern half of the Empire runs curiously parallel to that of the West. The crises appear even more serious; but they are successively surmounted. Let us trace the contrast. In the year 400 German influence at Constantinople reached its climax. Rufinus, the praetorian prefect, and Eutropius, the eunuch chamberlain, had been put out of the way; the Roman party, though supported by the empress, Eudoxia, was helpless. Gaïnas, the barbarian *magister militum*, was supreme; his troops were quartered in the capital; and the hopes of Stilicho, pursuing a similar and concerted policy in the West, might well be raised.

But thunder was in the air. The Gothic troops were insolent, and more odious still, they were Arian heretics. One summer evening the storm broke. A brawl developed, spreading rapidly through the city. The gates were shut, the soldiers hunted down and massacred by the populace, or burnt alive in the church where they had taken refuge. On that night German power was broken for ever. A few years later the Visigoth menace, which since Adrianople had hung like a cloud over the Balkans, moved westward when Alaric turned his steps towards Italy.

Arcadius and Honorius were succeeded by two equally incapable princes, Theodosius II and Valentinian III. Under the regiment of women, the Eastern court joined in the doctrinal contest between Constantinople and Alexandria, a battle big with political consequences.[1] Towards the close of the reign the Huns pressed even more heavily on the East than on the West; its provinces were devastated, its citizens crushed under ruinous taxation to provide subsidies. Once more, the peril passed westwards, and vanished at the death of Attila. The end of the Theodosian line brought more capable emperors on the scene; but in the West it was too late; a Majorian could do nothing against a Ricimer. In the East this dangerous power of the *magistri militum* encountered several checks. The supreme command of a Stilicho or Aëtius over all military resources, field army and frontier forces alike, was never permitted at Constantinople.[2] The threat of Vandal attacks in her rear increased Italy's dependence on her armies; Constantinople was not menaced so nearly. And when the German danger revived, effective counterforces were discovered by Leo and his successors.

The usual ambition of the barbarian *magister militum* was to marry into the Imperial House. This had been achieved by Aspar, the powerful Alan general, who on the death of the Emperor Marcian had contrived to elevate Leo, his creature, to the throne (457), and had forced him, after long temporizing, to give his daughter in marriage to Aspar's son, who might now expect to become the next Emperor. But Leo had other plans. Strong detachments of Isaurians, a fierce mountain race from one of the provinces of Asia Minor, were summoned to the capital,

[1] Cf. p. 35.   [2] Cf. Appendix A.

and their leader Tarasicodissa (the original name of Zeno, the future Emperor) became a rival *magister militum*, and was married to another daughter of Leo. A new bodyguard was created, consisting largely of Isaurians. The machinery for a *coup d'état* was now installed, but Leo hesitated to use it, and meanwhile Aspar's influence grew, while the State, weakened by the costly failure of the naval expedition against the Vandals (468) could offer no resistance. At last the moment came. Aspar was treacherously murdered at a banquet, and his party was broken up, an attack on the Palace being frustrated by the new guards (471). The Gothic tribes, however, on whom Aspar had depended, were still at large in Thrace, and under their leader Theoderic Strabo[1] continually menaced the safety of the capital. The Isaurians were unpopular, and when the court party, making use of Theoderic's troops, set up a rival candidate, Zeno, who had now become Emperor, had to flee back to his native Isauria. But here, too, a remedy was at hand. Theoderic the Amal (who was to become Theoderic the Great), king of the Ostrogoths in Macedonia, was ready to compete with his namesake for the titles and subsidies of Constantinople. By his aid Zeno returned to power; by playing off the two chieftains against each other, the ascendancy of either was prevented; and soon after the death of Theoderic Strabo, Zeno contrived to dispatch Theoderic the Amal to the conquest of Italy.

The German danger was gone; others remained. Isauria was a focus of rebellion. Bulgarian nomads had appeared on the lower Danube. Nationalism was growing in Armenia, Syria, and Egypt. Arabs raided the eastern frontier, Blemmyes the south. Vandal pirates held up the Mediterranean traffic. But these were minor difficulties. Persia, occupied with Hun invasions, was no longer troublesome. Barbarian influences within the Empire had been kept under. At the close of the century, the Roman Empire was still in being.

Not many years passed before the federate settlements in Gaul[2] sought to extend their boundaries. The Visigoths in Aquitaine, whose attempts on the precious Riviera coast were frustrated by

---

[1] Cf. p. 54.　　　　　[2] Cf. p. 47.

Majorian, had turned upon Spain, and by 476 had occupied the whole country with the exception of Galicia, where the Sueves still held out against them. About the same time a strong attack was launched upon Provence. Italy could send no help, and Euric's Visigoth dominion, now at its fullest extent, reached from the Straits of Gibraltar to the estuary of the Loire, and from the Atlantic to the Alps. Meanwhile the Burgundians in Savoy had captured Lyons, and the whole basin of the Rhone from Geneva to the neighbourhood of Avignon was in their hands. Hitherto the Salian Franks had apparently carried out their duties as *foederati*. The representative of Rome in northern Gaul was a curious figure, characteristic of the changing times. Aegidius had been, under Majorian, a commander of Roman troops in Gaul. Cut off from Italy, by the solid block of Visigoth and Burgundian territory, he became practically an independent ruler, and his son Syagrius succeeded him in this anomalous position. His capital was Soissons. The barbarians knew him as the *rex Romanorum*—a phrase meaningless to Roman ears. Childeric, a chief of the Salian Franks, had helped the Roman forces on the Loire in repelling Saxon raiders and the northward thrusts of the Visigoths. He saw clearly the advantage of keeping northern Gaul free for his own advance. Meanwhile the Ripuarian Franks, from their centres at Cologne and Mayence, were spreading to right and left of the Rhine.

In 482 Childeric died, and was succeeded by his sixteen-year old son, Clovis. The character of this strange genius has suffered from the sagas of his contemporary admirers. They worshipped a hero made in their own image; and so the brutality, cunning, and treachery of the Franks have been expressed in their highest common measure in the legendary figure of Clovis. The picture was probably more accurate than the Catholic presentation of him as pious Defender of the Faith, waging righteous war upon heretics and heathen. But neither does him justice. His full stature can be seen only in his achievements, which in less than thirty years transformed the face of Gaul. Federal obligations had ceased to have any force, and Syagrius was the first object of attack. Routed near Soissons, he fled to the Visigoths, but was surrendered by them under threats and

put to death by Clovis. All France north of the Loire (except
Brittany, whose Celtic tribes, joined by Romano-British refugees, remained independent) fell speedily into Frankish hands.
Meantime, by murder, conquest, or stratagem, Clovis had
gained supremacy over the rest of the Salians, and by the same
means finally added the Ripuarian Franks to his Empire,
and after heavy fighting hurled back the Alamans beyond the
Rhine.

Before the completion of this work a momentous event had
taken place—the baptism of Clovis into the Catholic Church.
The significance of this will be noticed later on. Its immediate
effects were to turn every Catholic priest in Visigothic or Burgundian territory into an agent working for the victory of Clovis, to
gain him the support of the Roman population in Gaul, and to
make him a desirable ally, from the Byzantine point of view,
against the Arian rulers of the West. Helped by these advantages
and by the weakness of Euric's successor, Alaric II, he attacked
the Visigoths, and after several unsuccessful campaigns finally
overthrew them at the great battle of Vouglé, near Poitiers (507).
Alaric was killed, and his Gallic dominions fell to the conqueror,
except the Riviera coast-line, which timely action on the part
of the Ostrogoths had secured for Italy. The Visigoths were
henceforward confined to Spain. Burgundy was the final victim,
but its conquest was not completed till twenty years after the
death of Clovis in 511. Many devices were employed; open warfare alternated with marriage alliances, support of factions,
treachery, assassination. Burgundy put up a gallant defence,
succumbing only to superior forces in 532.[1]

The union of two cultures is a biological process, and the result
is no more capable of exact analysis than the character of a man
can be explained on Mendelian principles. In the earlier stages,
however, a distinct duality can be observed. Most of these kingdoms fell long before it had been resolved, and even in the Frankish realm full unity was not achieved until the days of Charlemagne. Duality was inherent in the nature of settlement, which
was itself an inheritance from the Roman Republic. Troops

[1] See p. 76.

quartered in the provinces were lodged by the inhabitants, who gave up to their 'guests' a certain proportion (usually one-third) of their estates. Under this system of *hospitium*, bands of *foederati* ('allies', in theory), were found in almost every province during the fourth century, and the Goths and Vandals were probably regarded, at first, by the Romans of Italy, Gaul, and Spain, as a similar but temporary nuisance. Thus the population was sharply divided: on one side the civil inhabitants, carrying on the administration, agriculture, and trade, on the other, the soldiers—barbarian heretics for the most part, subject to their own laws and customs, having no abiding city and owing no loyalty save to their leaders.

Monarchy was universal; but it was not the Roman type, evolved from the 'republican' fiction of Augustus. The German king or chief had been elected of old by the assembly of freemen, who raised him on a shield, thus acclaiming him their leader. A king of strong character, sprung from a famous family such as the Amal, Balthid, or Meroving, could browbeat the circle of stubborn warriors, and with successful warfare or invasion his power increased. When Alaric, Gaiseric, and Theoderic led bands of mixed races into Roman territory, their rule ceased to be national, and became a personal lordship, resting on a military basis. The assembly disappeared; the racial aristocracy of lesser chiefs gave way to a new nobility of service, gathered round the king's person as seneschal, marshal, constable, or ruling the districts of his realm as counts (*comites*), holding both civil and military authority. This primitive system was very different from the Roman hierarchy of officials. Any Frankish courtier, for instance, could be called upon to undertake special missions. The Roman financial system survived in part, even in the Vandal kingdom. Indirect taxes remained—tolls on bridges and ferries, harbour dues and the like—and the Roman population continued to pay income-tax as long as the registers were kept. But the Germans did not understand direct taxation. It was not justified by their political system, as we see from the Franks. The king was absolute: the realm was his private property, inheritable by his heirs; its revenues went to his 'hoard'. He owed no duties to his subjects; there were no public services to be paid for. Viewed in this light, taxation was simply impious exaction, carried out usually by armed forces. When the king had an access of piety or a dangerous illness, the bishops would beseech him to save his soul by burning the accounts.

Another legacy of the old system of *hospitium* was that Germans and Romans continued to be subject to their own laws.[1] The inconvenience was, however, lessened by a certain degree of compromise. In the more Romanized kingdoms of Visigoths and Burgundians, the Teutonic law code had borrowed much from the Roman legislation; in the Frankish realm the Salic law, utterly different from the Roman, became general in the districts whose population was predominantly Teuton.

The main principle of German law was the superseding of the old family blood-feuds by the establishment of the 'King's Peace'. For this purpose a detailed tariff of compensation fees was laid down. Each individual had his *wergild* (price of a man), varying with his age and status, which was paid to his relatives by the man who killed him. Every finger had its price; each wound was carefully estimated. The Salic law is especially comprehensive; in thefts of cattle or pigs, the age and condition of the animal, the place and circumstances of the act, are all specified. These compositions are distinct from the penalty, and serve only to prevent the matter from developing into a feud. The importance of the family as a social unit is shown also in the most famous provision of Salic law, which bars the inheritance of females to an estate; the land is thus divided among the sons, but does not pass out of the family.

The amount of the *wergild* gives valuable information about the organization of Frank society. The courtier's *wergild* (600 *solidi*) was three times that of the free warrior; that of the free Roman (of all classes) was half the free Frank's, and equalled that of the Frankish *laeti*, a dependent class midway between freemen and slaves, corresponding in some ways to the Roman *coloni*, whose *wergild* was, however, less than theirs. The more skilful unfree workers, such as goldsmiths, had a higher *wergild* than the common labourers. The position of the Roman is significant of his degradation. But he could improve his standing

[1] Cf. p. 249.

by entering the king's service, as was done by many Gallo-Roman nobles.

It is probable that the full force of the invasion was confined to Belgium and northern France. The heart of the Frankish kingdom lay north and east of the Loire, and included the cities of Orleans, Paris, Rheims, Soissons, Cambrai, Cologne. One may picture this country as dotted with villages and farmsteads, groups of low, thatched houses and barns, of wood or wattle-and-daub, separated by a palisade from the gardens, orchards, meadow and ploughland. Practically all our modern meats, fruit and vegetables were known, as we see from the treatise on diet which Anthimus, a Byzantine doctor, composed for Clovis, to whom he had been sent by Theoderic the Great. Bacon and hard boiled eggs are favourite dishes. The latter are not recommended. Fresh cheese is good, but a man who eats it when old and hard 'needs no other poison'. Fish, poultry, and game, meat garnished with vegetables, sauces of wine and honey, preparations of milk, beer, and mead are mentioned. Agriculture had made progress. Besides hand-querns, big ox-driven mills were used and the Roman water-mill was becoming known. There was little commerce in this region; foreign imports were confined to luxuries, such as ivories, jewels, cloves, pepper, dates, and figs. The ruling class lived mainly in the country; over the narrow streets of the walled towns the bishops held sway, and gave staunch support to Clovis's régime. In return, rich gifts were made to the Church. Clovis and his sons built abbeys in Paris. Nicetius, bishop of Trèves, was able to bring Italian workmen to restore, somewhat shoddily, the old basilican church. Limestone pillars, their capitals carved with masks, replaced the Corinthian columns of granite, which had burst when the city was burnt by the Franks. Walls were painted to imitate the former marble facing. Other churches, however, were resplendent with mosaic, gilding and stained glass. In 470 the basilica which covered the tomb of St. Martin of Tours, a famous centre of pilgrimage, was rebuilt with a hemi-cyclic choir, modelled on the pilgrim shrines of the East, such as the Holy Sepulchre at Jerusalem. This form was to develop into the *chevets* of the Romanesque and Gothic cathedrals of France. Eastern influence—that of the Graeco-Sarmatian art of the Crimean region with its stylized animal forms, its dark glowing jewels or glass cubes set in gold filigree—is apparent also in the ornaments of Goths and Franks. Sidonius shows us a brilliant picture of a young Frankish noble and his escort in festal garb. Their striped, close-fitting tunics are covered by green cloaks with purple borders, and skin mantles over these; they have bare knees and skin boots; their horse-trappings glitter with jewels, and with baldrics, swords, throwing-axes, spears, and flashing shields with gold bosses and silver rims they march behind the prince, who is conspicuous in 'flame-red mantle, with much glint of ruddy gold and gleam of snowy silken tunic, and his fair hair, red cheeks and white skin according with the hues of his equipment'.[1]

Sidonius Apollinaris, Gallo-Roman noble, politician and poet, who later became bishop of Clermont in the Auvergne, is our chief authority for the conditions of southern Gaul at this time. It is a strange scene, a meeting-place of ancient and medieval manners. A few nobles had taken refuge in rock-perched castles, but most still lived in huge country-houses, spending their days, as in Hadrian's time, in their libraries, baths, ball-games, hunting or in rounds of visits to friends. They dine amid purple hangings, clouds of incense, massive silver plate, rose-wreathed cups, and are entertained by cithara, flute, and Corinthian dancing-girls. Elegant poems and letters are exchanged, in which the 'skin-clad' barbarians, in whose kingdoms they lived, are sedulously ignored. But Rome's degradation cannot be concealed. One may lampoon, in secret, the gross Burgundians or the manners of the Visigoth court, but in public one must pay them fulsome flattery. Some even, despairing of Rome, revived dreams of Gallic separatism, and put their faith in the semi-Romanized Burgundians and Visigoths. With a great wealth of detail, all the varied life of South Gaul passes before us. The Visigoth court, its tall king, his hunting, meals, devotions; Saxon, Herul, Frankish types; the Gallo-Roman squirearchy, literary, bucolic, or pious; the bishop, the monk, the merchant; vineyards and farms, inns, travellers and robbers, politics and epigrams, land-

---

[1] Mr. O. M. Dalton's translation.

a. MEROVINGIAN SCULPTURE. GRENOBLE

b. CAROLINGIAN ARCHITECTURE. LORSCH

III

BARBARIAN JEWELLERY

scapes, family scenes. Sidonius did not live to see the conquests of Clovis, but it is probable, from other evidence, that they did not produce radical changes here. Roman civilization was not rooted out; the barbarian, in childish admiration, plucked at the frail flower, already long past its bloom; and it withered in his grasp.

The Italian kingdom of Theoderic stands apart from those of the other German rulers. It is a unique attempt to use the system of *hospitium* to preserve Roman civilization entire. 'My kingdom', he wrote to the Emperor Anastasius, 'is an imitation of yours.' His own position was anomalous. He was king of his own followers, Ostrogoth and others. Over the Roman population of Italy he ruled, apparently, as the Emperor's vice-regent, holding the titles of *magister militum* and *patricius*, as Stilicho, Ricimer, or Odoacer had done. Theoderic avoided an explicit statement of this position; it would have admitted the right of the Emperor to control and even depose him, as a mere temporary official. But he acted in accordance with the theory. He struck no coins in his own name; his laws were *edicta* applicable only to the Italian provinces. The Emperor alone might place his head upon the coins, and make *leges* which held good throughout the Empire. The Roman civil service remained intact; at the Court were no seneschals or marshals, but praetorian prefect, *magister officiorum*, and the rest. The Senate continued to sit at Rome and was specially honoured by Theoderic. The provinces were governed and taxed, as before, by Roman officials. There was a deep cleft between Goth and Roman, military and civil. Inter-marriage was forbidden. The two sections met only at the top, in the person of Theoderic, who was himself a Roman citizen, though he could not confer this status on another. The Goths were subject to district *comites*, as in the other German kingdoms. New officials, the *saiones*, were created to protect the Romans from oppression by Goths, and inquire into abuses as the *agentes in rebus* had formerly done.

The 'Edict of Theoderic' gives a clear picture of his policy. It is a law code taken almost entirely from Roman legislation, with a few significant innovations. Special efforts are made, as in the

Salic law, to replace family blood feuds by recourse to legal expedients. The privileged position of the landowners is maintained, but so are the measures against oppression of the *coloni*. The shortage of labour is shown in the severe laws against kidnapping. The lower classes benefited indirectly, not only from the peace and order of Theoderic's strong rule ('the town gates were never shut!' exclaims an admiring contemporary), but also by the strict regulation of the markets and the control of food prices. Since it was to his interest to feed the army cheaply, profiteering by the landowners was checked, and very low prices prevailed. The general purpose of the Edict is conservative. There are no theories behind it. Roman civilization is to be preserved for ever, unchanging, safe within the ring of Gothic spears.

Theoderic was fortunate in his panegyrist, Cassiodorus, who presents his master's policy in rolling phrases which, though absurdly grandiose and pedantic, achieve occasionally a real eloquence, and display always a generous and honest spirit. But the measures speak for themselves. Taxes were remitted, Roman citizens ransomed from the Burgundian raiders. Frontier castles were fortified. Walls, aqueducts, and theatres in Rome, Ravenna, Verona, and other towns were restored. The 'bread and circuses' of the capital were zealously maintained. A magnificent palace, several churches, and a remarkable mausoleum were constructed at Ravenna, where the Court of Theoderic marked the centre of a strong government. It was also the mediator of culture, or at least of the toys of civilization, to the German kingdoms. Gundobad of Burgundy received a water-clock, while to Clovis were sent, with suitable compliments, a musician and a Byzantine doctor. Several poets from north Italy went to seek their fortunes at the courts of Gaul. A minor literary renaissance took place. One centre was Milan, whose grammar schools, attended even by boys from Gaul, flourished under the auspices of Bishop Laurence. Here, and at Ravenna, were the Romans who, like Cassiodorus and Ennodius, supported the Gothic régime. The opposition was to be found at Rome. The famous schools of the capital, with their long traditions and endowed professorships, were the stronghold of the ancient senatorial houses and the old learning. Many of these families had connexions with Constantinople; and Theoderic came later to suspect intrigues in that quarter against Arian and Gothic rule.

The greatest name here is Boethius, one of those rare figures who sum up in themselves all the knowledge of their time. Scientist, theologian, philosopher, and poet, he was consul at the age of thirty, and performed important services for Theoderic. But perhaps he represents his age most truly in the contrast between the appearance and the reality of his position. In a spiteful epigram, 'On Boethius girt with a sword', Ennodius brings out the inner contradiction between the high claims of the 'Roman' party and the hard actuality of Gothic supremacy in arms. And in his writings Boethius, master of the quadrivium, the 'realist' commentator on Aristotle and Porphyry, the lover of definitions and distinctions, the subtle theologian, appears not as the 'last of the Romans', but as the prototype of the medieval schoolmen. His most famous work, the *Consolatio Philosophiae*, was translated into English by King Alfred, and it influenced, as much as any other book, the thought of the Middle Ages. It was composed in prison. Theoderic saw, in the readiness of the nobles to accept the Emperor Justin's anti-Arian decrees, the ruin of his life-work. Unbalanced by illness and suspicion, he caused Boethius to be put to death with cruel tortures. He was regarded as a martyr by the Catholics, though it is truer to call him a martyr for the senatorial cause. For a certain antagonism existed between the Vatican party, with its plebeian notaries, who were now beginning to formulate the well-known curial style and methods, and the small circle of noble families attached by birth and education to older and more fastidious ideals.

The foreign policy of Theoderic falls into two periods; the division is marked by the rise of Clovis. His first plan was to secure the Italian frontiers by a series of alliances with the German kingdoms of the West. These Arian, barbaric powers had common problems in their orthodox Roman subjects, and their relations with their nominal overlord the Emperor. Theoderic's aim was to preserve a balance of power among these rulers, and to act as mediator between them and Constantinople. In this way he could assure himself the hegemony of the German kingdoms, and, while making himself useful to the Emperor, form a solid resistance to any orthodox or Imperial schemes for *reconquista* which might be brewing at Byzantium. (He had not forgotten the fall of his predecessor Odoacer.) Accordingly, he himself wedded the sister of Clovis; one of his daughters was given to Alaric II, the Visigoth king, another to Sigismund, prince of Burgundy. His sister married Thrasamund, king of the Vandals, thus removing the menace to southern Italy. The Danube region, through which Byzantine troops might pass, was made safe by driving the Gepids from Sirmium, the strategic centre.

The whole intricate structure was shattered at a blow, when in 507 Clovis and the Burgundians overthrew the Visigoths on the field of Vouglé.[1] All the arts of Theoderic, which had been used to warn Alaric of his danger, and isolate Burgundy, the buffer-state, were now of no avail. A great Catholic power, supported apparently by Constantinople, was supreme in Gaul, and had driven a wedge between the Arian states. At all costs it must be prevented from reaching the Mediterranean. Theoderic marches into Gaul and wrests Provence from the Burgundians. He becomes regent for his grandson, the Visigoth heir to Spain. New alliances are made with the Thuringians, powerful German neighbours of the Franks, and with the Heruls on the Danube. The Alpine fortresses are strengthened. The policy of harmony of interests is replaced by that of opposing powers. But it seems no less successful. Clovis dies in 511; and the relations with Constantinople, changing constantly with the varying winds of Papal claims, doctrinal issues, senatorial intrigues, and Imperial ambitions, appear to be set fair when Justin succeeds Anastasius (518). Theoderic had married yet another daughter, Amalasuntha, to Eutharic, a Goth of royal blood, and the succession seemed assured when Justin formally adopted him, and became his colleague in the consulship. Cassiodorus ends his chronicle with the gay festivities with which the occasion was celebrated in Rome. Yet before Theoderic died, storm-clouds had gathered on the horizon. Burgundy, under a Catholic ruler, had played into the hands of Clovis, and was making overtures to Byzantium. The conflict of Frank and Ostrogoth drew nearer as the buffer-state weakened. The Heruls were now *foederati* of the Empire,

[1] Cf. p. 64.

and menaced the north-east frontier. The Vandals, a far more dangerous foe, had become hostile. The schism between Rome and Constantinople being healed, Pope and nobles were united in support of the Emperor. The days of Ostrogothic rule were numbered, and Theoderic's ruthless measures to suppress sedition had no other effect than to set, beside the German hero of the *Dietrich*-saga, the complementary figure of Roman folk-tale and hagiology, Theoderic the monstrous persecutor, haunted by his victims at the hour of death, and hurled by their avenging hands into the volcanic fires of Hell.

Soon after A.D. 340 some of the Goths living near the mouth of the Danube were converted to Christianity by Ulfilas, whose grandparents had been carried off from Cappadocia in a raid, and whose remarkable work earned him the title of 'The Apostle of the Goths'. He translated the Bible into their language, but left out the Book of Kings; tales of Hebrew warfare were too exciting for these passionate people. Fierce opposition was at first encountered, perhaps owing to his pacific presentation of Christianity, but the Gospel spread rapidly, and passed westwards with the invading tribes into Italy, Gaul, Spain, and Africa. Ulfilas had been an Arian, and this heresy accordingly became the general form of German Christianity, though it had practically vanished from the Empire. The political consequences of this fact were enormous; it drove a deeper wedge than race or culture between Roman and Barbarian. Arianism itself, now identified with German civilization, underwent certain changes. It had begun as a theological difference, born of Trinitarian controversy. On barbarian soil it developed into a dislike of dogma, which was, no doubt, fostered by incomprehension of Greek subtlety, itself the fruit of a thousand-year-old tradition of dialectic; and this dislike of dogma issued in a return to the simpler pre-Nicene beliefs. Not only the Scriptures but also, to some extent, the Church services were rendered in the Gothic tongue, and it is probable that the organization of the Arian churches, cut off as they were from Catholic influence by the taint of heresy, as well as by the difference of race, was affected by German custom, while the isolation of the individual churches may also be ascribed to the pressure of constitutional habit. Within the Empire, a parallel is afforded by the Catholic hierarchy of patriarchs and bishops, which was largely based on the Roman system of provincial administration. Memories of the old heathen inter-tribal associations and local priesthoods may well have played their part in turning the Arian churches in each German kingdom into a kind of national institution, bounded by the frontiers of its people, subject to its king, and narrowly jealous of its national traditions.

Catholic subjects of the German kings were treated with tolerance; no organized attempts at conversion were thought necessary, owing to the complete separation of the German and Roman populations. A feeling existed that a man's creed should be that of his nation; and the saying of Theoderic is well known: 'We cannot enjoin religion; for no one can be forced to believe against his will.' Religion, however, could not be separated from politics, and on political grounds measures of repression were applied in all the kingdoms, when attempts were made by the Romans to conspire with their fellow Catholics, in or outside the realm, for the purpose of restoring Imperial rule, or of aiding the conquests of a Catholic ruler like Clovis. Suspicion of treachery and racial antipathy often sharpened these measures into real persecution, and, among the Vandals, Africa added the flames of religious fanaticism, though the effects of this must not be exaggerated. As long as Gaiseric lived there was no religious persecution, though hardship naturally arose from the conditions of Vandal conquest. Gaiseric's aim had been to create a central nucleus of his people, grouped round Carthage, which should preserve the national character.[1] The neighbouring Romans were therefore driven out from their properties, which became 'Vandal lots'; the Catholic clergy were likewise expelled from the district, in order that no Romanizing influence might creep in. Church property fell to the Arians. It was only in 483, under Huneric, the impossible son of Gaiseric, that systematic persecution of the Catholics, starting in the district round Carthage, spread to the

[1] For similar nuclei, cf. the Goths of Odoacer and Theoderic round Ravenna, Verona (Dietrich of Bern, in the saga, is Theoderic of Verona) and the north Italian towns; the Franks in north-east France and the Sueves in Galicia.

whole kingdom, and for all its intensity it ended with the king's death in the following year.

Among the Visigoths the political issue is alone considered. Euric, when extending his kingdom over Auvergne, found it necessary to imprison Sidonius, bishop of Clermont, the leader of the Gallo-Roman aristocracy; but it was not a rigorous confinement, and the chief annoyance appears to have been the endless gossip of two old crones outside his prison window. Smoking churches and ruined grass-grown altars might mark the trail of the invaders, but after the first onset, whether of Frank or Goth, the Roman population in Gaul, as elsewhere, was left undisturbed. The appearance of Clovis, a Catholic German, changed the whole order of things. The latent opposition between Arian and Catholic in the two great kingdoms of Visigoths and Burgundians now became evident. In Catholicism were centred all the traditions of Rome and her civilization. It was an international force, the last link with the Imperial capitals, headed by many of the senatorial families of Gaul; in its hands lay the organization for relieving famine or poverty. Against this, the Arian national churches of a ruling minority of barbarians, with their German spirit and decentralized system, could not finally prevail.

Parallel intrigues were carried on in both kingdoms by the Catholic clergy to further the supremacy of the Franks. Caesarius, bishop of Arles, scholar and statesman, played a great part in the events which centred round the famous siege of Arles, with its Visigoth garrison, by the combined forces of Burgundians and Franks. Suspected of an attempt to betray the city to Burgundy, he was exiled for a time. The city was actually taken by the Ostrogoths, and Caesarius so far failed in his purpose; but after the Visigoth defeat at Vouglé, it was only a matter of time before the whole of France acknowledged the mastery of Clovis. In Burgundy the most important see was likewise occupied by a consummate diplomat, Avitus of Vienne. Although carrying on close correspondence with Clovis, he contrived to stand well with Gundobad the Burgundian king, who treated him and the Catholics with great generosity; but regarding the interests of his Church as supreme, Avitus did not hesitate to work for the Frankish cause. The main facts may be given. Clovis had first sought to conquer Burgundy (500) by supporting the rebellion of Gundobad's brother; this had failed, owing partly to Visigoth support of Gundobad. Avitus, however, possessed overwhelming influence at the Burgundian Court, where most of the royal family were already Catholics, and Gundobad was induced to reverse his policy, and join the Frankish Catholic cause, deserting the system of alliances between the German Arian kingdoms which Theoderic the Ostrogoth had so carefully organized. This was the critical point in the downfall of Burgundy. Franks and Burgundians together overthrew the Visigoth kingdom at Vouglé; but by the intervention of Theoderic, who secured the Riviera coast,[1] Burgundy, the catspaw, lost almost all her increase of territory, while the Franks cynically divided the spoils with the Ostrogoths. Under the weak and pious Sigismund, Burgundy became officially Catholic, and the influence of Avitus and his fellow churchmen was supreme. When Sigismund murdered his own son, whose mother had been niece of Theoderic, an open breach with the Ostrogoths took place. The Franks at once seized the opportunity and invaded Burgundy. Sigismund was defeated, and his retirement to a monastery did not save him or his family from death. They were thrown into a well by the invaders. His brother Godomer succeeded for a time in repelling the Franks; with great energy and determination he reorganized the army and finances, checked the Catholic intrigues, and even succeeded in reversing Gundobad's disastrous orientation of Burgundian policy by allying himself with the Ostrogoths. But Theoderic was dead, and his kingdom in confusion. Visigoth power had vanished from France and there was nothing to stay the Frankish advance. In 532 the successors of Clovis once more attacked, and, fighting to the last, Burgundy went down before the onslaught of the victorious Catholics. The efforts of Avitus and Caesarius had succeeded, and the concessions made to their Catholic subjects had not appreciably delayed the ruin of the Arian kingdoms in Gaul. The Catholic problem continued to occupy the Visigoth rulers of Spain until Recared (586–601) united his subjects and secured his frontiers by adopting the orthodox faith.

In Gaul Clovis crowned his great work by the organization of a

[1] Cf. p. 72.

national church, which combined the political advantages of the Arian and Catholic systems. It was controlled by the king; its hierarchy gave valuable support to his régime; its frontiers were co-extensive with his own; the metropolitan at Arles, though acknowledged as the Papal representative, was not allowed more than an honorary position. At the same time the advantages of communication with Rome and Byzantium were assured; there was nothing to fear from Catholic intrigues; and (an important consideration) Clovis had not, like other German rulers, the Vandals especially, to guard against the submergence of national individuality by a Roman population, stronger both in numbers and culture. North of the Loire his Franks were very numerous; fresh reservoirs of Teutonic resources were at hand across the Rhine; and with the subjection of the Alamans the realm of Clovis received a German character, balancing the effect of the Gallo-Roman population of his latest acquisitions.

The relations of Theoderic to his Catholic subjects were complicated by the conditions of the Papacy, and especially by two schisms, one external and one internal, which affected his own attitude not only to the Romans but also to Constantinople. Broadly speaking, three conflicting claims were at work; the claim of the Pope not only to the primacy of the Apostolic Sees, but to universal authority in matters of dogma; the claim of the Byzantine patriarch to equality with Rome, and priority to the other patriarchates of the East; the claim of the Emperor to universal dominion. The inevitable clash of these claims resulted in schism between Rome and Constantinople, which lasted from 481 to 518. Theoderic naturally favoured the breach, which had given him the support of the Papacy. His influence was further increased when the papal elections produced rival candidates, each appealing to the Arian king for his support. The election of Symmachus, who was opposed to reconciliation with Byzantium, may have been due to the influence of Theoderic, but formally the choice was free, and in fact the Church enjoyed far more liberty under Theoderic than under a Clovis or Justinian.

So long as the heretical Anastasius reigned, Pope and Senate were, on the whole, united in their opposition to Byzantium. The accession of Justin in 518 and the return to power of the orthodox party produced a movement for reunion at Rome. The interests of Pope, Senate, and Ostrogoth were still identical, for Theoderic hoped for the recognition, long refused by Anastasius, of his son Eutharic as the successor to the lordship of Italy. His own position would thereby be greatly strengthened. This recognition was duly secured, and the schism ended. But all was not well. Eutharic died shortly afterwards. Justin renewed the measures against the Arian heretics—a direct blow at the Gothic kingdom. The *rapprochement* between the nobles of Rome and Byzantium became a thought too close for Theoderic's liking. His last years were clouded with suspicion and cruelty, though apart from the execution of the senators, Symmachus[1] and Boethius, no organized persecution either of Romans or Catholics was set on foot.

[1] This Symmachus, the father-in-law of Boethius, must be distinguished from the Bishop of Rome, who bore the same name, and also from the fourth-century senator, leader of the pagan opposition, patron of Augustine, and friend of Ambrose.

PART II

THE TRIUMPH OF JUSTINIAN

IV

CONSTANTINOPLE

THE centre of Constantinople was the Augusteum, a spacious marble-paved square, which in general effect must have resembled the Piazza San Marco at Venice. On the north side rose the dome of St. Sophia; on the east were the porticoes of the Senate House, while on the south side a low building with heavy iron gates formed the entrance to the Palace. Beyond this stood the lofty wall of the Kathisma, a structure whose upper stories, looking out on the Hippodrome on the opposite side, formed a royal box for the Emperor, and communicated directly with the palace buildings by galleries and a spiral staircase. In the square, besides the Milestone, a vaulted monument from which started all the roads of the Empire, stood a tall bronze column, bearing a colossal equestrian statue of Justinian, in full armour, holding the orb of the universe, his hand stretched towards the East, as if commanding the barbarians of Asia not to pass their frontiers. The Mesê, or Middle Street, lined with arcades, statues, and sumptuous palaces, led westwards from this square along the peninsula to the Golden Gate, a fortified entrance, after the Roman style, in the massive walls which ran across the isthmus.

Seen from the Bosporus the vast palace enclosure, which included the slopes between the Augusteum and the shore, was dotted with groups of gilded domes, white pavilions, baths, terraces, and chapels, set among trees and fountains, and connected by flights of marble steps.

The main entrance to the Palace led from the Augusteum to a large domed hall, decorated with mosaics displaying the wars and triumphs of Justinian. Behind it was the throne-room, and stairs led up from this to the palace of Daphne, with its airy terraces and chambers looking out across the blue waters to the snowy summits of the Bithynian mountains.

Several other Imperial residences existed, not only in this quarter, but outside the city, and on the Asiatic shore.

The group formed by palace, square, cathedral, and Hippodrome was the setting for many pageants and crises in the life of the capital. On New Year's Day, if the Emperor had deigned to accept the consulship, they saw the house-fronts gay with carpets, silken streamers waving from poles, the square filled with wooden hustings, crowded by the ranks of the city corporations and circus factions. Within the palace the Emperor received the homage of the Senate and the panegyrics of the orators, bestowing in return baskets full of gold pieces, silver cups, or ivory diptychs carved with his portrait. Then the gates opened, and marshalled by heralds the long procession of functionaries, courtiers, and guards filed across the square into the cathedral, where, in a blaze of candles, the Emperor offered his gifts at the high altar and received benediction, before proceeding in triumph to the Capitol. This was but one of many such ceremonies. Often they were confined to the Court, as when the Emperor held his solemn audiences (*silentia*) to confer dignities or promotion, or received Caucasian and Herul princes, or envoys from Persia and Abyssinia. Then the full splendour of Byzantine ceremonial was displayed. The little group of foreigners, guided by permanent officials appointed for this purpose, moved slowly between the lines of tall soldiers, through serried rows of golden shields and helmets, scarlet plumes and flashing spears, till they halted before the ivory doors of the entrance-chamber. A long wait ensued. Suddenly the curtains were flung back, and a brilliant tableau was revealed—the Emperor enthroned between the two Victories surrounded by white-clad guards with gold collars, the senators and high officials in their silk robes ranged about him. After a threefold prostration, the leader of the embassy was permitted to present his gifts to the Emperor before being dismissed with a few gracious words. Until the end of their stay the envoys would be sumptuously entertained, and shown carefully the more impressive sights of the city.

If St. Sophia, it has been said, belonged to God, and the Palace to the Emperor, the Hippodrome was the property of the people.

It formed the axis of Byzantine life, even as its orientation had determined that of both church and palace. Here the last liberties of the Roman people were expressed in the shouts of the circus factions, demanding from their ruler the redress of grievances or the downfall of an unpopular minister. Here the conquered Vandals of Africa, or in later times the Mahometan Arabs, were led round in triumph, and forced to prostrate themselves before the Emperor, while the Hippodrome rang with hosannas and songs of victory. Here, too, on occasion, took place the execution or mutilation of enemies of the state.

The central area of the Hippodrome, divided down the middle by a row of obelisks and columns, was surrounded by rising tiers of white marble seats, holding more than 60,000 spectators. At the far end the huge curving structure was raised upon massive arcades above the lower slopes. In the centre of the long south side stood the Kathisma, the lofty building on which the Emperor ventured forth from his palace, as on a projecting pier, into the angry sea of the populace. The Imperial box, with its adjoining rooms, was raised high above the reach of stones or storming mobs.[1] Below it, on a balcony, were guards and musicians. The rectilinear end, which was both goal and starting-point for the charioteers, was formed by tiers of stone boxes, occupied by the aristocracy of Byzantium. Below were the chambers, fitted with barriers, from which the chariots burst forth down the course, wheeling sharply round the *meta*—the monument which marked its farther end—to dash back along the other side of the central axis, or *spina*, under the shouting ranks of frantic onlookers.

The open spaces and arcades round the Hippodrome were filled with obelisks and famous statues, transferred from Rome, or torn from the cities of Greece, Egypt, and Asia Minor, whose glory they had been. Some of these were the vulgar colossi beloved of the late Empire; some were the dignified equestrian figures of Roman Emperors. Others were of the purest Hellenic style, a few the actual handiwork of such sculptors as Phidias and Lysippus. The superstitious populace of the Middle Ages gave them magic powers, and read the secrets of the future in the

---

[1] It could, however, be entered by stairs from the Hippodrome, as the Nika Riot shows.

hieroglyphics of the Egyptian stelae. The Frankish crusaders
melted down the bronze for coin; but one of them was moved
with compassion for the melancholy, dreaming Hercules and the
loveliness of Helen's beauty. 'Her mouth, half-open like a flower,
seemed to speak, her enchanting smile ravished the soul of him
who beheld it. But who could portray her deep eyes, the curve
of her brow, the grace of her delicious body?'[1]

From the upper porticoes of the Hippodrome the eye ranged
over the clear waters of the Sea of Marmora on the south, covered
with the sails of the shipping of three continents, and beyond
them the groves and country houses and the far mountains of
Asia Minor; eastward lay the cupolas and terraced gardens of the
Palace, the narrow strait and the houses and churches on its
farther side, and in the foreground the Augusteum, backed by
the great dome of St. Sophia. To the north the roads and squares,
the aqueducts and triumphal arches of the city, the shining roofs
of countless churches, and high bronze pillars with spiral friezes,
rising above the serried housetops, led the eye onwards to the
line of square towers and massive walls, and the open country
that lay beyond.

All these attractions, however, counted for nothing beside the
frenzy of the contest between Greens and Blues. The circus
parties were an inheritance from the Early Empire; they were
now, in every great city of the East, the most important fact in the
lives of its excitable populace. Every citizen was a member of one
of the factions, which sat on opposite sides of the Hippodrome,
wearing their blue or green colours, praying passionately to the
saints for the victory of their party, or shrieking insults at the
opposing ranks. All the civic patriotism, all the local loyalties of
race and class, all the venom which had in earlier days fomented
the Greek *staseis*, those internecine party-struggles of the City
State, now flowed into this curious channel. Even the arts were
affected; statues and epigrams celebrated the beauty and prowess
of those darlings of the public, the charioteers. The cosmopolitan
mobs of Antioch or Constantinople cared less for the victory of
Roman arms on distant frontiers than for the triumph of Green
or Blue. It is difficult to trace any real political or religious

[1] Nicetas of Chones, 864.

antagonism behind the strife of parties. Accusations of heresy and treachery, of witchcraft or immorality, were scattered indiscriminately by both sides; they were merely the current coin of Byzantine abuse. But the dangerous freemasonry which linked up the Blue or Green parties of the great cities of the Empire, and the passions aroused by the chariot-races, which might culminate in a sudden riot, if not a revolution, made the circus factions a powerful force in politics. In the interests of the State careful organization was necessary. At the head of each party were numerous officials, elected by a sort of Jockey Club, composed of some hundreds of wealthy men, whose subscriptions supported the training establishments, and in addition to the racing provided the bear-baiting and acrobats for the intervals. These officials had special privileges and duties in the Court ceremonies, especially those connected with Imperial births and marriages, and were responsible also for keeping order in the Hippodrome. Their followers formed a guard of honour in State processions, and the bands of the citizen militia, which policed the capital and defended the various portions of the walls allotted to them, were closely connected with the party organizations. The strangest feature of all, though not without Roman precedent, is that the Emperor himself belonged to a faction; and the result was that while one party was favoured, and allowed to murder or terrorize its opponents, or to form bands of Mohocks, fantastically dressed, whose outrages made the streets of the capital unsafe, in the other were concentrated, at a crisis, all the elements of opposition to the reigning house, personal or religious, racial or dynastic, kindled, perhaps, by the final sparks of Greek democracy, flickering out in a world which knew only absolutism.

Anastasius had favoured the Greens, but Justin and Justinian reversed this policy. While his position was still uncertain, Justinian's partiality for the Blues had gone to all lengths, and even the courts of justice had been corrupted by party feeling. By the beginning of 532 he felt more secure, and orders were issued to the great cities that disorders of either faction should be put down. The City Prefect of Byzantium had consequently decreed the execution of seven Greens and Blues, convicted of murder in a recent disturbance. Unfortunately the rope broke twice; two of the condemned men were rescued by an indignant crowd, and both parties petitioned the Emperor for a reprieve. When this was refused, the parties united, and with the watchword *nika* (conquer!) the Green-Blues began the famous rising which is known as the Nika Riot.

In a few days the movement developed a more serious character. The buildings round the Augusteum were set on fire. The country folk, enraged by ruinous taxation, joined in the fray, and the faction riot became a popular rising. Demand was made for the deposition of the three most unpopular ministers. Alarmed at the disorder, Justinian complied, and even appeared in person in the Kathisma, swearing on the Gospels to grant redress and amnesty; but it was too late. He retired into the Palace, followed by gibes and insults. The popular rising had now become a revolution. Various nobles, who had always hated the upstart house of Justin, were backing the rioters, and a nephew of Anastasius was crowned Emperor, against his will, and conducted to the Kathisma by the excited mob which swarmed into the Hippodrome. The position of the real Emperor, besieged in his Palace, seemed desperate. The loyalty of the senators, apart from his own creatures, was doubtful; the guards were wavering, and he could count only on the personal retainers and barbarian troops of two of his generals. A hurried council took place, and Justinian prepared for flight. The situation was saved by Theodora, whose famous speech, even in the Thucydidean garb which Procopius has given to it, has an authentic ring. 'Though safety should lie only in flight, yet will I not flee. Those who have worn a crown should never survive its loss. Never will I live to see the day when men no longer hail me as Empress. Escape then, if you will, Caesar; you have money; the ships await you; the sea is unguarded. As for me, I stay. I hold with the old proverb which declares that the purple is a fair winding-sheet.'

Vigorous action followed. The Blues were to be bribed to desert the Greens; meanwhile the two loyal generals had forced their way into the Hippodrome by different gates, and an appalling massacre ensued. More than 30,000 dead were left lying there when night ended the slaughter.

The unhappy nephews of Anastasius were promptly put to

death—Justinian was too frightened to spare them—and several of the nobles were banished. The measures taken, though not vindictive, were sufficient to ensure that there should be no repetition, either from senators or circus factions, of the activities which had so nearly deprived the ruler of his throne. While his position was thus actually strengthened, on the ashes of the ruined quarter extending from the Forum of Constantine to the Palace Gates there rose a magnificent series of buildings, crowned by the great church which, together with the legislative code which bears his name, constitutes the most lasting monument of Justinian.

Saint Sophia, the Church of the Holy Wisdom, has been acknowledged ever since that day to be, in the words of Sir John Mandeville, 'the fairest church in all the world'. Procopius rises to its description in a noble passage, and Paul the Silentiary, a distinguished courtier and poet, in the hexameters composed for the reopening of the edifice by Justinian, has fused poetic imagery and exact architectural detail into a glowing picture. Ethereal lightness was the main impression given by the building. The dome appeared to be 'hung from the sky', and all the parts were 'surprisingly joined to one another in the air, suspended one from another, and resting only on that which is next to them'. This effect was produced by the daring semi-domes which supported the great central cupola on east and west, and by the admirable proportions of the whole, and was increased by the light and sunshine poured into the church through forty windows in the dome, and by the soft radiance of the many-coloured marbles which clothed the walls and floor. Cloistered courts and fountains formed the approach. When the double narthex, with its nine doors, was passed, the whole length of the building became visible. The square central space, with its dome resting on four massive piers rising 'like sheer cliffs', was flanked by the two-storeyed arcades behind which were the seats of the members of the Court, the upper storey, with delicate latticed grills, being reserved for women. Beyond this space stood the ambo, rising like an island of ivory and silver from swirling seas of marble, streaked with deep green or glowing red, powdered with gold stars, or splashed with milky streams on glittering black, or 'like blue cornflowers in grass, with here and there a drift of fallen snow'. The eastern end was formed of three apses; the central one contained the sanctuary, shut off by a great silver iconostasis, on which stood figures of martyrs and pairs of winged angels with bowed heads. The altar was of pure gold, hung with silken figured curtains, and both the pyramidal ciborium which surmounted it and the curving tribunes beyond it for the patriarch and his clergy shone with silver, elaborately worked. At night, hundreds of perfumed lamps, in clusters, or shaped to resemble silver ships or crowns, lit up every part, and shone even through the openings in the dome, forming a beacon for the sailor entering the adverse currents of the Hellespont, and anxiously 'awaiting with taut forestay the onslaught of a storm from Africa'.

In St. Sophia purely Christian architecture reaches its highest point; the abstract theology of the East has found its incarnation in stone. 'Whoever enters there to worship perceives at once that it is not by any human strength or skill, but by the favour of God, that this whole work has been perfected. The mind rises sublime to commune with God, feeling that he cannot be far off, but must especially love to dwell in the place which he has chosen.'

As its dome, 'like a watch-tower', rose high above the city, so 'The Great Church' overshadowed in importance the countless other edifices which came into being at this time. Among these, the Church of the Holy Apostles, with its tombs of the Emperors, was hardly inferior to St. Sophia in lavish decoration, and is also of interest as having been the model from which St. Mark's at Venice was taken. All through the Empire, buildings of every description, many of striking and original design, were being erected—aqueducts and cisterns in Mesopotamia, stone bridges where the roads of Asia Minor crossed above the mountain torrents, baths and fountains in Syria, huge fortresses on the African frontier, walled monasteries on Mt. Sinai, and churches all round the Mediterranean, and along the Adriatic shores to Parenzo and Ravenna. Byzantine influence was, in the following century, to become predominant even at Rome, and while its architecture can be seen from the domes of Périgueux to the

a. ADORATION OF THE MAGI.　　　　*b.* DIPTYCH OF THE SYMMACHI.
SYRIAN SCHOOL　　　　　ALEXANDRIAN SCHOOL

cupolas of Kiev, from the Aix of Charlemagne to the oases of Upper Egypt, its types of ornamental motives and its typical presentation of sacred events and personages spread even farther, carried by ivories, textiles, and miniatures, to Ireland, Northumbria, and Germany.

The origins of Christian Art have been hotly debated, not without religious and patriotic bias. The question has recently taken a new form. The old antithesis of 'Orient oder Rom' has been given up, and methods of approach have altered, owing to the enormous increase of material brought forward for comparison. Broadly speaking, the changes of these centuries are seen no longer as a catastrophic flood, washing away all landmarks, but rather as the manifold interlacing tributaries and currents in a continuous stream, whose importance is to be gauged by the momentum with which they surge through old channels. The forms, no less than the spirit, of Christian Art had their sources in the East; but it was not the first appearance of Oriental influence. Nile and Orontes had for centuries past poured their waters into the Tiber. Alexandria, the centre of Hellenistic traditions of modelling, ornament, and ideal presentation of the human form, was the place of origin, for instance, of the Roman house-decoration which is reflected in the Catacombs. Antioch, representative of the realistic Semitic style, behind which lay the great traditions of the figure-sculptors of Babylon and Assyria, became prominent when Christianity was made the State religion, and Christian Art changed its character to suit the new conditions. The simple gaiety and pathos of the Catacomb frescoes, the playing Cupids, the anchor, fish, and dove, the suppliant figures and Orphic symbols of rebirth, were replaced by the awe and grandeur of historical and dogmatic scenes. Christ was no longer a graceful Greek youth, or a shepherd carrying a lamb, but a divine king ruling his Oriental Court among the clouds, or a dolorous, bearded Semitic figure, sharing the sufferings of the countless martyrs whose legends were depicted in full detail along the walls of the basilicas. Constantine's famous buildings, especially those at Jerusalem, influenced both structure and decoration of the churches which were rising in every province, and miniatures, ivories, and pilgrim 'souvenirs' disseminated through the West those types and figures, picturing, for instance, the various Apostles, the Days of Creation, or the parallels between Old and New Testaments, which formed the subject-matter of medieval art.

Behind these twin influences of Antioch and Alexandria lies a third, older and more mysterious, the importance of which it has been the great achievement of Strzgowski to display, the far-spread tradition of the Asiatic nomad cultures, with its surface patterns, its formal designs of vine-tendrils, flowers, and animals, its abstract, non-representational character. Just as the nomad-folk, suddenly appearing from the unchanging steppes of Asia at all periods of history, have left their mark upon the countries which they overran, so their artistic influence has made itself felt at the hands of Scythians, Turks, and Arabs; and at this time especially, through the medium of northern Persia,[1] it was exercised largely upon Armenia, one of the oldest seats of Christianity, with flourishing bishoprics, churches, and monasteries. Both Syrian and Coptic art were profoundly affected by these Asiatic forms, and through them the West; but they penetrated more directly by other routes. The Goths sojourned for a time in the steppes of South Russia, long enough to acquire a taste for the sombre, formal jewellery and the interlacing ornament of Iranian type which in their subsequent wanderings they spread over North Italy, West Germany, France, and Spain, where the style developed among Visigoth, Merovingian, and Lombard, and can be traced, for example, in the grotesque animals of certain Romanesque sculpture. It may be that its abstract form appealed to the kindred tastes of the northerners, just as in Ireland, which lacked a figure art, the introduction of Christianity was soon followed by the appearance of Eastern ornamental motives, which combined readily with the whorls and trumpets of Celtic patterns into the complicated designs of the Book of Kells.

The Iranian artist, if he used forms of men, animals, or plants, employed them only as constituent parts of a decorative design, as in a Persian carpet. His designs were flat; there was little or no sense of modelling or perspective, either in painting or sculpture.

---

[1] The Sasanian figure-art of the *southern* district was derived from Mesopotamian and Hellenistic sources.

Degrees of distance were represented by placing the figures in zones one above the other, and bright colours were laid side by side without gradation of tone. His ideal was a continuous pattern, marked out by opposing tints or alternating light and shade, rather than a symmetrical scheme leading the eye up to some central point. The art of the Scythians, and that of the later Turco-Mongolian peoples, have the same peculiarities. When we look at the change which came over Christian art, and contrast the cool Roman basilicas, their bare surfaces and ordered structure, their strongly moulded relief and deeply cut capitals, with the rich and glowing churches of this time, with the brilliant colouring of mosaic and fresco, the flat, sharp-edged figures of processing martyrs, the covering of every surface with arabesque designs, punctured ornament or marble lattice-work, the impost-capitals like blocks of frozen lace, it is not difficult, even without recourse to the evidence of architectural forms, of ivories and miniatures, to realize the significance of this third aspect of Byzantine Art.

The name 'Byzantine' art is justified, for the great city was at this time the meeting-place and crucible of all these influences. She was also the centre of commerce. 'Into her harbours sailed expectantly the vessels of the world's trade, and the winds themselves conspired to bring merchandise to enrich her citizens'.[1] From South Russia and the Danube came furs and hides; but it was from the East that she drew her chief riches. The Court and upper classes consumed vast quantities of silks, spices, and perfumed woods; and Byzantium became for the West a city of magic and strange luxury when the Emperor sent gifts of silk-stuffs and precious stones to the Courts and churches of the barbarians.

There were two main routes between the Far East and the Mediterranean. By the older and shorter route caravans crossed the great deserts of Central Asia, and by Samarkand, Bokhara, and the oases of Sogdiana reached the Persian frontier in 150 days. Another 80 days' journey through Persia brought them to Nisibis, the Roman frontier town. The other route, used extensively since A.D. 150, was by sea. Ceylon was the great

[1] *Paul the Silentiary*, ii. 232–5.

central market, to which silk and cotton, aloes, pepper, cloves, and sandalwood were shipped from China, Malay, and the East Indies. From this point two lines of shipping radiated to the West. One, the most important, led up the Persian Gulf to the mouths of Tigris and Euphrates and the great markets of Hira. The other rounded Arabia and passed up the Red Sea to the ports of the Yemen on the eastern shore, and those of Abyssinia on the west, or to the Roman cities at the head of the gulf, Clisma, near Suez, and Aila on the eastern branch. A few merchants from Syria or Alexandria actually visited the East, and saw the amethyst, as big as a pine-cone, glittering on its temple-summit in Ceylon, or the Indian monarchs with their immense armies and herds of elephants. Stories were current about the Isle of Satyrs, which is Borneo, home of the orang-utan, and Chinese sources tell of Western traders in their ports. Some had sailed down the African coast, and seen the stockades and 'dumb barter' of the caravan-trade with the interior. But they did not venture too far; for, Cosmas tells us, outside the four great gulfs of the world, the Mediterranean, Red Sea, Persian Gulf, and Caspian Sea, ran the circumambient Ocean, with its deadly mists and fierce currents, and there was constant danger of being sucked into it. One day, not far from Zanzibar, a number of albatrosses appeared. The sky grew threatening, and passengers and crew shouted in terror to the steersman to port the helm, and turn back into the Gulf, for the surf of the Ocean was already visible. The albatrosses followed them, flying high, a sign that the Ocean was near.

Cosmas the monk, a retired Alexandrian merchant, has entertaining and reliable tales of his travels, of seals and giraffes, musk-deer, coco-nuts, pepper-trees, and other rarities. His cosmology is equally entertaining but less reliable. In Gibbon's phrase, 'the nonsense of the monk is mingled with the practical experience of the traveller'. By methods still familiar, he interprets the Scriptures so as to confound the pernicious Pagan doctrines that the world is round, and that Antipodes exist. For him the universe was an oblong box of two storeys, made in the proportions of the Ark of the Covenant, as set forth by Moses, 'The Great Cosmographer'. Stars are carried by angels; the sun sets behind a great mountain. He is a good example of popular monastic speculation; but his particular theory was not widely accepted.

Most of the overseas trade was in the hands of Persians; they commanded the markets of Ceylon, and enjoyed special privileges. The Red Sea traffic was handled by the sailors of Abyssinia, who also visited the Eastern ports. The whole of the silk trade passed through Persian hands, and the inconvenience of this was obvious. Justinian's trade policy was governed by this fact. Attempts were made to establish the northern caravan route, which passed through Turkestan, north of Persian territory, round the Caspian, and down to the eastern end of the Black Sea. Another scheme was the employment of State bargaining with Persia. By a commercial treaty permission to import silk was limited to three frontier towns, Callinicum in Osroëne, Nisibis in Mesopotamia, and Artaxata in Armenia. Smuggling was severely punished, and the cost of raw silk, which was purchased by Imperial officials, was fixed by law, while at the other end a maximum price was laid down for the finished products from Tyre and Beirut. The measures taken were not entirely successful, for sometimes Persia refused to sell at the price offered, and the Syrian silk-merchants were faced with ruin. The Byzantine government had eventually to pay the higher price, but it took advantage of the opportunity to make the industry a State monopoly.

Justinian's main efforts were directed towards the Red Sea trade. The Ethiopians of Aksûm (Abyssinia) had become Catholics, and therefore allies; Justinian had helped them to regain their power over the opposite coast, the Yemen. Their trade was extensive—incense, spices, emeralds, ivory from the interior, and gold and slaves from farther south; they handled also the Arabian and much of the Asiatic commerce. Justinian's favours were bestowed with a purpose; Abyssinia was to compete with Persia for the silk trade of the West. The Persian hold, however, on the markets of India and Ceylon was too firm, and nothing much came of this. A romantic episode provided the solution. Two monks succeeded in smuggling silkworms' eggs out of China, where the secret was jealously guarded, by concealing them in the hollow of a bamboo. Syria was soon covered with mulberry-trees, and after a time the Empire ceased to depend wholly on Chinese imports.

In spite of the rigorous control exercised by the State, and the numerous duties exacted, Byzantine trade flourished exceedingly. Syria and Egypt were hives of industry, and the Mediterranean was thronged from end to end with the ships of traders, bringing all the exotic fruits, jewels, stuffs and spices, the curious enamels, embroidery, and metalwork of the Near and Far East into the seaports of Western Europe; while the gold Imperial *nomisma* was current coin in all the markets of the world.

In the foregoing pages some attempt has been made to sketch a background for the Imperial policy of Justinian by using as symbols the great buildings which surrounded the Augusteum. To complete the picture, it would have been necessary to describe the social life of the various classes of Byzantine society. The silk-clad nobility, with their town houses and country seats, their posts in the administration, the army and the church, their intrigues for power and struggles for precedence, their hunting and horse-racing, their literary pursuits and eclectic culture. The middle class, the University circle, with its State-paid professors, its efficient schools of law and rhetoric, closely connected with the machinery of the civil service, whose corruption and nepotism John Lydus paints in such lively colours. Then the sober luxury and more homely manners of the rich merchants, bankers, and shopkeepers; and the whole public life of the city, its parishes, police and firemen, its law courts and schools, its hospitals with their house-physicians and separate wards, its orphanages and almshouses, its public bakeries, water-supply, cisterns, aqueducts, and drainage. The splendid squares and broad streets, colonnades and triumphal arches of brilliant white marble, thronged with statues, the shops displaying their flaming silks and gleaming metalwork for sale, and the roadways kaleidoscopic with the many-coloured throng, nobles in rich cloaks, long-sleeved tunics, and brocaded sleeves, followed by slaves with short jerkins and cowls, or mounted on white horses with gold-embroidered saddle-cloth; women with brightly patterned gowns and shawls, or *dévotes* in grey and black; monks and pilgrims; courtesans, beggars, and pickpockets; guards and mercenaries; Slavs, Germans, Huns; merchants of Syria and Egypt; jugglers, astrologers and quack doctors at street corners, story-tellers in the bazaars, recounting the old folk-tales of Asia or the latest marvel or witticism, often coupled with the names of the great, even of the Emperor and his consort. Or the steep, narrow lanes, with overhanging balconies and dark shops and brothels, leading down to the crowded harbour—the haunts of the foreign sailors, and the home of the plague, which from time to time sweeps over the city, killing five thousand a day. Ghosts walk the empty streets then, and glide even through barred doors, terrible voices warning the victim of his approaching end.

And running like a cross-section through the whole of Byzantine life, the Church with its many activities, from the Patriarch and his clergy, the preachers in the great churches, the fashionable confessors, the scholarly clerics, down to the peasant monks and wandering ascetics. The city and its environs swarmed with monasteries and convents, some founded, and often inhabited, by senatorial nobles and their women-folk, others the refuge not only of the needy but of fugitives from justice. They are an integral part of the State, as Justinian's detailed legislation shows. Here, as elsewhere, he follows the traditional theory of Rome. Just as the due performance of the *sacra* secured good harvests and kept the enemy from the gates of the Republic, so now, it is announced, 'if these pure hands and sanctified souls pray for the Empire, the army will be strengthened, the prosperity of the State increased, agriculture and commerce will flourish, under the assured benevolence of God' (*Nov.* 133. 5). It is impossible to over-estimate the importance of religion in Byzantine life. Our topic of conversation is the weather; theirs was theology. Our internal crises are social and economic; theirs were doctrinal. Their wars were crusades, their Emperor was God's vice-gerent. In settled periods the monasteries with their armies of monks and troops of dependants played a great part in the formation of popular opinion; stylite hermits swayed the populace, and Emperors bowed before their demands and solicited their counsel. In times of stress the churches were thronged with suppliants, and the Virgin herself was to be seen defending the battlements of her holy city.

Byzantium had need of all her spiritual armoury. She was essentially a beleaguered city, and the suppressed excitement of a state of siege pervades the outlook of her inhabitants. Omens and prodigies are everywhere; pagan statues speak or sweat, ancient inscriptions foretell imminent calamities; icons and relics heal the sick, avert misfortune, or remove one's private enemy by sudden death. Wild rumours fly; the Emperor is a magician, he walks headless by night, his queen is possessed by a demon. Earthquake or plague drives the population frantic; they seize their belongings, bury their valuables, rush through the streets. And the enemy is always at hand; less than thirty miles away was the great land-wall, beyond which, during long periods, it was not wise to venture. Many a hunting-party failed to return at evening; and villages, monasteries, and country houses round the capital flamed in the path of successive invasions. Constantinople is a bastion thrust out into Asia, exposed to the surging of the barbaric hordes issuing from the great steppes or the Arabian deserts. Like some pinnacled city in a medieval miniature, Tsarigrad of the Slavs, Micklegarth of the Northmen, it lies bathed in the sunshine of Western dreams. But from the Eastern aspect it glows with a more baleful light. Under a stormy sky the domes glitter, the walls are tipped with spears; before the ramparts stand the long rows of Avar tents, and bands of Arab horsemen scour the desolate plains. The relentless ring of barbarians edges closer, burning to ravish 'the city of the world's desire'.[1]

[1] Constantine the Rhodian. Cf. *Rev. des Ét. Grecques*, ix (1896), p. 38.

V

JUSTINIAN AND THE WEST

JUSTIN died in 527 and was succeeded by his nephew Justinian, who had been for several years the virtual ruler of the Empire. He was a man of moderate height, spare, middle-aged, rather bald, with curly greyish hair, ruddy and round-faced, affable, accessible, and complacent. Immensely industrious, with an aptitude for detail, he dictated the tactics of a distant campaign, the architecture of an African fortress, the exact programme for the consular games, or arguments for compulsory fasting in Lent. He was dignified and self-controlled in general demeanour, but action sometimes found him wanting. In the Nika Riot he displayed a fundamental weakness, and the influence exercised over him by Theodora and John the Cappadocian hints at an indecisive character—in Diehl's words, *une âme de valeur plutôt médiocre*.

Yet the achievements of this man have earned him the title of Justinian the Great. He stands in history as the builder of St. Sophia, the founder of European Law, the restorer of Roman dominion from the Pillars of Hercules to the Euphrates. *Imperium Romanum*—it is the secret of his success. The Macedonian peasant, when he assumed the purple, put on also the greatness of those heroic rulers whose superhuman efforts had for five centuries kept the Empire in being.[1] In the holder of the Imperium were centred all the powers of Church and State, of the law, the army, the administration. He was responsible for the welfare of his subjects, whether in the Eastern parts or in those Western provinces which had been for a time committed to the charge of his viceroys, the Germanic kings. He was the protector of all Catholics, within or without the Empire, and the merciless enemy of all heretics and pagans. This is the theory which underlies all the actions of Justinian. The codification of Roman Law perpetuates the expression of a civilization handed down from Republican times, and emphasizes the constitutional position of the

[1] Cf. F. W. Bussell, *Constitutional History of the Roman Empire*, vol. i, p. 217. 'The sovereign himself in succeeding lost much of his own capricious individuality, and became an inheritor and a simple exponent of the undying policy of Rome.'

Emperor as *fons iuris*. Elaborate ceremonial at Court exalts the Imperial office, and throughout the Empire the inscriptions on his buildings and the nomenclature of his cities record for posterity the name and glory of Justinian. The administration is to be purified, not only because the Emperor owes a duty to his subjects, but also because they must be placed in a position to pay the heavy imposts necessary to finance his imperialist schemes. Above all, the reconquest of the Roman provinces of the Empire—Africa, Italy, Spain, if not Gaul and Britain—is the great dream of Justinian. Danube and Eastern frontiers are neglected, drained of troops for Western campaigns. Monophysite Egypt and Syria are persecuted and alienated, while support is given to the Papacy and to the Catholics of Africa and Italy. The provinces, both in East and West, are crushed by intolerable taxation to provide money for armies and fortresses, and corruption and extortion creep back under the shadow of Imperial bankruptcy. It is easy to point to the end of the long reign, the depleted coffers, the starving peasantry, the dwindling armies, the West falling away, the East threatening, the Empire defenceless and its senile Emperor concerned only with theological disputation, and to say that Justinian's policy was disastrous, that the resources of the State were not more than sufficient to protect its Danubian and Persian frontiers. All this is true; but it must be remembered that Justinian had the defects of his qualities. The Great Age of Byzantium, which fixed her impress indelibly upon the laws and arts of Europe, was due to his Roman conception of Empire, which demanded the recovery of the West and the headship of the Catholic Church, no less than the creation of the Code and of St. Sophia.

The Empress Theodora presents the strangest contrast to her husband. Luxurious, haughty, dominating, revengeful, clearsighted and unscrupulous, she exercised continual influence either by persuasion or intrigue over the mind and decisions of the Emperor. In modern jargon, a realist, a 'believer in direct action', a salutary counterforce to the cloudy imperialism and the elaborate paper schemes of Justinian. It is impossible to determine how much truth lies behind the scandal retailed with much gusto by Procopius in the *Anecdota*. Her illegitimate son, her interest in measures dealing with the traffic in women, and her Monophysite leanings certainly agree with the main facts of the story that she had been a courtesan in Byzantium, and afterwards in Alexandria and Antioch, where she had come under the influence of leaders of the Monophysite party. It is, perhaps, not fantastic to see, in her exaction from the courtiers of ceremonial prostration, and her studied insolence towards them, a revenge for her own more unceremonious treatment at the hands of their class.

Until her death in 548 she was practically (though not, of course, constitutionally) co-ruler of the Empire. Her favourites became prefects, generals, patriarchs, and popes. Her enemies were disgraced or destroyed; even the all-powerful John of Cappadocia paid the penalty at last. Possessed of vast estates and revenues, she controlled her own secret service, and sometimes even thwarted the Imperial agents, never failing, however, to conciliate Justinian after the event. Most striking of all was her influence upon Eastern policy. She was naturally attracted to the Monophysite Church, and even when it was proscribed at Byzantium she harboured its priests and monks; but she saw also, more clearly than Justinian, the political danger to the monarchy if the essential provinces of Asia, Syria, and Egypt were driven to revolt by persecution of their faith. Her counsel produced the opportune concessions and toleration which were necessary to prevent the occurrence of this disaster.

The Conquest of the West began in 533 when Belisarius, the Empire's best general, set sail for Africa with 10,000 infantry and some 5,000 horsemen. With him went his assessor, the historian Procopius, who has left us a detailed account of the campaign. The pretext for war was the fact that Hilderic, the weak Vandal king, whose sympathies lay with Catholicism and Byzantium, had been driven out by Gelimer, who represented the anti-Byzantine party. A similar pretext offered itself when the time came for the invasion of Italy; and the similarity extends also to the course taken by the fighting. In both cases sudden initial success proved unstable, and years of confused struggle followed

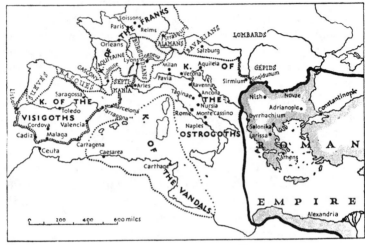

ROMAN EMPIRE, A.D. 526

ROMAN EMPIRE, A.D. 533-600

CONQUESTS OF JUSTINIAN

before the conquest was complete. In Africa everything favoured Justinian's bold plan. The Vandal fleet and a large part of the forces had just been dispatched to Sardinia to quell a revolt. The Byzantine troops landed without difficulty on the African coast, and marched towards Carthage along shady roads, camping by night among delightful orchards. They were received with open arms by the Roman population. The Vandal forces consisted of light cavalry, and the proper tactics would have been guerrilla warfare against the armoured horsemen and slow-moving infantry of their adversaries. But Gelimer chose to engage in two pitched battles. In spite of serious mistakes Belisarius was victorious in both, and in a short time Carthage was in his hands, and the Vandal king, whom Procopius makes into a curiously temperamental and romantic figure, had surrendered himself in order to spare the sufferings of his dependants. All seemed over; a small army of occupation was left, while Belisarius returned to enjoy his triumph at Byzantium, taking with him the Vandal nobility, who were formed into a cavalry corps stationed on the Persian frontier. Everything was done to restore the old conditions in Africa. The Catholic clergy were favoured, and severe measures taken against Donatists, Arians, and pagans. The Roman landowners were to receive back their estates; but legal claims going back over a century presented serious difficulties. Moreover, discontent soon arose when it became apparent that their contributions to the Imperial revenues were the chief cause of Justinian's solicitude for their welfare.

Greater troubles, however, were in store for the African provinces. While medals were being struck in Constantinople, and hymns of triumph resounded in the Hippodrome, the Roman power in Africa was threatened by the attacks of Berber chieftains, who swept down from their mountain-fastnesses in continual *razzias*. Solomon, the Byzantine general, succeeded finally in driving them back, and even pursued them into the hills, but the Byzantine tactics (and they fought always according to rule) were not suitable for dealing with these light horsemen and camel-mounted raiders. The heavy armour of the Roman troops was designed more for defence than attack, and the increasing use of the bow produced an addiction to long-distance fighting which did not improve the morale. Insubordination also was rife, and continual mutinies took place, the commander-in-chief being sometimes obliged to flee for his life. A succession of heroic figures—Solomon, Germanus, John Troglita—enabled the Roman power to surmount these crises, and thanks to the fact that the Moorish chieftains, divided by perpetual feuds, were incapable of united action, by 548 the Imperial authority was permanently established, and the ravaged provinces had rest.

In a vigorous passage of his Secret History, Procopius denounces the African conquest, which cost, he says, the lives of five million men, and left the country impoverished and depopulated, a prey to Moorish inroads, grinding taxation, religious oppression, and military insurrection. There is reason to think that this picture is overdrawn. The vast ruins of noble cities still visible in that region bear witness by their walls and aqueducts, many of which date from this period, to the forethought of Justinian. The frontier fortresses are interesting not only in themselves, as displaying many of the features—moat, keep, bailey, flanking-towers, crenellation, &c.—usually associated with medieval fortification, but also as forming part of a huge defensive system, extending to the slopes of the Aurasian Mountains and the uplands of Numidia, of walled refuges for the peasants during Moorish raids. The churches and spacious monasteries in the interior continue the Roman basilican style, embellished with Byzantine ornament, while on the coast Greek influence is paramount, and has left traces in delicate capitals and mouldings. Mosaic floors display in vivid colours the excitements of the hippodrome and the fashions of the period. The activity of the Church is shown by an efflorescence of councils and controversial literature. Numerous remains of farmsteads, irrigation works, and oil-presses indicate the widespread fertility of the country. To the Mahometan invaders, a century later, the coastline from Tripoli to Tangier seemed one continuous orchard set with scattered habitations.

In Italy Imperial intervention was even more opportune. The equipoise of Theoderic's dualistic state had been destroyed by the death of the strong personality who had held the scales. His daughter, Amalasuntha, had acted as regent for her ten-year-old son, who had been proclaimed king immediately on the death of his grandfather. The rule of a woman produced problems which hastened the break-up of Theoderic's system. Her Roman education made her suspect to the Gothic warriors, while Byzantium used her as a pawn in the Imperial game, and perhaps even connived at her death. Regarding the throne as an Amal prerogative, she was determined to keep it even after the death of her son, while still in his minority; but, like the rest of her people, she had small sense of national unity, and did not hesitate to negotiate secretly with Justinian when her position became critical.

It is an illuminating fact that each successive Gothic leader—Theodahad, Witiges, Hildebad, Erarich, Totila—regarded his relations with the Emperor as something purely personal, not unlike the bargaining of Theoderic, the semi-independent *magister militum*, with the Emperor Zeno, before setting out for the conquest of Italy. But at the same time they appealed, inconsistently, to the arrangement made with Anastasius[1] as forming a sort of legal foundation for the Romano-Gothic State. They failed utterly to perceive that the position of Theoderic, deliberately unformulated, had in fact only been preserved by a network of foreign alliance without, and religious and political harmony within, which enabled him to show a firm front to Byzantium. The ascendancy of the Franks, the intrigues of the Catholics, and the discontent of the senatorial class had already undermined this structure before the death of Theoderic.

Amalasuntha, unable to maintain herself against the Gothic opposition, decided to share the throne with her cousin Theodahad, another type, even more remarkable, of Romanized barbarian. Platonist and pacifist, he had one more consuming passion, the acquisition of landed property. He was ready to exchange Italy, he secretly assured Justinian in later negotiations, for an estate and a position at the Imperial Court. By his orders Amalasuntha was imprisoned on an island in the Lake of Bolsena, and subsequently put to death. This was the signal for the Byzantine

[1] See p. 69.

attack. Italy was to be invaded by land from Dalmatia, and by sea from Africa. In 536 an Imperial force seized Salona, the capital of Dalmatia, while Belisarius led an army of about 7,500 men into Sicily. The smallness of his forces is remarkable, considering his aims and his achievements. It was to some extent set off by the superior organization and strategy with which he opposed the incoherent barbarian masses. But it made him practically unable to fight a pitched battle, and this determined the nature of the war, in which castles and sieges play a prominent part.

The military genius of Belisarius is seen at its highest under these conditions. As an exemplary professional soldier, brave in the field, resourceful in tactics, he had secured the devotion of his motley troops in the campaigns of three continents, and he was invaluable to Justinian for the same reason, since he had no political ambitions and was unswerving in his loyalty to the throne. Yet his very success aroused constant suspicion in the Emperor's mind; he was stinted of men and money, and harassed by hostile colleagues in the command. His lack of political sense led occasionally to grave blunders, and his subservience to his wife Antonina, bosom friend of the Empress, drew him into the complicated intrigues of the Palace. He falls short of heroic stature; yet a balance struck between his limitations, external and internal, and his astonishing achievements shows him clearly the greatest general of his century.

Sicily fell almost without a blow; it had been barely occupied by the Goths, and its landowners received the Byzantine troops with open arms. Naples, the Gothic centre of Campania, was the next objective, and after an exciting siege it yielded to assault, not without the occurrence of some regrettable incidents. The commercial population was less ready than feudal Sicily or Bruttium to welcome the Imperial forces, whose Huns, Isaurians, and Slavs seemed to it more to be dreaded than the Goths.

Theodahad, meanwhile, futile and desperate, had been treating with the Emperor; but a success in Dalmatia nerved him to repudiate the offer already mentioned, and no result was reached. The fall of Naples sealed his doom. He was deposed by the Gothic army, and Witiges, one of Theoderic's generals, elected in his stead. The main Gothic settlements were in North Italy, and Witiges immediately withdrew to Ravenna to organize his forces, leaving Rome open to the Byzantines. Belisarius occupied the city, and spent the winter of 536–7 in repairing the ruined walls. He realized the importance of holding the capital, though to many Romans it seemed a fantastic notion to defend with 5,000 men a circuit of over twelve miles against the attacks of ten or twenty times their number. The story of the siege is a succession of picturesque and thrilling incidents, beginning with the escape of Belisarius, on his iron-grey charger with the white blaze, from the pursuing cavalry, and his arrival before the city gates, which would not open at first to the riders covered in dust and blood. Treachery and panic were rife within. More than once the Goths seemed on the point of forcing an entrance by storming some weak point, or creeping up under the portico of St. Peter's, to be assailed by broken statues torn from Hadrian's mausoleum. Belisarius held on grimly until tardy reinforcements arrived, and in March 538 the year-long siege was raised. The way was now open for further advance, and the Gothic strongholds of Central Italy were attacked; by the end of 539 the Byzantine troops were closing in on Ravenna. A curious episode follows, which brings out forcibly the Gothic and Byzantine characters. Justinian, faced with the prospect of a Persian war, was ready to grant terms to the Goths, leaving them in possession of the lands north of the Po. Belisarius, however, would not be baulked of his victory, and refused to ratify the agreement. The Goths, in dismay, seeing themselves landless, offered him the crown, and Witiges consented to abdicate. Belisarius accepted, but once inside Ravenna he threw off the treacherous pretence. The Goths were helpless, and no further resistance was possible. Witiges and his retinue were sent to Byzantium. Justinian added the name 'Gothicus' to his other titles, and a praetorian prefect was dispatched to govern the reconquered province, while most of the troops were transferred to the East.

What followed was, in the eyes of Byzantium, mere rebellion. But it was a very formidable rebellion. Fourteen years of warfare were needed to complete the subjugation of Italy. Under the resolute leadership of Totila, the Goths reduced the Byzantine hold on the peninsula to the garrisons of coastal towns and isolated strongholds. Their purpose was to dominate the plains, and in this way secure for themselves the tribute which would otherwise have gone to the Byzantine exchequer. At the same time skilful use was made of the unpopularity of the 'Greeks' and their administration, and the *coloni* were supported against their masters. By the expropriated landlords, and the Catholic clergy who supported their régime, Totila was looked upon as tyrant and heretic; to the peasants, relieved of many of their feudal *corvées*, he came as a deliverer. The small Byzantine armies could not oppose him in the field; Rome was taken and retaken; Belisarius, after a hopeless struggle carried on with insufficient means, was finally recalled, a confessed failure. In 549 Totila presided in state at the Roman Hippodrome, and began to restore the buildings of the capital, while his fleet ravaged the coasts of Dalmatia. 'The whole of the West', according to Procopius, 'was in barbarian hands.'

At this point, moved perhaps by the influential Roman *émigrés* at his Court, Justinian decided to send out, for once, a really adequate expeditionary force. After some delays in Dalmatia, Narses, the veteran eunuch, easily evading the defensive system of Totila, entered Ravenna by the coastal road. His barbaric troops—Lombards, Heruls, Huns formed the greater part—were sufficient in number to face the enemy in the field, and the military science of Narses gave them the advantage. A decision was now imminent. Totila hastened from Rome, and at the great battle of Busta Gallorum (552), in the Apennines, the Gothic forces were crushingly defeated. Totila himself was killed. With their backs to the wall, the Goths put up a desperate fight; the garrisons of South Italy capitulated in 555; Brescia and Verona, aided by Frankish forces, held out till 563.

Narses, says a naïve chronicler, restored to Italy 'its former joy' (*pristinum gaudium*). The 'Pragmatic Sanction', issued in 554, is a deliberate attempt on the part of Justinian to set the clock back, if not to 476, at least to the period before Totila had dispossessed the Italian landholders and liberated their serfs. An Exarch was henceforth stationed at Ravenna, holding supreme command over the province; all the old civil machinery was replaced, and Justinian believed that by his efforts the Roman Empire had finally regained the country of its origin. What he had actually done was something very different. By destroying the Gothic power he had removed the only possible barrier against the barbarous Lombard hosts, who poured into Italy a few years after his death.

Justinian's tax-gatherers had completed the ruin of a devastated country. The rural districts were depopulated, the cities in decay. Rome, five times captured in the wars, was a desolate place of vast ruins; her trade was gone; her people must depend henceforward on pilgrims' alms and papal charity. The aqueducts were cut, and the huge baths stood idle, while the fertile Campagna was fast becoming the melancholy and malarial plain which until recent times surrounded the capital. 'Bread and circuses' were no longer. The last games had been held under Totila; Justinian finally put a stop to the supplies of free corn. Consuls and Senate gradually disappeared. Many nobles migrated to Byzantium, leaving their palaces to crumble into ruin.

Over all Italy crept the shadow of resignation and apathy. For the man of quiet life there was nothing left to hope for in this world. His refuge was the cloister, and the new system of Benedict of Nursia, which met this need, soon spread over the West, supplanting the earlier form which had been brought from Egypt to the monasteries of southern France. Although the rule of Benedict borrows much from its predecessors, its spirit of self-subordination, of regular, moderate living is very different from the fiery, individualist, competitive asceticism of the Thebaid. Sufficient food, sleep, exercise, and clothing are allowed, while excessive effort, whether intellectual or physical, is not exacted. The services to learning, agriculture, and building rendered by the later Benedictines were still to come.[1] Cassiodorus, however, had introduced the copying of manuscripts into the monastery

---

[1] Dom Cuthbert Butler, O.S.B. clearly distinguishes Benedict's original idea from the subsequent developments (*Benedictine Monachism*, 2nd ed., chap. iii, London, 1924).

at Squillace which he founded in his old age, and his devotion to classical literature and to the vanishing purity of the Latin tongue has preserved for posterity, beside the curiously alembicated tincture of antique thought and letters which Lactantius and Jerome, Ambrose and Augustine furnished to their medieval readers, the poetry of Virgil and Horace and the prose of Cicero, Livy, and Quintilian. The Benedictines, not long after the death of their founder, seem to have taken over the practice of reproducing manuscripts; but Benedict himself, *scienter nescius et sapienter indoctus*,[1] did not encourage it. *Summa quies* is, indeed, the keynote of his rule, and this was to be found (to quote the exquisite closing cadences of Newman's well-known passage) 'in the *nil admirari*; in having neither hope nor fear of anything below; in daily prayer, daily bread, and daily work, one day being just like another, except that it was one step nearer than the day before it to that great Day which would swallow up all days, the day of everlasting rest'.

The success of Justinian in the Western adventure was chequered by deep shadows. Brilliant conquests, achieved by wholly disproportionate forces, were set off by equally striking weaknesses and dangers. Broadly speaking, the Byzantine hold on the western Mediterranean was that of a sea power. Although the western provinces of Africa had been abandoned, the coastal towns were held as far as the Straits of Gibraltar. The maritime cities of southern Spain were reconquered from the Visigoths. Provence was now in Frankish hands, and the Italian prefecture was reduced to the actual peninsula, for Raetia and Noricum were Roman no longer, and Corsica and Sardinia, as a result of the Vandal conquests, were now grouped with Africa, while Sicily was under the direct control of the Emperor. The course of the Gothic War had foreshadowed the fate of the inland parts of Italy; the Imperial forces were not sufficient to protect them from northern inroads, and they were destined before long to be carved into Lombard duchies. But the districts round Venice, Ravenna, Naples, and Rome, as well as southern Calabria, remained in Byzantine hands, and the Imperial government, or

[1] Greg. *Dial.* ii, Praef.

exarchate, at Ravenna was not extinguished for two centuries.[1] The increased importance of this city is shown by the magnificent churches which date from this period, while the effects of the half-century which had transformed Rome, the most glorious city of the West, into a decayed provincial town, a humble dependency of her eastern rival, are strikingly displayed by the contrast between the intense and noble figures of the apsidal mosaic of SS. Cosmas and Damian (c. A.D. 530), the final expression of centuries of Roman art, and the flat, lifeless scenes depicted in the mosaic of S. Lorenzo fuori le Mure (c. 580), the production, it is probable, of inferior Byzantine craftsmen. The Papacy itself had lost all independence. One pontiff had been summarily deposed, another carried off to Constantinople to face insult and imprisonment.[2] The 'Caesaropapism' of Justinian was continued by his successors, and even Gregory the Great was obliged to lavish flattery upon the tyrant Phocas. Yet the power of the Church was steadily growing; its bishops exercised increasing civil jurisdiction, its patrimonies swelled. It had a permanent organization, and could afford to wait while the means were being prepared for that extension of Papal influence in Western Europe which is the work of Gregory.

[1] 'Imperial and Lombard possessions in Italy', it has been said, 'were left so intertwined that no sort of national unity was possible'. Thus the Byzantine conquest is partly responsible for the lack of national feeling which determined so much of the subsequent history of Italy.

[2] See below, p. 116.

VI

JUSTINIAN AND THE EAST

IN the West Justinian had pursued an offensive policy; in the East his aims are deliberately defensive. Stability on the frontiers was to be maintained by immense systems of walls and fortresses; if other means failed, the barbarian must be bought off. Stability inside the Empire was to be secured by administrative reform; besides lessening the chances of disorder, this would, by increasing the prosperity of the inhabitants, and by improving the fiscal machinery, guarantee for Justinian his all-important revenues. It was not that he deliberately sacrificed the welfare of his subjects to his own financial needs; in his philosophy, ruler and people had equal duties to the Empire of which they formed a part—his to conquer, theirs to enable him to do so by paying cheerfully the taxes demanded of them.

In two great ordinances of A.D. 535 Justinian began his work of reform. Detailed instructions were given for the arrangements of each separate province; only the leading principles can be mentioned here. One of the chief abuses consisted of the excessive fees (*suffragia*), amounting really to premiums, which officials had to pay for obtaining their posts; as a result, they were driven to recoup themselves by extortion and dishonesty of all kinds, and from the great ministers of the capital down to the humblest police and soldiers of the provinces the whole administration was riddled with corrupt practices. Crowds of petitioners flocked to Constantinople; the central officers could not get reliable information about the provincial governments, and the officials, if brought to book, pleaded the exigencies of the *suffragia* as their excuse. This excuse was now removed; in future, only light fees were to be paid on entering office. Rigorous orders were given for the cleansing of the administration. The governors are to have 'pure hands'—the phrase runs like a *leit-motif* through all the ordinances. They are to render equitable justice, to protect their subjects from the violence of the military or the exactions of subordinate officials; to hold the balance between rich and poor, to respect equally the rights of Church and State. But their first duty is 'to increase the revenues of the fisc, and do their utmost to defend its interests'. The orders were reinforced by a terrible oath, which each new governor was made to swear; if he failed in his duty, he would incur 'the rigours of the dreadful judgement of God, the fate of Judas, the leprosy of Gehazi, the palsy of Cain'. In some parts of the Empire, important simplifications were made in the administrative system. Provinces were combined into larger units, dioceses disappeared, and military and civil powers were occasionally united—a change foreshadowing the 'themes' of subsequent Byzantine history. Legal procedure was also simplified; it was made easier to carry an appeal to the governor of the province, but harder to appeal directly to Constantinople; this gave speedier local justice, while preventing congestion in the law-courts of the capital.

By these 'splendid conceptions' Justinian hoped that he had given the State 'a new flowering time'. The next twenty-nine years were to prove him wrong. They show an incessant renewal of the same edicts, an endless repetition of the same threats and recriminations. The case was hopeless, and the reason lay partly in the system itself, partly in the Imperial policy. The vast and complicated machinery of government, with centuries of corruption behind it, offered a dead weight of resistance to any reform. And Justinian's continually growing need of money proved too strong for any real improvement to be possible.

Contemporary writers are full of the miseries of the unfortunate subjects of Justinian. Each province had its tales of injustice, its notorious oppressors. A regular cycle of legends about such men was current in the bazaars. John 'Puffycheeks', governor of Asia, had insulted the bishop, driven an old man to suicide, violated the children of the notables. John 'Scissors' in Italy was famous for his skill in clipping the coinage. In the capital itself, John of Cappadocia, when head of the financial administration, had installed a torture-chamber for recalcitrant taxpayers in the dungeons of his official residence, while Tribonian, when minister of justice, trafficked openly in legal decisions. As need grew, fresh taxes were imposed; monopolies and tariffs were added to the traditional burdens of the land-tax and those connected with the transport and provisioning of troops.[1] The cities of Asia Minor, whose stable conditions and flourishing trade during the preceding century had enabled the Empire in the East to avoid the bankruptcy which had overtaken the West, now felt the full pressure of Justinian's demands: for the Balkans were ravaged by Huns and Slavs, and Syria had been devastated by Persian inroads; from neither of these regions could increased revenue be extorted. And, in spite of everything, the revenue was insufficient: the close of the long reign saw fortresses neglected, the soldiers' pay in arrears, the frontier garrisons cut down; and the vicious circle closed when the defenceless empire had to pay ruinously for these false economies, in swelling subsidies to its barbarian neighbours.

Justinian's passion for order and uniformity found a more successful outlet in the abstract sphere of legislation. The task before him was enormous, and the achievement, considering the difficulties encountered, a very notable one. Roman Law consisted of two masses which were usually distinguished as old law (*ius vetus*) and new law (*ius novum*). The old law consisted principally of the statutes of the Republic and early Empire, the decrees of the senate during the same period, and the comments of contemporary jurists. These formed a vast conglomeration: some of them were inaccessible, others had become obsolete, and there were numerous discrepancies and contradictions. One jurist might be quoted against another, and no judge or lawyer could feel sure that some obscure opinion might not be produced against him in court which would upset his arguments. The new law comprised the ordinances of the Emperors in subsequent times. Here, too, there were uncertainties; one decree might repeal another, and no complete collection of the decrees had yet been made. But it was an easier problem than the other, and so in 528, the year after his accession, Justinian began his great work by appointing a commission of ten to go through the *ius novum*, removing contradictions and redundancies, and gathering the most valuable part of the rest into one volume of ten books. This was the famous 'Codex Iustinianus', and its success encouraged the Emperor to proceed to the *ius vetus*. A new com-

[1] See above, p. 8.

mission was appointed in 530 to deal with the enormous mass
of literature involved, which consisted of no less than 2,000
treatises. Out of the writings of all the recognized jurists, one
statement of the law on each point was to be selected; and the
expressions of the author were to be changed wherever clearness
demanded it, or the requirements of the time. The results of this
process were the fifty books which comprise what are known as
the *Digest* or *Pandects*, the most remarkable and important law-
book that the world has ever seen, both in itself and in the influence it has exercised on all subsequent legislation. It is open to
criticism in several respects. The work was done in haste, and the
arrangement is by no means ideal. It is not, properly speaking,
a codification, a reduction of previous laws to an organic system.
It is more like some of the buildings of the time, where the delicate
mouldings and reliefs of an earlier age are thrust in among coarse
rubble and hasty brickwork, to serve as common stones in the
clumsy fabric. In the time of her greatness Rome found her
most perfect aesthetic expression in the art of legislation, and the
'elegance' of her legal formulae, the brilliance of her solutions,
have never been surpassed. The jurists of the sixth century were
not content merely to abstract from their illustrious predecessors.
Subtle interpretations were misunderstood, and in consequence
perverted, essential phraseology was cut and mutilated, Hellenistic and Oriental conceptions were introduced into the Roman
system.

These defects were perhaps inevitable. A more perfect re-
daction could not have been accomplished in the time, and under
the conditions of Justinian's reign. As it stands, it is the complete
expression of the period. In its insistence on the Latin language
and the Latin heritage, in its doctrines of Imperial absolutism it
looks back to the long roll of Caesars. In its increased humanity,
its recognition of the rights of the individual, its checks on the
patria potestas, it records the long progress of ancient thought.
And the influence of the Church is plainly visible in the increasing
severity of laws concerning divorce and sexual offences.

In order to complete his legislative work Justinian published
the *Institutes*, an elementary text-book for the use of students.
Legal education was also reorganized, and detailed regulations

were issued for the three great universities of Rome, Constantinople, and Beirut. Nothing was to be left to chance or change. No further commentaries were allowed; translations must be strictly literal. Only to the Emperor himself was further legislation permitted; and it is curiously ironical that, in spite of the insistence on Latin as the official language, most of these later laws are written in Greek, that they may be 'better understanded of the people', while no penalties could prevent the appearance of a flood of Greek paraphrases of the 'immutable' Pandects and Constitutions.

In the West the direct influence of Justinian's legal code was hardly felt. Roman law was known mainly through the code which Alaric, the Visigoth king, had produced some thirty years earlier, a practical compilation for the use of his people in Gaul and Spain, in which the simpler of the Roman legal conceptions were skilfully harmonized with the conditions of the time and the tribal customs of the Goths. It was not until the eleventh century that Justinian's code began to be studied systematically in Provence, Lombardy, Ravenna, and Bologna. But Roman law made itself felt not only in the regions containing a predominantly Romanized population, but also wherever the growth of trade, the claims of the Church, or the revival of legal thought demanded nicer distinctions and more logical categories. It became, in later times, a powerful weapon in the hands of an ambitious prince or grasping bishop, seeking to override the limitations of feudalism by assuming the absolute prerogatives of a Justinian.

The absolutism in question found perhaps its most striking expression in the ecclesiastical sphere, where it resulted in what has sometimes been called 'Caesaropapism'. Justinian was not content to regulate the Church by detailed legislation; in doctrinal disputes he exerted to the full his Imperial prerogatives of convoking councils and assigning limits. Imperial ministers presided, messengers hurried to and fro from the Palace, and if the decision were in doubt the Emperor would occasionally intervene in person. Though formally distinct,[1] Church and

[1] *Nov.* 6, praef. (A.D. 535).

State were actually one, and political considerations guided Justinian along the road into which his theological interests had already led him. Foremost among these considerations was the unity of his empire; and this was to be obtained by two means— force and conciliation. The treatment accorded to heretics illustrates both methods, and furnishes at the same time an example of the way in which politics and dogma intermingled in the Imperial policy. In theory the heretic had forfeited all rights, public and private. 'It is just', said the Emperor, 'to deprive of their worldly goods those who do not worship the True God.' In practice there were many distinctions and degrees. Politically insignificant heresies could be crushed. For Manichees, death was the only punishment; usually they were burnt alive. Paganism, for the most part a dwindling remnant of scattered superstitions, was severely handled. In isolated valleys and lonely hill-towns the old beliefs still lingered; at Baalbek immemorial rites were still celebrated in the temple, and in the Libyan desert Jupiter Ammon still gave his oracles, though he had at this time retired to a more inaccessible oasis, where he was worshipped in company with Alexander, now become a god. This shrine was transformed into the Church of St. Mary, and the temple of Isis at Philae, on the Nubian border, was also made into a Christian centre. Paganism still had its adherents among the educated classes, and stringent laws were accordingly directed against them. They might not inherit, or enter into contracts; they were debarred from holding any office, except those which were in themselves a penalty, like the *curia*. An inquisition at Constantinople discovered a number of distinguished pagans, including university teachers and doctors; many of them were scourged and imprisoned. In Palestine the Jews had lost their centre of revolt, and submitted, under protest, to the regulation by Imperial decree of their text of the Scriptures; but the Samaritans, goaded by excessive taxes and Christian persecution, broke into riot on their hill-tops, and were almost exterminated by severe punitive measures. In the West political considerations were even more apparent. The Donatists in Africa were deprived of their property and churches; they had been in league with the anti-Imperial forces. The Arian clergy were solidly organized, and

Justinian would have allowed them to remain on condition that they embraced the orthodox faith, but the hatred of the Catholics, who had suffered much from them, was implacable, and these latter were supported by the Pope. Justinian accordingly acceded to their demands for vengeance. In Italy other causes favoured the spoliation of the Arian churches. Their Gothic sympathies were an excuse, their great riches an incentive to the hand of the spoiler.

The Monophysites were on an entirely different footing. Up till 541 they are called 'the hesitants', and Justinian reasoned with them as erring brethren. Sterner measures followed, but conciliation was always in view. The problem was fundamental to the safety of the Empire. On one side were the prosperous and powerful Monophysite cities of Egypt and Asia Minor, the backbone of the Imperial budget. On the other was the Catholic opposition at Constantinople, and above all the Pope, supported by the great majority of the Western bishops. To retain the allegiance of the East, already threatened by conflicting interests and national animosities, without losing the support of the newly conquered West, was a difficult, possibly a hopeless task. At all events, Justinian's complicated policy was not unworthy of a great Emperor. In this policy he was ably seconded by Theodora, whose Monophysite sympathies were well known. The early years of his reign showed that he was prepared to recede from the extreme Catholic position taken up by Justin. In 529 persecution of the Monophysites ceased, and the exiles were recalled. In 532 a conference was called at Byzantium. It failed to reconcile the two parties, but Justinian did not abandon hope, though he felt it wise to publish a rescript declaring his orthodoxy, in order to reassure the Pope. In 535 the Monophysites were in the ascendant. Anthemius, one of their number, was made bishop of Constantinople, and at once got into touch with the patriarchs of Alexandria and Jerusalem. Meanwhile John of Tellas, a fiery preacher, spread Monophysite doctrines in his wanderings over Asia Minor. Monophysite monks flocked to the capital, and fashionable people would have their children baptized in Monophysite churches, and entertain Monophysite chaplains at their board. The following year saw a remarkable change. The Pope,

Agapitus, arrived in Byzantium on an embassy from the Ostrogoths. He lost no time in excommunicating Anthemius, and, supported by the Catholic party, convoked a synod which deposed him and other bishops. Justinian was induced to ratify the decision. Persecution began again. In Syria, Armenia, Mesopotamia, Monophysite monks were hunted down, starved, whipped, and burnt alive in market-places. John of Tellas was captured and put to death with slow tortures by Ephraim, bishop of Antioch. The Pope died shortly afterwards, but his able legate, Pelagius, exercised great influence at Court. Even in Egypt temporary submission to the decisions of Chalcedon was imposed upon the cowed populace.

Theodora now played a dramatic counter-stroke. Rome, occupied at the moment by Belisarius, was forced to accept her nominee, the supple deacon Vigilius, as the new Pope. Justinian's hopes of the unity of East and West were raised anew. The Monophysite party at Byzantium regained its lost ground, and Jacob Baradaeus, the strenuous Monophysite monk from whom the Jacobite church derives its name, took up again the missionary work of John of Tellas in Asia Minor, meeting with even greater success than his predecessor. Monophysite influence grew steadily from this time until the death of Theodora in 548. The culmination of the struggle was the famous affair of the 'Three Chapters', which lasted from 543 till 554.[1] Apart from the intrigues connected with it the controversy can be regarded as a stage in the long series of efforts to conciliate East and West which began with the Henoticon of Zeno and ended with the proposed Monergetic solution of Heraclius. Soon after this the Monophysite provinces passed under Moslem domination, and the necessity for combating the separatist tendencies of Syria and Egypt ceased to exist. The means employed by the emperor in pursuit of the policy, inevitable for any Byzantine ruler, of political and religious unity are not without interest. Justinian opened the contest in 543 by issuing a condemnation of the Three Chapters. He hoped for the acquiescence of the Pope, but Vigilius, on his native heath, was not to be browbeaten. It was necessary to kidnap him, take him to Byzantium, and subject

[1] See Appendix B, p. 272.

him to various threats and indignities before he consented, in 548, to condemn the Three Chapters. The publication of his *Judicatum* to this effect raised a storm of protest among the bishops of Africa, Dalmatia, and Illyricum, and in 550 Justinian allowed him to withdraw the *Judicatum*, in hopes of succeeding by less violent measures. But his hopes proving abortive, he resorted again to coercion, harrying the African bishops, and ill-treating Vigilius, who was practically a prisoner in Byzantium, to the great scandal of the faithful. In 554 Vigilius, broken in health, gave way, and in his second *Constitutum* finally condemned the Three Chapters. Justinian now endeavoured to enforce his will upon the Western bishoprics, but Italy proved obdurate. Vigilius was succeeded in the Papal chair by Pelagius, the legate at Byzantium, who had receded somewhat from his Catholic position in order to placate Justinian. The North Italian bishops, already jealous of the encroachments of the Roman see, seized the opportunity to break off relations, and this minor schism lasted till the end of the seventh century.

On the whole Justinian had failed. The East remained un-reconciled; the West was subdued, but sullen and discontented. Ominous murmurs began to make themselves heard. 'Only Christ is King and Priest', declared Facundus in Africa. 'The Emperor should execute the canons of the Church, not fix or transgress them.' Yet Justinian's ideal of unity was a great one; and in an estimate of his ecclesiastical policy one should not forget what is perhaps the most brilliant aspect of it, namely the foreign missions, which carried the faith and culture of Byzantium from Central Europe to the Far East, and created a tradition which, persisting throughout the Middle Ages, gave to the Slavs of Russia and the Balkan States a heritage of art and learning as essential to their civilization as that which the Western nations owe to Rome.

The combined use of commerce, missions, and diplomacy was the peculiar creation of Justinian's statecraft. It is well seen in Arabia, where, incidentally, the Byzantine policy bears a striking resemblance to that recently pursued by certain Great Powers in the Near East. From Damascus to the Gulf of Akaba stretched a long line of bishoprics, of which Bostra and Petra were the metropolitan sees. Then came deserts and the Red Sea coast, the Hedjaz, and farther south the Himyarite country. There were many Jewish colonies here, and the Himyarites had mostly abandoned their primitive cults for the Jewish faith. On the Persian Gulf Christianity had gained a firm footing, having spread from Persia, where several bishoprics flourished, and had even penetrated into Yemen and Nejd in the interior. The interests of Persia and Byzantium clashed in these regions, for both were interested in the coastal trade and the Indian traffic. Well before the end of the fifth century Byzantium had reinforced her diplomatic actions. The ruler of Aksûm (Abyssinia) was encouraged to claim the kingdom of the Himyarites. He became a Christian, and the foundation of the still existing Church of Abyssinia dates from this time. With Byzantine support the Aksûmite power extended for some years over the Himyarites, but the country was too distant for this support to prove really effective. About the year 570 Persia tired of the Byzantine intrigues, and conquered the district, which until the coming of Islam was ruled by Persian deputies. In Upper Egypt Christian missionaries played an equally important part. The Nobades, a wild tribe, were converted about 540 by a Monophysite mission, and were used as a check to their still more troublesome neighbours, the Blemmyes, who were thrown back into the desert, while the Nobades took their place on the frontier. Longinus, a remarkable personality, seems to have penetrated about the year 578, on his evangelizing journeys, to the upper waters of the Blue Nile. On the outposts of Empire, sectarian differences are felt less strongly, and Justinian knew how to choose the best men, and gave whole-hearted support to Monophysite workers in this field which he would have hesitated to bestow nearer home.

The monk was an integral part of his diplomacy. At many a barbarian court Byzantine priests became the trusted counsellors of the king, and obtained ascendancy over the women, eager to embrace a mystic faith, while in the train of Christianity came a new culture and a new world of ideas. More material methods were not lacking. The Berber chieftain was proud to wear the ceremonial *burnous*, the diadems, medals, brooches, and purple boots bestowed upon him in reward for his loyalty. The King of Lazica, in the Caucasus, for similar reasons, was made an officer in the Imperial Guards. To other rulers were given wives from the Byzantine nobility, and their sons were often sent to receive their education in the Palace. Nor were the traditional Roman ways forgotten. Political exiles, rival princes, pretenders, and adventurers were encouraged to visit the capital, and provided a ready excuse for Byzantine interference in the internal affairs of their countries. Lands and subsidies were bestowed with a lavish hand, and the well-tried policy of setting a thief to catch a thief[1] was assiduously practised, Moorish sheikhs being incited against each other, Franks supported against Goths, Gepids checked by Lombards, Bulgars by Huns, and Huns by Avars.

The defence of the long Eastern frontier gave occasion for all these methods. Behind it lay the great Persian Empire, the only state with which Byzantium treated on equal terms. Age-long antagonism had resulted in mutual understanding, and there were even suggestions of a kind of concerted 'Weltpolitik'. The Roman and Sasanid Empires, declared a Persian ambassador on one occasion, were like two lighthouses illuminating the world. Instead of attacking, they should support each other. Chosroes wrote to the Emperor Maurice, 'They are to the world what his two eyes are to a man'. From a brief survey of the geography of this region it will be seen that physical conditions contributed to maintain for centuries a fairly stationary frontier-line, and to standardize, as they do to this day, the methods of protecting it. On the north the key of Justinian's defensive system against the menace of the steppes was the Crimea, which was strongly fortified and garrisoned. From this centre radiated lines of commerce, and Byzantine influence was exercised upon the tribes of South Russia. The Tetraxite Goths, immediately to the north, round the Sea of Azov, had long been Christians, and fear of the Huns bound them to the Empire. Westwards, between Don and Danube, were the Kutrugurian Huns, whose king, Grod, had received baptism, Justinian himself standing sponsor at the font. But their presence on the Black Sea was a danger, and so the

---

[1] Cf. pp. 48, 54, 62.

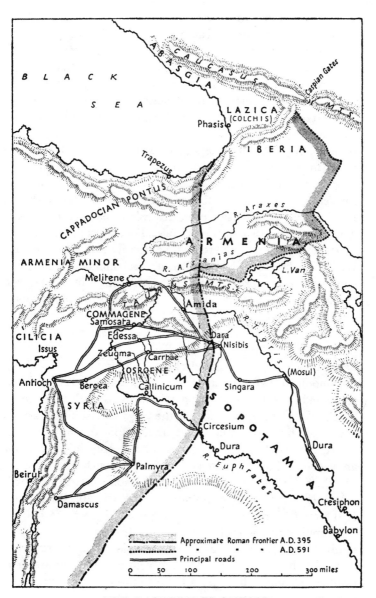

THE EASTERN FRONTIER

Utrigurian Huns, who lived east of the Don, and were considered more harmless, because more distant, were encouraged by Byzantium to attack their kinsfolk. At the eastern end of the Black Sea was the land of Colchis, whither Jason had once fared in search of the Golden Fleece. This myth has been interpreted as a poetic account of the rich merchandise from India and China brought down to the Black Sea at this point. Whether or not such a caravan route was in use across Central Asia at so early a date, in the sixth century A.D. Lazica, as the region was called, was of prime importance as guarding the bridge-head of the northern-most connexion between Europe and the Far East. It was coveted by Persia, whose role in the great silk trade was only that of middleman, and who saw even this role threatened by a route which passed north of her dominions. For corresponding reasons Justinian was determined to retain a decisive influence over 'our Lazica', as he proleptically called it. Its commercial value was considerable; it supplied the Empire with furs, skins, and slaves, and took from it salt, wine, and corn. From a military point of view it was admirably suited for defence. With its wooded mountains and narrow passes it provided a barrier to the northern inroads of the Huns, and effectively kept Persia from access to the Black Sea. Already in Justin's time its king, Zathios, had come to Constantinople for baptism, had married a Byzantine wife, and had consented to admit Byzantine garrisons to his castles. Justinian continued this policy, supporting the kings against unruly nobles and combating Persian influence, and, in spite of temporary set-backs, managed to maintain control not only in Lazica but among several of the other Caucasus tribes, such as the Abasgi and the Sabirian Huns, who held the 'Caspian Gates', by which a northern invader might threaten both Persia and Byzantium. In Iberia (the modern Georgia) he was not so successful; its geographical position rendered it dependent on Persia. Farther south the two Empires marched side by side along the stretches of the Euphrates frontier. The problem of the Euphrates had troubled Rome for five and a half centuries. Was it really the best frontier-line? Its course was very different from those of Rhine and Danube, which, roughly speaking, together enclosed Rome's European possessions. The Euphrates does not flow round and protect Armenia; on the contrary, the Armenian *massif* envelops the head-waters of both Tigris and Euphrates, making a frontier-line very difficult. Again, the border-lands of Rhine and Danube were cultivated, open to Roman influence, and accessible from the capital. The Euphrates, on the other hand, is separated from Syria by a wide expanse of desert; it is therefore harder to convey troops to it, and the advantage is all on the side of the Eastern power, which has a shorter journey, through fertile country, and a wider choice of routes to the frontier. Finally the Euphrates, instead of curving round the outskirts of the Roman Empire, flows straight down, until it sweeps away into the heart of the Persian dominions. To control the river from source to sea was plainly impossible, and Rome never attempted to do so. The southward limit of her influence came eventually to be fixed at the confluence of the Aborras (Circesium), where the Euphrates entered the desert. Various efforts were made to find other solutions, such as the Tigris line, for example; but the only real alternative was the conquest of Persia. Alexander the Great was the only Western commander who had succeeded in this. Augustus seems to have contemplated it at one time, and Trajan, Julian, and other emperors had pursued a forward policy in these regions. But from the end of the fourth century up to the Arab conquest the frontier remained practically stationary. Rome realized that the southern, desert half of Mesopotamia was untenable by a Western power. The northern part, however, had to be held, since this district was bisected by the perpendicular frontier line from Amida on the Tigris to Circesium on the Euphrates. The key to the situation was Armenia, and geography proved in the end the deciding factor. Here, too, various solutions had been attempted by both Empires, ranging from complete annexation to veiled sovereignty by means of resident officers or princes educated in the Imperial capitals. A partition finally took place;[1] Rome now held only a quarter of Armenia, but it was the most essential part for her purposes, since it formed a valuable hinterland for Cappadocian Pontus, and at the same time constituted a base for the control

[1] Cf. p. 18. In the ninth century Armenia once more became a bone of contention, between Byzantium and the Arabs.

of Lazica. The partition did not put an end to the intrigues of either side; Armenia, with its flourishing Church, its great fairs which drew merchants from Europe and Asia, its warlike people and ambitious nobles, provided opportunities in plenty for the clash of interests and the resources of diplomacy.

It is evident that occasions for friction were not wanting on the Eastern frontier, and internal troubles were always an invitation to the opposing Empire to renew hostilities. Since the middle of the fifth century Persia had lost prestige. Rival claimants disputed the succession, while the royal power itself was threatened by the aristocracy and priesthood, and the stability of the country undermined by the religious and socialist agitation of the Mazdakites. On the north-east frontier the depredations of the Huns were causing serious trouble. Justin, accordingly, took the offensive. Payments to Persia for the upkeep of the Caucasus forts were discontinued; the Lazi and Iberi were tampered with, and an open attack made on the great frontier stronghold of Nisibis. Hostilities were inevitable, and 527 saw the outbreak of the First Persian War. Apart from the ravaging of Syria by Persian troops, no serious damage was done, and when Kabad, the 75-year-old Persian king, died in 531, the young Chosroes, bent on securing the succession, was glad to make an 'eternal peace' with Byzantium. The situation, however, was now completely altered. Chosroes was the type of a successful Oriental monarch. Energetic and pugnacious, with a keen brain capable of appreciating the details of organization or the subtleties of Oriental medicine, he extended the boundaries of his empire during the course of a long reign (531–579) to the Oxus in mid-Asia, and the Yemen in southern Arabia. In 540 he saw his chance. Justinian had denuded the frontier to raise troops for his Western conquests, while Armenia and Lazica were becoming impatient of Byzantine hegemony. The Second Persian War lasted from 540 to 545. In successive years Syria was raided and Antioch sacked; Lazica was occupied, and Commagene, Armenia, and Mesopotamia felt the full weight of the Persian onset. A five-years truce was finally negotiated, Justinian paying a large indemnity, but scattered fighting continued in Lazica and among the vassal

Arabs of Syria. No decision was reached, and in 555 another truce was made, followed in 561 by a fifty-years peace, under which the Persians were to evacuate Lazica in return for heavy subsidies. On the whole the *status quo antea* had been maintained.

The ways of Imperial states alter little in this region, and the tactics of Rome and Persia are strangely similar to those of Turkey, Britain, and Russia in recent times. A notable instance is the Byzantine handling of the Arab sheikhs in Syria. Harith-ibn-Gabala, chief of the Ghassanids, became by Byzantine help the ruler of an Arabo-Roman state (a counterpoise to the power of the King of Hira, who was a Persian vassal). Arethas, as the Byzantines called him, was made Patrician, and received a handsome subsidy; Bostra, his capital, was created a metropolitan see, with jurisdiction over parts of Arabia and Palestine. The same methods were used by Persia, and to read the histories of Ammian or Procopius is to realize that the similarity extended also to the actual fighting. We find the same tactics, ruses, siege-craft, fortification, and even armament. The parallelism is seen likewise in the results of the great campaigns. The conquests of a Trajan or a Julian do not endure; the Persians take Lazica, which geographic fatality has denied them; in a few years they are forced to evacuate it. Chosroes ravages Syria, and even reaches the Mediterranean, and carries off a fragment of the True Cross. He has soon to restore it, and to repel invaders from his own territory. A deadlock had arisen; the defences were stronger than the attack, and it was not until the entrance of Islam upon the scene that the equipoise of the two Empires was upset.

The end of Justinian's long reign is a period of deepening gloom. Theodora died in 548, and deprived of her inspiration the aged emperor became irresolute and negligent of the affairs of the Empire, and concerned only with theological disputes. 'His thoughts were all on heaven', sang Corippus, the discreet African poet, celebrating the accession of the new ruler. His last ordinance, published in 565, relates to ecclesiastical matters, and is stuffed with quotations from the Scriptures and the Church Fathers, evidence of intensive study. Since 555 there had been no regular wars, and the army had been dangerously reduced in numbers and efficiency owing to financial straits. The Persian frontier lay practically open, and Byzantium itself was defended only by its decorative guardsmen. In 558 the Danube strongholds were abandoned, and the Long Wall of Anastasius was crumbling into ruin. The Kutrugurian Huns, provoked by the double-dealing of Justinian, poured into Thrace, and advanced to the walls of the capital. Panic ensued, and the situation was only saved by the prompt action of the veteran Belisarius. Four years later a similar attempt by the Avars was with difficulty repulsed. The enormous cost of the buildings of Justinian, his wars, his Court expenses, had drained the treasury. The coinage was debased, the taxes increased in number and severity. The misery of the population was heightened by a succession of serious earthquakes, followed by an outbreak of plague. In Byzantium itself the city services were failing. One year there would be a scarcity of provisions; in another, the water-supply would be deficient. The Greens and Blues once more began to make the streets unsafe, and there was talk of a plot to murder the Emperor, while two rival Justins openly intrigued for the succession.

In his palace sat Justinian, eighty-two years old, in the shadow of approaching death, caring for none of these things. Far into the night, with senile iteration and remorseless ingenuity, he was pursuing, in the company of a few aged priests, the absorbing problems of the charnel-house, the macabre riddle of Divine corruption.

VII

THE AFTERMATH

THE ruin of Justinian's handiwork was nowhere seen so speedily as in northern Italy. A few years after his death the Lombards burst into the plains that lie between Alps and Po, and in a short time had possessed themselves of the district. From their original home in the Elbe region they had travelled across Europe by stages. By the end of the fifth century they were the ruling power in Hungary, and soon afterwards, by crushing the Heruls, they became Rome's neighbours on the Danube. Their conversion to Arian Christianity, and the introduction of more settled conditions, led to an increase in the royal power, as was usually the case with German peoples when thus exposed to Roman influences. But the culture which they acquired here was very slight; a century later they appeared to the Romans to be typical 'barbarians'. Their king, though absolute, was little more than a war-leader chosen for a single campaign. They possessed no magistrates or constitution; the blood-feud still reigned supreme, and the real bond of society was the clan. Since their departure from the Elbe they had rarely remained settled on the same land for more than one generation, and their agriculture was consequently primitive, since even in Hungary they had left the field-work to be done by slaves and subject peoples, while they themselves plundered the territory of their neighbours.

Hitherto the Lombards and Gepids had been the leading forces on the Danube frontier, and Justinian had, in Rome's customary fashion, retained Sirmium, the key-point of the district, for the Empire by playing off one people against the other. The entry of the Avars, a fierce tribe of Asiatic origin, broke up this situation. Using the Lombards as their catspaw, they destroyed the Gepid kingdom, taking most of the territory and booty for themselves. The Lombards were now in sorry plight; their independence was threatened by the Avars, and the hoped-for increase of land was not forthcoming. In desperation they embarked upon what was to prove the final stage of their migration. In 568, under the leadership of Alboin, the Lombard host set out for Italy, its numbers swollen by adventurers of various races. Narses, governor of Italy, had just been recalled, and the frontier defences seem to have offered no effective resistance. Cividale fell, and the Friuli region was soon overrun; the Patriarch of Aquileia left his doomed city and fled to the lagoons of Grado. The Imperialists retained Padua and Mantua, holding the Po line, and preventing the Lombards from streaming down the eastern coast; but Vicenza and Verona were lost, and the frontier region of the southern Tirol was now cut off from Ravenna. A year later Alboin entered Milan, and finally, after a long siege, captured Pavia, which became the Lombard capital. Northern Italy had been torn from the Empire, but worse was to come. In succeeding years Ravenna and Rome itself were continually threatened, and Byzantine counter-attacks successfully beaten off, while two independent Lombard bands pressed southward to found the great duchies of Spoleto and Benevento.

The death of Alboin was followed by a kingless period of more than ten years. The conquest had been carried out by means of subordinate leaders, who were placed in command of garrisons in the principal towns. Gradually these 'dukes', about thirty-five in number, became settled in the districts they had originally occupied, and the 'duchies' developed into hereditary domains, largely independent of the central power. The weakness of the kingship, which permitted this independence, is the determining factor in Lombard history. A strong monarch might reduce to obedience his recalcitrant dukes, and even, on rare occasions, control the powerful duchies of the South. But the initial period of freedom had done its work. Lombardy was always a kingdom divided against itself. Its enemies—Emperors, Popes, or Frankish invaders—could always count on the support of some rebellious Lombard noble. And it was due to this lack of cohesion that the conquest of Italy was never brought to completion. Byzantium could spare few troops to reinforce her garrisons; the power of the Papacy was, as yet, undeveloped. It was only the weakness of the Lombard monarchy that saved the Imperial forces from being swept from the shores of Italy, and the Pope from being reduced to the level of a Lombard bishop.

Preceding invaders of Italy had, as we have seen, regarded the Roman inhabitants as fellow-partners in the Empire. The Lombards, on the contrary, looked upon them as subjects, and treated them like the Slavs in Hungary who had tilled the soil for their warrior overlords. The Roman landlords were expropriated, and their land, cattle, houses, and *coloni* became the booty of the conquerors. But it was not land, as such, that the Lombards wanted, it was rather the means of living in idleness, or in economic freedom to make war. The Roman land-organization was therefore retained; it was merely the ownership that changed hands. The *coloni* became identical with the Lombard half-free class, the *aldiones*, and some of the poorer landholders seem to have shared their fate. Church property was seized without scruple, for the Arian invaders were not inclined to respect the rights of Catholics. By this process every free Lombard came to be both soldier and landowner, though the size of the holdings was not uniform, much of the land being retained by the dukes for their private estates. Under the combined influence of continued settlement and Roman organization the clan gradually disappeared, and was replaced by territorial ties. The unit was the duchy, and the extent of these duchies coincided, on the whole, with the districts (*civitates*) previously governed by magistrate and bishop, the chief town remaining the centre of administration. The duchies of Spoleto and Benevento, however, covered a much larger area, and were practically independent principalities, being isolated from the northern Lombards by a belt of Imperial possessions.

By the end of the sixth century the Lombard kingdom was firmly established in Italy. The monarchy had been restored under Authari, and owing to this reassertion of the central power the Lombards had not only held their own, but even increased their territory at the expense of Byzantium. Their chief danger at this period was the aggression of the Franks, who made continual raids into northern Italy in concert with the Imperial attacks from Ravenna. Authari (584-90) succeeded in ending this Franco-Byzantine alliance, which was, it is true, already undermined by the mutual suspicions of both parties, each of which accused the other, with considerable justice, of playing for its own hand. For a century and a half, thanks to Authari's achievement, Lombardy was free to concentrate its defence upon a single front.

Defence, however, was not enough. The king's position depended upon the size of his personal following, which enabled him to cope with the more powerful of his dukes. Owing to the lack of a regular financial system, this following had to be rewarded by grants of land, and this, in turn, necessitated further conquest. Any increase in the Lombard population worked also to the same end, since, as in ancient Sparta, each free warrior was economically dependent on his plot of land, tilled for him by servile labour. The result was a continual series of raids upon the neighbouring territory, and under this pressure the internal organization of Byzantine Italy transformed itself, during the two centuries which followed, into a military system of defence. Justinian had been careful to restore to Italy and Africa the administrative conditions of the fourth century, under which the military and civil powers were strictly separated. In the East, however, he had in some provinces favoured the union of both powers in the hands of a single officer, a practice which developed into the 'theme' system of later times. This policy was inevitable, and before long it was extended to the West. Every year the barbarian menace became more terrible, and there was no corresponding increase of the resources wherewith to meet it. Military considerations, in consequence, became paramount. Continual war conditions transformed the civil machinery of ancient Rome into medieval feudal dispositions. The soldier is now the most important member of the community, and in Italy a soldier class finally emerges as one of the chief divisions of the free population. The same principle is reflected both in central and local government. The Exarch, an official combining the supreme military and civil powers, is appointed at first in cases of special emergency, but soon becomes the regular governor of Italy, overshadowing the civil prefect, whose sphere is confined to duties of financial supervision. In the towns the municipal council and officers slowly disappear before the growing power of the military commander, the *tribunus*, who adds judicial and executive roles to his original authority.

Italy was now a frontier march, and every walled city became a fortress to be held against the enemy. From his head-quarters at Ravenna the Exarch directed the defensive system, elaborately centralized, whereby Byzantium, hard-pressed as she was by Avars and Bulgarians on one side, and the gathering storm of Arab invasion on the other, contrived nevertheless to keep her hold upon Italy for nearly two centuries. A notable achievement, in view of the peculiar difficulties presented by this province. Its interests were no longer identical with those of the capital. It mattered little to the Roman nobleman or the Italian peasant that Byzantium needed soldiers and money for the Eastern front. What immediately concerned them was the Lombard danger; and the Imperial forces were inadequate to deal with this, though troops and subsidies were from time to time dispatched for the purpose. It was necessary to make Italy depend on her own resources, and to this end the citizen population became a militia, stiffened at first by Byzantine detachments of regulars, but later drawn almost entirely from native sources. Under the Exarch were *duces*, controlling the new divisions into which the remnants of Imperial Italy had been grouped, and *tribuni*, commanding the city garrisons. Armies were maintained at strategic points, Ravenna, Rome, Naples, Calabria, while the fleets of Ravenna and Sicily secured communication by sea. On land, the main artery of a defence made difficult by geographical conditions was the road connecting Ravenna with Rome, and this was carefully guarded by a line of castles, and by a special force stationed at Perugia to control the crossing of the Apennine passes.

Centralization went farther. Determined efforts were made to assimilate Italy in every way to the other provinces of the Empire. Greek officials were placed in charge of the administration, and Greek methods adopted. Byzantine titles were bestowed upon members of the Italian aristocracy, and when their loyalty had been proved, executive offices were entrusted to them. A host of Oriental merchants, craftsmen, pilgrims, priests, and monks made its way into Italy. Byzantine manners and dress prevailed among the upper classes. Gregory of Tours describes the Roman noblemen whom he saw clad in silk dresses studded with jewels, and the mosaics of Ravenna tell the same

story.   At Venice eunuchs and separate women's quarters recalled the customs of Constantinople, and the ceremonial robes
of the Doges betray a similar origin.   In the churches of Italy
Eastern saints and martyrs received special attention at this time.
Dedications, for instance, to S. Michael, S. Theodore, SS. Cosmas and Damian, became common, while Byzantine ritual and
art were freely employed in the ecclesiastical buildings and
services. Bishops and even Popes bearing Greek names are
recorded; the Greek language became familiar once more at
Rome. From his palace on the Palatine the Roman *dux*, representative of the Exarch, and through him of the Emperor, dominated the city with his Byzantine troops, and in every large town
a Greek quarter was to be found, which was prepared to support
any measures taken by the central power to restore the obedience
of the Italian population. Most remarkable of all was the reconquest of southern Italy by the speech, manners, and institutions
of Greece, as classical Hellenism had conquered it fifteen centuries before. This process continued until the eleventh century,
surviving even under the Norman kings, and traces of it remain
to this day.

In spite of this intensive organization the Byzantine power
in Italy rested on unstable foundations. The Lombards were to
prove the immediate cause of its downfall, but the institutions
themselves contained the seeds of their decay. The actual com-
pleteness of the centralizing process contributed, when the weakness of the directing centre became manifest, to the emergence of
local forces. The Greeks had never, even when they came to
deliver Italy from the Ostrogoths, received the whole-hearted
support of the populace, and the exactions and rapacity of the
Byzantine officials did little to increase their popularity. The
antagonism between East and West, fostered by the fact that
their interests were becoming increasingly divergent, was brought
to a head by religious controversy. The rulers of Byzantium,
bent at all costs on preserving the unity of the Empire, made
continual efforts during these centuries to impose compromises
in religious matters, a policy which aroused fierce antagonism in
a Catholic Italy, careless of the problems of Imperial statesmanship. Finally, the same decentralizing tendencies which for the

past three centuries had been concomitants, if not causes, of the break-up of the Roman Empire were now accentuated in Italy by the needs of the time, which placed military considerations in the forefront. Under the stress of the invasions and of the economic ruin which they produced the old city life, and with it the middle-classes, had gone under. The great machine forged by Diocletian and Constantine had confined the lower classes in corporations, working for the service of the State. The upper class had ended by controlling the machine for themselves, and the bankruptcy of the State left them yet more powerful. Great landlords took over the local jurisdiction and tax-collection. They became responsible for the *coloni* on their estates. When Italy became an armed camp, and every citizen a militiaman, the military organization fell naturally into the hands of these nobles. The landowner became the leader of his retainers, as the tribune was the leader of the town contingents. And when the soldier class, owing to lack of Byzantine reinforcements, became predominantly Italian, local patriotism was bound to develop. The process was completed by the gradual identification of the Byzantine officials with the Italian aristocracy, since the former endeavoured to add to their powers by acquiring estates in Italy, and the latter, by holding Byzantine titles and executive offices, secured official standing and social distinction. Thus with the waning of the central power arises a feudal system, replacing the Imperial machinery by a number of local dominations.

The remaining functions of the central government were filled by the Church, the growth of whose temporal power was the last great factor in the formation of medieval Italy before Charlemagne. The Theodosian Code, and more recently the Pragmatic Sanction, had given to the ecclesiastical hierarchy not only special privileges but also a large measure of political power, especially in the sphere of municipal government. The tribune and the bishop now shared most of the rights and duties of the old municipal officials; and the power of the Church was further increased by her status as the largest landholder in Italy. In many of the towns it was the bishop who controlled the city-gates and saw to the proper garrisoning of the walls, as well as providing for the urban water-supply and other services. Hospitals and charitable offices had long been the care of the Church; and even in matters of jurisdiction and taxation she had been able, by her superior organization and her moral prestige, to secure for herself a definite standing in the Imperial system of government.

The increasing power of the Papacy is shown by the growth of the estates of the Church, which not only assured the revenues of the See of Rome, but also provided a means of exerting moral and material influence throughout Italy. Since the time of Constantine the Church had been legally empowered to hold property, and this property had shown continuous increase owing to the legacies of wealthy Christians and the donations of Roman nobles. A further cause was the working of the universal tendency of the smaller landowners to place themselves under the protection of a powerful landlord, freeholders often becoming mere life tenants in return for the advantages of security.

The letters of Gregory the Great, written at the close of the sixth century, provide valuable information concerning Rome's efficient and detailed management of her various 'patrimonies'; they serve also to show the part played by Gregory himself in developing the material resources of the Church. In his instructions to the 'rectors', ecclesiastical officials who combined the duties of bailiffs, magistrates, and poor relief officers in their several districts, attention is paid to the minutest details of stock-farming, leasing, slave-holding, and all the matters which concerned a landlord. Saddles are supplied from Campania, and wooden beams from Bruttium, for the use of the Roman Church. From Sicily, where lay the richest and most extensive of the patrimonies, came large contributions of corn, which secured the provisioning of Rome herself—a symbol of the replacement of Imperial functions by ecclesiastical activity in the former capital of the Empire. The vast revenues obtained in this way were applied to all manner of uses—ransoming of prisoners, relief of famine, maintenance of hospitals, support of various churches which had suffered by Lombard ravages. *Douceurs* finally, on a princely scale, seem to have been given to the various Byzantine officials whose co-operation was found necessary, apart from the funds employed in more indirect diplomacy. An interesting light is thrown on these relations of Gregory with the Imperial administration. His letters are full of accusations, couched in the plainest terms, of rapacity and injustice. It is clear, moreover, that he speaks as one having authority, and in the full expectation that his warnings will not go unheeded. Preceded and followed by obscurer pontiffs, Gregory holds already, in some degree, the position which the Papacy was destined to occupy in later centuries. Head of a strong central organization, unquestioned arbiter of justice, armed with the Keys of Peter and the old majesty of Rome, he is an almost superhuman figure, beside whom, in the eyes of the suffering population of Italy, the Emperor is but a far-off potentate, and the Exarch merely an ineffectual general or an unjust governor.

It must, however, be emphasized that this power lay rather in the personal prestige and moral authority of Gregory than in the material force at his command. To meet the many-sided opposition to the claims of the Roman See, untiring diplomacy and careful combinations were necessary. Even within the confines of Italy and Istria, the great archbishops of the North—Milan, Aquileia, and Ravenna—refused to accept the domination of Rome, and though the schism was eventually healed, their independent attitude was maintained, not without secret encouragement from Byzantium, which welcomed such checks on the undue growth of Papal influence.

But Gregory's aims were wider than the boundaries of Italy. In the functionaries whom he appointed to superintend the Church estates, in Italy and elsewhere, he had ready to hand a corps of diplomatic and intelligence officers, through whose agency he was able to establish contact with all the governing forces of the West, lay or ecclesiastical. He did not hesitate to invite (with incomplete success) the aid of the Imperial power in reducing Illyrian bishops to obedience, in repressing Donatists and pagans in the African exarchate. In Spain, where the Visigoth kingdom had recently become Catholic, Gregory lost no time in entering into close relations with the royal house as well as with the hierarchy of the new Church. In France a determined though fruitless effort was made to exercise, through the Papal Legate at Arles, that authority over the national Church to which the Roman bishops had long laid claim. The correspondence of Gregory with various Frankish sovereigns, in particular the notorious Brunhilda, urges the suppression of simony and other abuses in the Church, and proves his intimate acquaintance with the conditions prevailing in the various dioceses, as well as with the course of political events. The Papal claims were received with respect rather than admission, for the Merovings were not inclined to surrender the advantages of ecclesiastical control; but the personal influence of Gregory was recognized throughout France, and a still further extension of his activities is shown in Augustine's mission to England, which was destined to have such important consequences.

Meanwhile, the primacy of the Roman See was stubbornly maintained against Eastern encroachments, a bitter controversy being carried on with the bishop of Constantinople, who claimed, as Metropolitan of the capital of the Empire, the title of Oecumenical (or 'universal') Patriarch. Relations with Byzantium were strained still further by the diverging theories of Papacy and Empire. To Gregory, the Pope was above the Exarch, the Church above the State; to the successors of Justinian, on the other hand, the Italian province, like other parts of the Empire, was subject to the Emperor and his subordinates, for 'it is not the State which is within the Church, but the Church which is within the State'. To Gregory, convinced that the sole path to Heaven lay, for those called thereto, through priesthood or monastery, the decree of the Emperor Maurice, forbidding ordination or the cloister to his civil servants or soldiers, became a crime which would have to be answered for at the terrible Judgement of the Last Day. A Byzantine bishop, closer to the Eastern frontier and consequently more aware of the desperate peril of the Empire and its need of every possible recruit if civilization itself were to be saved from destruction, would perhaps have been more understanding than Gregory. As it was, relations between Rome and Constantinople were practically broken off at one period; and the paean of rejoicing with which Gregory greeted the assassination of Maurice shows the depth of his conviction that the interests of the Church had been gravely menaced by the policy of the dead Emperor. No thoughts, however, of a possible separation from Byzantium can have entered his mind, and indeed the Italian situation forbade it. The enemy was at the gate; and though he underestimated the difficulties that confronted the Exarch, Gregory fully recognized the value of his protection, and the necessity for co-operation in dealing with the Lombards—though even here hints of a separate policy foreshadow the future course of Papal diplomacy.

The character of Gregory was admirably fitted to deal with the peculiar situation. By birth a Roman noble, he had filled the office of Prefect of the City before entering a Benedictine monastery. In his subsequent career as Papal Legate at Constantinople he had enjoyed opportunities of observing the Imperial diplomacy at first hand, in that city which was still the centre of European politics. Nothing is more marked in Gregory's activities than the clear-sighted realism with which he interprets the current of affairs both in the Empire and in the barbarian kingdoms, and even diverts it on occasion to the service of the Church. Succeeding to the Papacy at a time when all Italy was in utter confusion and distress, he found himself at the head of the only stable institution in a changing world. His surroundings reinforced the teaching of his legal and administrative training; only by material means, in such an age, could the Church perform fully its work of spiritual salvation. Stress is accordingly laid on the practical doctrines of penitence and purgatory, on the atoning power of benefactions to the Church. Unworthy instruments—Brunhilda in France, Phocas at Byzantium, stained by many and notorious crimes—are nevertheless hailed as champions of the Church, for the civil power lies in their hands, and only through them can justice be enforced. Gregory's realism shows itself also in his disregard of literary style, of classical education, even of orthography. He frowns upon any extraneous studies that may hinder the interest of, or create a spirit critical towards, a Church whose unquestioning obedience constitutes its true strength. Gregory openly professed ignorance of Greek; his acquaintance with Church history is curiously slight, and his most characteristic production is his Commentary on the Book of Job, with its fantastic interpretations and strained allegorical conceits. It is sufficient evidence of the decline in cultural standards which had taken place since the days of Boethius and Cassiodorus that the medieval reputation of Gregory, apart from his *Pastoral Rule*, rests mainly on his dogmatic learning.

But we are still on the threshold of the Middle Ages. Gregory is the last great personality of the transition period in the West. There is little indication that he realized the new paths which the Papacy was destined to tread. It was sufficient for him to deal with each emergency as it arose, to preserve the Catholic faith from compromise or error, to protect the suffering population of Italy, and, above all, to maintain intact the powers and privileges of the Bishop of Rome. He is a Janus-like figure. One aspect foreshadows (at least, to later eyes) the Papal domination of the West, the temporal power of the Church, the peculiar blend of legalism and mystic doctrine which characterizes medieval thought. The other aspect shows us the greatest of those Roman nobles turned bishop, who, in Gaul, Africa, or Italy, through the wreckage of the Empire, led their retainers in a desperate fight against the swamping deluge of barbarian invasion, owing what success they gained less to the material forces at their command than to the unwilling respect accorded by their enemies to strength and nobility of character, and to the glamour of an ancient civilization.

As his epitaph proclaims him, Gregory is 'God's Consul'—a Roman statesman, last of his line.

Justinian bequeathed to his successors an Empire burdened with debt, distracted by religious controversy, extortionately governed by a bureaucracy more corrupt than ever, and inadequately protected by a dwindling army against the new dangers that threatened its frontiers. To make matters worse Justin II had taken over, with this *damnosa hereditas*, an equal, if not increased, share of the imperialist ideas which had actuated Justinian. Insolent demands on Avars and Persians, reinforced by no military or financial strength, ended only in ignominious withdrawals, or worse, in the outbreak of ruinous wars. In spite of Chosroes's desire for peace, Justin provoked hostilities with the Persian Empire (a *casus belli* was never wanting on the long frontier), and temporary success for the Roman arms was speedily followed by the disastrous fall of Dara (573), one of the chief defences of the Mesopotamian line. Justin's megalomania now issued in madness; Tiberius, an able general, became his successor, and a policy more suited to the needs of the situation was inaugurated.

Fully realizing the critical position of the Empire, Tiberius was prepared to concede lands to the Avars in the Danube region, taking care only to retain Sirmium, the essential point. But things had gone too far, and shortly before his death the great fortress was surrendered to the Chagan of the Avars, while a flood of Slav invaders poured resistlessly into Northern Greece. The action taken by Tiberius had anticipated the future course of events. Byzantium, separated from Western Europe by a solid barbarian block, must concentrate henceforward upon her Asiatic provinces, where a definite policy of conciliation in religious matters and alleviation of fiscal hardships was laid down for the reassurance of her wavering subjects. Meanwhile, despite every effort made to terminate hostilities, the war with Persia dragged on, ruinous but inconclusive, into the reign of Maurice, who succeeded Tiberius in 582. A lucky chance to end it occurred in 591, when a new Persian ruler, placed in power by a palace revolution, was forced to seek Roman aid to maintain himself upon the throne. Peace was the price exacted by Maurice, and a general westward movement of the Byzantine troops was at once set on foot, with a view to restoring the Danube frontier. The tide seemed to have turned in favour of the Empire; but another reversal of fortune was destined to plunge it immediately into the lowest depths. Anxious to follow up his success against the Avars, Maurice refused to allow his troops to return to the capital for winter quarters. A mutiny broke out on the Danube. Phocas, an uneducated centurion, was proclaimed Emperor, and the rebels marched upon Constantinople. Maurice's stern measures had made him generally unpopular, and Phocas found no difficulty in entering the city. His coronation was followed by a general massacre of the former reigning house.

The strong hand of Maurice was now removed, and under the purposeless rule of his successor it seemed that chaos was come again. The circus-parties of the great cities were at each others' throats; persecution of Monophysites and Jews, expressly ordered by Phocas, was rapidly alienating the Eastern provinces, while Persian armies steadily advanced along the whole frontier-line from Armenia to Palestine. In 608 they were at Chalcedon, facing Constantinople across the narrow strip of sea. Plague raged in the capital, and shortage of food added to the miseries of the inhabitants. Even the Greens, the Emperor's own party, taunted him in the Circus and resisted his officers, in consequence of which they were deprived of political rights.

Salvation was to come from an unexpected quarter. Africa, at this time perhaps the most flourishing of the Imperial possessions, was governed by Heraclius, a brilliant and successful veteran commander. Disaffected nobles at Constantinople had entered into correspondence with him, and he finally consented to dispatch an expedition to place his son, another Heraclius, on the Imperial throne. In 610 the fleet sailed from Carthage, and the fresh spirit of enterprise, the battlemented ships, the picture of the Virgin, 'not made with hands', which the leader carried at his masthead, bring us into a new atmosphere. Medieval Byzantium is before us. The city on the Bosporus is no longer the true centre of the Mediterranean world. Her territory is narrowed down to the surrounding districts of Asia Minor, Thrace, and Macedonia. Spain has driven out the Imperial garrisons. Byzantine power in Italy steadily diminishes in face of the development of Papal and Lombard organization. After 604 no Roman troops are found in Dalmatia. Slav invasions have driven a wedge between East and West, and the rift grows continually wider. Gradually the Balkan States are coming into being. The Empire now looks eastwards, and its forces are concentrated on the Persian front.

Heraclius encountered few obstacles in overthrowing Phocas, the hated tyrant, whose death immediately followed his downfall. But this was only the beginning of his task. Twelve years were to elapse before the Empire was sufficiently restored to be able to undertake aggressive operations of any size against its Eastern enemies. Order and discipline had to be re-established in the armies; the insolence of the nobles and the turbulence of the factions must be abated, the financial resources of the State must be repaired, and the religious conflicts of the provinces appeased, before Heraclius could deliver Constantinople from the twofold menace of Avars and Persians, and restore to the Empire its lost provinces. In the meantime the Persian advance continued. By 614 Damascus had fallen; Jerusalem itself was captured soon afterwards, and the True Cross, the holiest relic of Christianity, carried off to Persia. Egypt now became for ten years a Persian province, and her invaluable resources of food-stuffs and revenue were lost to Byzantium. Worse still was to come, for the Persian forces advanced again through Asia Minor, and pitched their camp at Chalcedon, facing the capital across the waters of the Bosporus, while simultaneously on the land-ward side the Avars, descending in force, ravaged the northern suburbs. In despair, Heraclius actually thought for a moment of transplanting the seat of Empire to Carthage, in order to make a fresh start in a new environment, where precedent carried no weight. This remarkable plan was not realized, but its concep-tion indicates the originality of its author, an originality that marks the solution which he ultimately found.

By 622 much had been achieved. Careful appointments to important posts had surrounded the Emperor with members of his own family or trusted dependants. Economy in administra-tion and reorganization of the available troops had restored the Imperial machine to working order. Religious discord presented a more obstinate problem. Mere tolerance was not enough, since in this age even tolerance had to be imposed by force. A formula of compromise was found to patch up the differences of Catholics and Monophysites, but the long-continued efforts of Heraclius to secure its acceptance met with repeated failure.

In the capital, however, all were of one mind in face of the common peril, and the forthcoming campaign against Persia began to take on the aspect of a crusade. For nearly a century this point of view had been gaining ground; the wars of Byzan-tium were coming to be regarded as holy wars, undertaken in defence of the Christian faith, whose existence was indissolubly bound up with that of the Roman Empire. The strange genius of Heraclius sharpened the religious consciousness of his subjects;

Church and State were at one in furthering the great enterprise. Sergius, the Patriarch, allowed Church money to be borrowed to finance the operations. Sacred vessels of gold and silver were melted down to provide additional funds. Blues and Greens were reconciled for the nonce, and even the free distribution of bread—the prerogative of the capital since the days of the Gracchi—was able to be suspended without serious disturbance.

The strategy of Heraclius was bold in the extreme. Constantinople was menaced on two sides. He resolved to buy the Avars off, while he concentrated his attacks on Persia. Further, instead of attempting to regain the lost provinces of Syria and Egypt, he decided to strike at the very heart of Persia, and to lead southwards into the Tigris valley all the Christian peoples of Armenia and Trans-Caucasia. In less than six years (622–8) he had accomplished his daring project. In the first campaign (622–3) the chief object was the freeing of Asia Minor. Heraclius landed at Issus, near the 'Cilician Gates' which form the entrance from Syria into Asia Minor. Advancing into Cappadocia and Pontus he drew off the Persian troops from their threatening position at Chalcedon, and defeated them in a decisive battle. The next two years (623–5) saw a further advance. Heraclius occupied Armenia, and busied himself with recruiting the Colchian and Iberian tribes. Successful raids were made into the northern districts of Media, but the Persian armies, in spite of repeated reverses, were still able to prevent a definite invasion.

The year 626 was the turning-point of the war. Chosroes determined to put forth all his strength to crush this dangerous adversary. One army was to hold Heraclius, another was to advance on Chalcedon and attack the capital. Meanwhile the Chagan of the Avars had collected an enormous host, and was preparing to invest Byzantium simultaneously from the north. There had been loose alliances on former occasions between the European and Asiatic foes of the Empire; but this was the first example of a strictly co-ordinated effort, and the double menace was overwhelming. With sublime courage Heraclius held to his plan. Part of his forces was dispatched to Constantinople, where Bonus the Patrician and Sergius the Patriarch were placed in charge of the defence. Another part was to oppose the Persian

containing force, while Heraclius himself held Armenia, and proceeded with his preparations for an attack on Persian territory.
All through July the siege of Byzantium continued. Each day
saw some fresh attack upon the walls, while Slavonic vessels in
the harbour threatened the sea defences. Filled with religious
enthusiasm the inhabitants put up a desperate resistance. A
concerted attack was repulsed with heavy losses; the plan having
been discovered beforehand, many of the Slavs were trapped by
Roman ships, and the Avars, panic-stricken at the disaster to
their forces, retired from the siege. Meanwhile the other Persian
army had been defeated, and Heraclius himself was nearing the
end of his long preparations. Towards the close of the next year
the final blow was struck. Heraclius descended into the Tigris
valley, routed the last Persian army, which fled southwards in
disorder, and seized for himself the residence of Chosroes, seventy
miles north of the capital. Persian resistance was at an end. The
armies revolted, and Chosroes was deposed, and put to death
with lingering tortures. His son made peace with Heraclius, and
the Persian Wars of the Roman Empire were over for good and
all. By the terms of the agreement Rome regained all her lost
provinces, and the prisoners in Persian hands were restored to
her. The most striking symbol of victory was the return of the
True Cross, which figured largely in the joyful pageantry which
greeted Heraclius on his return to Constantinople. Old and new
persisted side by side in this closing ceremony of a passing world.
The triumph of the Roman Imperator, whom his people saluted
by the name of Scipio, found its conclusion in the cathedral of
St. Sophia, where the Patriarch raised high the sacred relic of the
Rood to bless the Christian Emperor, Head of the Church and
Defender of the Holy City.

The brilliant ceremonial was the celebration of a real and
startling revival of the fortunes and prestige of Rome. On north
and west the Avar domination steadily declined after its check
before the walls of Byzantium. Slavs and Bulgars revolted from
its hegemony, and the next few years witnessed the foundation of
the first Slavonic power in Moravia, speedily followed by the
establishment in Dalmatia of an independent Croat principality.
In the East the Persian Empire, hereditary foe of Rome, had

received the heaviest blow ever dealt it by a Roman Emperor. All its recent acquisitions had been torn away, and permanent civil war was now implanted in its territory. Once more the Mediterranean civilization had claimed for itself the populations of Asia Minor, Syria, and Egypt. The final chapter of Graeco-Roman history had been written.

It was actually the last triumph of the ancient world. Rome and Persia, the age-long combatants, had destroyed each other in a final death-grapple. Their weakened and rebellious provinces lay open to the onslaught of Islam, which in a few years was destined to break forth from the Arabian deserts. Behind the barrier of the Balkan states, now rapidly coalescing, Western Europe was assuming new forms. The growth of feudalism in Italy and France can already be discerned, and signs are not wanting of the future expansion of the Papal power. The missionaries of Rome have carried her message to the far West, and England is slowly becoming Christian. Out of the chaos of invasion, the medieval world of Europe is beginning to take form and substance.

PART III

THE ONSLAUGHT OF ISLAM

VIII

THE FAITH

THE beginnings of Islam are made more difficult of comprehension not only by the obscurity which surrounds the birth
of any religion, but also by its later developments, which tend to
transform the primitive characteristics, and even sometimes to
replace them by opposite qualities. Islam, in its earliest stages,
was a personal faith; Islam to-day, as a world-force, is a faith and
culture uniting the most diverse peoples; Islam as a conquering,
nationalist principle is the connecting link between the two. In
summary outline, then, three aspects of Islam may be distinguished—the Faith, the Conquest, and the Culture—and it is
convenient, if not strictly accurate, to label by these names three
phases in its historical development.

In the case of all three, it was inevitable that misconceptions
should exist in the current view taken of them. The 'paynim
followers of Mahound' still suffer from their medieval reputation,
and are seen through the eyes of a crusading Europe. Only in
recent years has intensive criticism sought to discover what facts
may lie embedded in the mass of legend and tradition which is
virtually all that remains, in Christian or Moslem sources, of the
earlier history of the movement. It used at one time to be thought
that the Faith of Islam was a new Faith, an original Arabian
religion. It is now certain that the Faith was not new, neither
was it Arabian. Arabia, it is true, was its cradle, and Arab cults
and social habits imposed certain limitations upon its outlook,
and influenced its ritual; but the creed is actually the offspring
of Judaism and Christianity, with a later admixture of Zoroas-
trianism. It was not new, but rather the assertion of continued
revelation to the Peoples of the Book; Abraham, Moses, Jesus,
Mahomet—the line of prophets is unbroken. The teaching of
Islam may, in one sense, be regarded as a re-emphasis of the
Semitic elements in Christianity, which had become submerged

by Hellenistic influences.[1] The Conquest of Islam, moreover, can no longer wear the aspect of a fierce crusade of fanatical and visionary warriors, bearing the sword in one hand, the Koran in the other, intent on forcible conversion of the unbelievers. It was in reality a nationalist movement, caused largely by food-shortage,[2] and led by a sternly realist aristocracy of military adventurers, in whose view the conversion of the subject races was politically inexpedient. Finally, the Culture of Islam was not, as is often supposed, an Asiatic civilization, irreconcilably opposed to that of Europe. It was, on the contrary, a product of the same elements as those which formed the background of early Christian thought, the union, namely, of Hellenistic and Semitic culture which pervaded the Near East; and this common basis accounts largely for the extensive influence exercised by Islam upon the medieval culture of Europe. The religious hostility of Christian and Moslem has obscured their common origin, their co-heirship in the legacy which the conquests of Alexander bequeathed to mankind; but this community can, none the less, be traced throughout the history of Islam, although with the spread of the faith into Asiatic regions, and the shifting of the capital from Syria to Iraq, Oriental characteristics become more prominent. Let us now see how these apparent paradoxes can be explained.

The sudden movement which in the seventh century A.D. launched upon the world a conquering Arab nation is one of the surprises of history. Arabia is a country peculiarly ill-suited to unified control, as Rome and Persia, Turkey and Great Britain have, each in its turn, had good reason to remember. By far the greater portion of its territory is desert land, patrolled by Bedouin nomads, stubbornly individual by nature and training, acknowledging no bond or loyalty outside the tribe, or in some

---

[1] In the eyes of medieval writers, Islam was not a pagan religion but a Christian heresy. Thus John Damascene in the eighth century compares it with previous heretical movements, and Dante (*Inf.* xxxviii. 31–6) regards Mahomet as a heretic, *seminator di scandalo e di scisma.* (Cf. A. Vasiliev, *Histoire de Byzance*, vol. i, p. 274.)

[2] Whether or no Caetani's theory of a steady process of *inaridimento*, or desiccation, in the Arabian peninsula be accepted, the importance of the economic factor among the causes of the Arab migrations cannot be overlooked.

cases the family.[1] A striking contrast to his wandering brethren is the sedentary Arab of the fertile fringes, accustomed to an urban life, engaged in commerce or agriculture, maintaining regular contact with civilized nations, the middleman of commerce on the great trade-routes between East and West. Yet a nationalist point of view is hardly to be expected here. In the extreme south-west, the population of the Yemen, profiting by the Red Sea trade, had attained a certain unity, as their ruins and inscriptions attest, under the rule of the Sabaean kings. But Abyssinian invasion, a century before,[2] had destroyed their political importance, though it could not alter the conditions which gave them so large a share in the traffic of the Far East. In the north, Rome and Persia had found it worth their while, as great powers have done in more recent times, to encourage a settled hegemony among the wandering tribes of Transjordania and the desert parts that stretch from Palestine to the Euphrates. The Ghassanid suzerainty, on the Syrian borders, was supported by Rome, while the prosperous kingdom of Hira, the trading centre of the lower Euphrates, was used by Persia as a buffer state. Both vassal kingdoms, however, had ceased to exist shortly before this time. On the west, the Arabs of the Hedjaz, though not politically united, had adopted settled conditions of life. Agriculture was practised in the northern part, and the settlement of Yathrib, known subsequently as Medina (*Madīnat an-Nabī'*, City of the Prophet), possessed a flourishing date-palm industry, and a considerable population of Jewish and Arab cultivators. Two hundred miles farther south on the great caravan route which passed up the shore of the Red Sea lay the town of Mecca, which owed its prosperity entirely to commerce. Its merchants provided the markets of Syria and the West not only with the incense and aromatic woods of South Arabia, but also with commodities from India and Further Asia which the hostility between Rome and Persia had prevented from taking the shorter Euphrates route. It was also a religious centre, for here was the Kaaba, with its mysterious black stone which drew pilgrims from all parts.

---

[1] 'I and my brother go against my cousin, and I and my cousin against the stranger.' Arab proverb.   [2] See p. 117.

Religion in Arabia was no more organized than politics; local shrines, sacred pillars and enclosures, hereditary ritual, and a large number of primitive and ill-defined deities were its constituent elements. The Jewish and Christian communities in the coastal districts had introduced their faiths, often in a debased or heretical form; but the bulk of the population remained attached to their ancient practices, which were probably, for the most part, on the level of the baetyl-worship of early Crete or Palestine. Such cults survived more by traditional usage than from genuine religious feeling; no attempt at theology was made, though a certain movement towards monotheism seems to have arisen, which may have influenced Mahomet in early life. Mecca was perhaps the most important of all the tribal sanctuaries. It was surrounded by a sacred territory, and the annual *Hajj*, the pilgrimage and festival which centred there, increased its prestige and contributed also to its commercial prosperity.

Mahomet was born at Mecca about A.D. 570. He was a member of the trading community, and by the age of thirty seems to have become reasonably affluent. It is impossible to determine the stages of his religious evolution, nor can we draw from the sources available to us a convincing account of his character. Many of the qualities attributed to Mahomet, whether attractive or the reverse, appear to belong to a generalized 'Prophet'—a type familiar to the East—rather than to an individual. The 'Mecca period', during which his secret propaganda slowly gathered round him a band of devotees, is shrouded in obscurity. The main subjects of his thought were bound to arouse opposition among the materialist and conservative merchants of Mecca, among whom ancient custom and tribal morality reigned supreme. His doctrine of the Unity of God met with no challenge or resistance, but the denial of the efficacy of local deities as intercessors, the emphasis laid on the universal duties of charity and pity, and, above all, on the imminence of the Last Judgement, which Mahomet preached with apocalyptic fury, were bound to be held suspect and subversive by respectable members of society. Under their scornful criticism, his wild utterances and confused thought were forced to justify themselves by argument, and his principles, borrowed largely from half-understood scraps of Christian and Jewish legends, were fortified by examples and analogies, drawn chiefly from the Scriptures. Such reasoning deepened the gulf that separated him from his ancestral worship, and he began to denounce its polytheism and idolatry, though the cult of the Kaaba was, by a true political insight, allowed subsequently to form an essential part of the new religion.

The turning-point was reached in 622, the date of the Hegira or migration, when Mahomet forsook his native city and turned to the more congenial surroundings of Medina. As his following grew, the necessity for laws and regulations became evident, and the new political importance of Mahomet is reflected in the series of 'revelations' embodying a civil and penal code and a number of ritual observances. In spite of opposition from the Jewish population, he succeeded before long in dominating the community, and attaching to himself a large body of believers who had, as the name Islam implies, 'submitted themselves to the will of Allah', and therefore to his Prophet. But their economic needs had next to be supplied, and a momentous step was taken when Mahomet determined to plunder the Meccan caravans, justifying his aggressive policy by representing it as God's vengeance on the unbelievers. Nothing was better calculated to persuade the Arabs of the truth of his teaching than the success of the Medinese raids, and when not even a powerful coalition of the Meccans and other victims had prevailed against them, the way was prepared for the triumphal return of the Prophet to Mecca (630). When Mahomet died, in 632, his political authority was supreme in the Hedjaz, and the respect accorded to his conquering arms throughout the peninsula was a sign that a new centralizing force had arisen in Arabia. God had abundantly justified his Prophet.

It is clear that the origin of Islam was purely religious. The urgent need to convert his fellow men was the motive of its founder in gaining his earliest adherents. Political elements emerge after the migration to Medina. From now on, the guiding principle is no longer conversion to the will of Allah, but submission to his Prophet. Individual conversions may still have been based on religious conviction, but tribe-conversions were political

in character. The spread of Islam is henceforward closely connected with the supremacy of Medina. All, however, were
Moslems, so long as its growth was confined to Arabia. When the
Arab forces spread over the Near East and northern Africa, the
home of ancient civilizations, the case was different, and Islam
is clearly seen as State rather than Religion. So far from enforcing
their beliefs at the sword's point, the conquerors left their subjects free to practise their own religions, provided they acknowledged the Arab supremacy, and paid the necessary tribute.
Inferior in culture, the Arab had no wish to throw away his only
advantage, that of belonging to the True Faith, by sharing it
with others. He preferred to live as a conqueror among a crowd
of helots. The final stage is reached when this military aristocracy
can no longer maintain its exclusive existence. The old bureaucratic and commercial system of the conquered states has been
taken over, and economic motives come into play. Social equality between conquerors and conquered is achieved in this way,
and the common elements of the Christian and Islamic religions
lessen the obstacles to conversion. This, however, was a gradual
process; the political conquest of the Near East by the Arabian
armies is separated from its 'Islamization' by a space of two or
even three hundred years.

IX

THE CONQUEST

RELIGION, as we have seen, had made possible the organiza-tion of Medina. This organization united the scattered Arabs in military conquest; out of this community grew a state. The key to the movement is to be found in the character of the imme-diate successors of Mahomet. His death was followed by a general rising in Arabia against the domination of Medina, and Islam seemed destined at this time to succumb before an overwhelming reaction of tribal feeling and particularist tendencies. The situa-tion was saved by the strong and ruthless generals who led the Medinese forces against the peoples of Central Arabia; they, and not the contemplatives of Islam, directed the course of the move-ment. In swift and merciless campaigns they gained ascendancy over the whole peninsula, uniting the warring elements in a loose confederation, organized for aggressive action. But before the subjection of Arabia was complete, the earliest raids on Syria and Iraq, undertaken only with small forces, and with little idea of regular conquest, had carried all before them, and the over-whelming victories of the Yarmuk and Kadesíya[1] had made it possible for the newly formed confederacy to avoid disruption by launching its masses upon the neighbouring territories. The time was ripe for such an adventure, and the nearest outlet for the surging forces was the land that lay immediately north of the peninsula, between the empires of Rome and Persia.

Neither power was in a position to offer organized resistance. A period of anarchy in the Sasanid domains had followed the triumphs of Heraclius, and when order was finally restored, it came too late. The situation of the Roman Empire, apparently so brilliant, needs more explanation. Her victories had not only rendered Persia a defenceless victim; they had at the same time so weakened her own resources that in less than eight years all her newly regained territory in Syria and Egypt was lost to her. One important reason for this speedy reversal of fortune was the decadence of her military power. Long campaigns had spoilt

[1] See p. 151.

the discipline of her troops, and the aged Heraclius, preoccupied by religious controversy, no longer exercised the same authority over them. The composition of the army was very mixed. Armenians and Trans-Caucasians had been enrolled in great numbers, and these unassimilated elements helped to provoke disorder, while their leaders, drawn in many cases from the feudal nobility of their own countries, proved equally insubordinate. The military value of the two armies in Syria was gravely impaired by these shortcomings, while in Egypt things were even worse. Here the defence was entrusted to a landed militia, inexperienced in warfare, while the command was shared between five equal chiefs, the consequences of which can easily be imagined. Serious as the military position was, a more formidable danger was the growing disaffection of the population. A determined policy of conciliation, relief from the burden of taxes, a tolerant religious attitude, might conceivably have kept Syria and Egypt loyal to the Byzantine administration, but the measures taken by Heraclius, inevitable though they may have been, alienated all sections of the populace. The Imperial treasury had been drained by the wars of conquest, and the provinces just regained were immediately compelled to take their full share in providing revenue. In Syria the situation was complicated by the mutual hatred of Jews and Christians which showed itself in riots and massacres in the big towns. In 634 orders were given for the forcible baptism of Jews, while the refusal of the Monophysites to subscribe to the Imperial formula was followed by persecution in Syria and Egypt alike. The result is seen in the help given by Jews to the Moslem invaders, and in the evidence of contemporary chronicles and lives of Coptic monks, where the defeats of the Empire are a subject for rejoicing, and a sign of celestial vengeance on the 'Chalcedonite heretics'.

Raids on the Syrian frontier cities had long been a regular practice of the border Arabs, and the first attempts of Islam can have created no consternation at Byzantium. In 629, well before the death of Mahomet, an attack on southern Palestine had been beaten off; but five years later a more formidable movement took place. Two armies entered Palestine from south and east, and inflicted a serious defeat upon the Byzantine forces. Next year

they were encamped before Damascus. The valiant efforts of
Heraclius to relieve the city were of no avail, and six months later
it was forced to open its gates. One after another, the remaining
towns succumbed to the invader; only Jerusalem, Caesarea, and
the coastal districts still remained intact. With undaunted
courage, Heraclius prepared to strike a decisive blow for the
defence of Syria. With the spring an overwhelming Byzantine
force, feverishly recruited during the winter, advanced upon
Syria. Damascus was retaken, and the Arabs retired before
superior numbers to the farther side of the Yarmuk. A number
of engagements took place in this region, culminating in a
terrible Byzantine defeat on the Yarmuk (Aug. 636), which
sealed the fate of Syria. Heraclius had thrown his whole strength
into the campaign, and its utter destruction removed all hope
of meeting the invaders in the field. One by one the fortresses
surrendered: by 637 the coastal towns, Acre, Tyre, Sidon,
Beirut, were in Arab hands; the next year saw the fall of Jerusalem and Antioch, and when Caesarea, the administrative
capital, was taken in 640, the country as a whole had already
accepted the domination of Islam.

The main force of the invasion had been directed against
Syria; expeditions to Iraq had been on a small scale, and not
markedly successful. The victory of the Yarmuk made it possible
to divert the stream of conquest, after a great battle had taken
place at Kadesíya (637), which for the future of Persia proved as
decisive as that of the Yarmuk itself had proved for Syria. The
Persian troops, utterly routed, fell back in disorder, while the
king fled precipitately from his capital. The Arab forces advanced
on Ctesiphon, which was taken and pillaged. Mesopotamia was
soon overrun, and Moslem bands pushed up the Tigris and
Euphrates valleys, and penetrated the Armenian mountain-
ranges. Meanwhile in the south and east the remaining provinces of the Persian Empire were steadily reduced to obedience,
and the last of the Great Kings, fleeing eastward before the
invader, found a miserable end at Merv, on the confines of
Turkish territory. It is noticeable, however, that the non-Semitic
culture of Persia proper, with its brilliant and individual traditions of over a thousand years, offered a far more stubborn

THE ISLAMIC WORLD

resistance than Syria or Iraq. Even after ten years the conquest was incomplete, and Persia succeeded in permanently retaining her national speech and ways of thought.

By 650 the Persian Empire was no more, but the impetus of its conquerors was not spent. Further Asia was now to feel the onrush of the Arabian avalanche. As in the West, its progress was made easy by the weakness of the opposing empires. The Turks, who had for about a century been masters of Central Asia, were in a state of anarchy, and the massive empire of their Great Khan had dissolved into a chaos of conflicting tribes. The Moslem cavalry now pressed onward into Herat and Balkh (651). Stayed for a time by internal dissensions in Iraq, the advance began again, and twenty years later, Bokhara and Samarkand fell before the victorious onset. Early in the next century, a new wave of invasion swept north-eastward to the borders of China, where the brilliant T'ang dynasty was at this period in full decline. Chinese Turkestan seemed destined to succumb: but new forces in China reasserted themselves, and by the middle of the eighth century equilibrium had been reached. Islam was now firmly entrenched at Balkh and Samarkand: it held control of western Turkestan, and commanded the passes of the Pamir. Meanwhile its raiding horsemen had already penetrated North-West India. The great empires of this region —Sind, Kashmir, Punjab—had been dominated by the Gupta rulers further south. Towards the middle of the seventh century, however, this hegemony had collapsed, and the full tide of Moslem conquest which set in at the beginning of the following century carried the Arab standard victoriously through the Indus basin, and laid the foundation for the future magnificence of the Punjab princes.

Of more immediate importance to the West was the conquest of Egypt, which followed closely on that of Syria. As in other cases, the permanent occupation of the territory was preceded by a plundering expedition, whose sudden success led to more extensive operations. But the campaign was inevitable. Apart from its rich cornland and its key-position in commerce, Egypt was a standing menace to Moslem Syria, a permanent naval base for Byzantine counter-attacks. Alexandria was the chief centre of ship-building in the eastern Mediterranean, and during the following centuries it was to be the cradle of the growing sea-power of Islam.

The details of the conquest are not clear. Two great figures stand out. The leader of Byzantine resistance was the patriarch Cyrus, who had also been placed in charge of the civil administration. The Moslem forces were commanded by 'Amr, a general who had already distinguished himself in Syria. The conquest centres round the siege of Babylon, not far from the modern Cairo. The complicated policy of Cyrus is difficult to estimate: his main purpose appears to have been to save useless bloodshed and destruction of property by timely compromise. Babylon, after holding out for several months, surrendered in 641. Alexandria, by a treaty of which Cyrus was the author, was handed over in the following year, and the subjugation of the rest of Egypt was systematically pursued. As we have noticed above, the Moslem policy in these early days was to segregate the Arab element from the conquered population, and make of them a ruling and privileged class. A new capital was therefore chosen, near the ancient Babylon, and Old Cairo came into being, as the central point of the Arab domination, just as in Iraq the seat of government had been placed, not at Ctesiphon, but at Kufa (near Hira), to form the citadel of Moslem Arabianism against foreign Persian culture. In the same way, the permanent conquest of North Africa may be said to begin with the foundation of the great city of Kairawan.

This further conquest was a slow process, impeded by two main factors, Berber resistance and the struggles for the Caliphate. Justinian's great wars had destroyed the Vandals, and restored prosperity to the coastal regions, but had failed to check the power of the Berber chieftains: whole districts remained in their hands, and only continual vigilance along the network of military roads and fortresses, supplemented by diplomacy and timely subsidies, preserved the cultivated lands from tribal razzias. The resources of the Empire had been drained by the Persian wars of Heraclius and the attacks of Islam; the capital was consequently unable either to help or to control its African province, and the governor of Carthage had actually raised the standard of revolt. In these conditions, Arab raids, which began to be made as early as 642, met with little organized resistance; but the permanent occupation of the country was delayed till the end of the century. This was due largely to the hostile attitude adopted at first towards the Arabs by the Berber chieftains. Once the tribesmen had been won over to Islam, the situation was changed. The African dominion of Carthage and Rome had centred in the coast-towns; that of Islam drew its strength from the Moorish inhabitants of the interior; from these masses emerged the flood of warriors which poured down on the maritime districts, driving out the remnants of Byzantine rule, and spreading across the sea to Spain and Sicily. The Berber element is decisive in the Moslem attacks upon Western Europe.

The other factor which has been mentioned as an obstacle to the advance of Islam was of less importance here than in the East. The struggles for the Caliphate, however, delayed the consolidation of Egypt, and thus hindered further progress; further, the leader of a successful raid was always liable to arouse the jealousy of the Caliph and was frequently recalled or superseded for this reason. The coast of the Pentapolis, which lay immediately to the west of Egypt, was secured as early as 642, in order to safeguard the left flank against Byzantine attacks; but not till 670 was the great camp founded at Kairawan, in Tunisia, as the base for extended operations in Proconsular Africa. About twelve years later, a general rising of the Berbers, who still sided with the Byzantine cities, drove the invaders back upon the Pentapolis, and the final conquest of North Africa, which took place in the early years of the eighth century, was only accomplished when the Berbers of the Aurasian mountains had been subdued and conciliated, and the growth of Arab naval power had made possible a concerted attack upon the coast towns.

But the Berber problem remained: subsidies were not enough to keep them loyal, and the conquest of Spain, which immediately followed, was due to the necessity of providing booty and occupation for the new allies. The attack on Spain which took place in 711 appears to have been at its inception one of those summer raids which throughout the Middle Ages descended upon the coasts and islands of Southern Europe, carrying off women from the countryside and jewelled images from the plundered monasteries. But unexpected success awaited the invaders. In their march along the southern coast, they encountered and scattered the forces of the Visigoths, and a triumphal progress began. The unpopularity of the Goths, and the treachery of the Jewish population, seeking to avenge their recent persecution, prepared the way. In two months Cordova had surrendered, and some weeks later Toledo followed suit. The Visigoth kingdom, weakened by dynastic changes and internal dissension, collapsed like a house of cards. These swift and surprising successes of the Moslem forces were consolidated the next year, when the governor of North Africa crossed over into Spain with reinforcements and in a series of systematic operations drove the Gothic chivalry into the Asturias mountains, and proclaimed from Toledo the sovereignty of the Caliph of Damascus. The advance continued across the Pyrenees, and in a few years the Arab-Berber troops were in possession of the southern French coastline as far as Narbonne. From this centre they were destined to harass the neighbouring towns, Toulouse, Arles, and Avignon, for the next forty years. But the left horn of the encroaching crescent had neared its limit. Eudo, Duke of Aquitaine, stoutly defended the walls of Toulouse, and the culminating point was reached in the great battle of Tours or Poitiers (732), in which Charles Martel decisively routed the Saracen forces. This battle has become a symbol of the salvation of Western Christendom from the infidel terror, and its legendary fame is not unjustified. But in fact the force of the invasion was spent, and it is doubtful whether any permanent conquest of southern France would have been possible. The Arab troops were by this time strongly diluted with Berber elements, and the antagonism between the two races, which was to show itself more clearly in Spain and Africa, had already appeared. The Kingdom of the Asturias, moreover, in the north-west corner of Spain, the magnet of all the forces of resistance to the invaders, was daily growing in strength, and a barrier was thus being placed along the Pyrenees, preventing reinforcements from the south.

A far more formidable menace to European civilization was developing at the other end of the Mediterranean. Byzantium was the real objective of Islam, and this right wing thrust was all the more powerful, since it came from the very heart of the new empire.

In 642 the plundering bands were in Cappadocia, in 646 in Phrygia, and in 651 and 653 they penetrated to Angora. In Armenia the situation was even more serious; between 646 and 666 a systematic occupation of the country was undertaken. In slow movements, alternated with sudden rushes, the tide was creeping towards Byzantium. In 668 it had actually reached Chalcedon. Meanwhile the Saracen sea-power had steadily developed. Stealing out from the African ports, the corsair fleets ravaged Crete, Lycia, and the Aegean islands, and Cyprus soon became an important naval base. As the fleets grew bolder, they pressed closer on the capital, and actions took place in the Hellespont itself. In 673 a determined assault by land and sea was made upon Constantinople, repulsed only by the utmost effort, and by the efficacy of the terrible 'Greek fire'. A twenty years' breathing-space was granted to the hard-pressed Byzantines, owing to civil war in Islam, and for a moment Armenia was regained; but in 693 the forward march of the Arabs was resumed, and again the Bosphorus was threatened. Finally in 717 came the great siege of Constantinople, and its heroic defence by Leo 'the Isaurian', whose brilliant victory set bounds for over three hundred years to the progress of Islam.[1]

This may well rank as one of the decisive battles of history. When the discomfited invaders turned homewards, after a year-long siege which had seen their transports burnt or captured, their troops numbed by the bitter weather or ravaged by plague and famine, they relinquished their last serious enterprise, for many centuries, against the capital of the Roman Empire. The reorganization carried out by the Isaurian rulers, which strengthened the internal resources of the Byzantine dominions, destroyed any possibility of concerted action on a similar scale. Henceforward the naval operations in the eastern Mediter-

[1] The advance of Islam began again with the Seljuk Turks after the battle of Manzikert (1071).

ranean were limited to summer raids, until the western Arabs, who had become possessed of Sicily and Crete, began to take a hand in the game. But it is the crowning glory of Byzantium to have stood alone against the full force of Islam, at the moment of its greatest strength and unity, the saviour not only of the ancient Imperial traditions but of the future of medieval Europe.

X

THE CULTURE

Mahomet had left no succession schemes, and his death removed the very mainspring of the movement. All had depended on him; the word of God, issuing from the mouth of his Prophet, had been paramount. Fierce dissensions at once sprang up among his immediate followers, and simultaneously the Arabian tribes, still unreconciled to the supremacy of Medina, raised the standard of revolt, while in various parts of the peninsula arose rival prophets, seeking to emulate the successes of Mahomet. As we have seen, the bloody 'Ridda' wars, which reduced Arabia to obedience, led directly to the foreign conquests of Islam. They had, however, another effect, namely the healing up of discord, in face of the common peril, among the factions of Medina. The venerable and respected Abu Bakr was chosen as Caliph, or 'Successor' (of the Prophet), and was succeeded, two years later, by Omar, a political genius of the first rank, whose skilful direction of the Syrian campaign laid the foundation of the Moslem Empire. In 644 he fell by the hand of a Greek or Persian assassin, and Othman, a member of the Umayyad family, became Caliph. The rivalries of Medina, however, still smouldered, and its autocratic power provoked opposition in many quarters. A movement of reaction against the central government started among the semi-nomadic troops of Kufa and Egypt, and was fostered in the name of religion by Othman's rivals. Obscure negotiations with the Moslems of Medina resulted in the murder of Othman by a party of troops from Egypt. Ali, the Prophet's son-in-law, who had probably been concerned in the movement, imprudently allowed the murderers to invest him with the Caliphate, the other claimants having withdrawn to Mecca. Since these claimants were supported by Basra, it was natural that Ali should be favoured by Kufa, the rival city, and the victory of Kufa over Basra secured him the temporary control of Iraq. Ali had now, however, to face the army of Moawia, governor of Syria; and though the first results were inconclusive, the balance of military strength and public opinion gradually turned in favour of Moawia. But before a decision could be reached, Ali had been assassinated, early in 661, by the adherents of a third party. His son Husain was proclaimed at Kufa, but abdicated in favour of Moawia a few months later. The fortunes of the Umayyad dynasty, which was to govern the Empire until 750, were henceforward secure.

Apart from the innovation of hereditary succession, which it was no mean achievement to have imposed on the individualist Arabs, important changes now began to be made in the system of government.[1]

The capital was fixed at Damascus, and the old religious authority, emanating from Medina, was replaced by political control, which borrowed its machinery from the Byzantine administration. Early in the eighth century the power of the Umayyads reached its zenith. The supremacy of Syria was assured, and powerful viceroys in other parts enforced the rulings of the Caliph. The attacks on Byzantium were renewed with increased vigour: in the West, Spain was added to the Empire, while in the East, Moslem arms penetrated to the Punjab, and far into Central Asia. A brilliant court flourished at Damascus, poetry and learning revived, and the Umayyad mosque in that city, together with the mosque of Omar in Jerusalem, display the second flowering, under the stimulus of Arab wealth, of Byzantine architectural tradition.

At this point, however, a decline set in. The history of the last Umayyads is a succession of brief reigns, a series of intensive feuds and outbreaks of revolt. Opposition to the dynasty arose from several sources. The old elective theocracy of Medina had never countenanced the ascendancy of the nationalist generals and statesmen of Syria, and continual intrigues in this quarter had to be encountered. Local feuds developed into a struggle between 'North Arabians' and 'South Arabians', which spread throughout the whole Empire. Africa and Spain, no less than Iraq and Khorasan, were torn by dissension, and even within the Umayyad house echoes of the dispute were heard, producing, as a result, palace murders and dethronements. The most formidable enemies of the régime, however, were the Shiites,

[1] Cf. p. 164.

members of the Shia, or party, of Ali, whose head-quarters lay
in Iraq. During the brief caliphate of Ali, Kufa had been the
capital of the Empire, and the memory of those golden days still
remained, to sharpen the resentment felt against the more
civilized and powerful Syrians. Gradually the movement took
on the emotional colours of a religious cult. Ali and his son
Husain, who had fallen in the cause of the Kufa people, were
venerated as saints. They were the martyrs of Islam, the son-in-
law and grandson of the prophet himself, and the depositaries of
the true faith. Their descendants, or certain of them—this point
gave rise to further discord—were the only rightful heirs to the
Caliphate. But it was not from Iraq that the revolution was
destined to take its birth. Though Persia, as a whole, had proved
itself loyal to the Umayyads in the time of their ascendancy, and
still remained, after their downfall, more faithful to their memory
than any province outside Syria, its north-eastern parts were the
scene of a Shiite outbreak which changed the whole face of the
Mahometan world.

Beginning in Khorasan, a great anti-Syrian movement swept
westwards, supported by the South Arabians, and dominated by
Persian influence, whose nominee, Abul Abbas, founder of the
Abbasid dynasty, was proclaimed Caliph as 'As-Saffah', the
Shedder of Blood, and proceeded forthwith to justify his name.
One by one the members of the Umayyad house were hunted
down; the only survivor fled westwards into Spain, where he
succeeded in gaining the supreme power. Meanwhile the ashes
of former Umayyads were thrown to the winds, their palaces and
aqueducts ruthlessly demolished. A new age was to begin; such
was the watchword of the conquerors.

They were right. The Abbasid victory marks the transformation of the Moslem Empire, as will be seen later in connexion with
the administrative and social spheres. From now on the Arab
conqueror yields up his exclusive position; the growth of converts, the exigencies of government and trade, the superior
numbers and civilization of the conquered peoples have done
their work. Islam is no longer the religion of the Arabian overlord; it is becoming the force that binds together Moslems of all
races. And the representative of that force is the Caliph. He is

no longer, as in Umayyad times, the director of schemes of conquest and exploitation by an imperial race; in spite of the increase in system and complexity of the administrative machinery, the provinces of the Moslem Empire successively free themselves from the political control of the central power, while remaining loyal to its religious authority. Spain was the first to go. In 756 Abdalrahman, last Umayyad survivor, was proclaimed Emir, and governed as an independent prince. Africa was not slow to follow suit. In 788 Idris ben Abdallah, a descendant of Ali, founded in Morocco a similar emirate, that of the Idrisites, with Fez as its capital. Here too the religious authority of the Caliph was not questioned, but in practice the ruler was independent. A more important emirate was centred at Kairawan, in Tunisia. Ibrahim ibn Aghlab, about 800, laid the foundations of the Aghlabite dynasty, whose naval power dominated the central Mediterranean throughout the ninth century. The conquest of Sicily, steadily pursued, was accomplished in 902. South Italy was continually ravaged, and in 846 Rome itself was the scene of one of their daring exploits. By 870 Malta was in their hands, the key to Western commerce, while the cities of the Adriatic were constantly at the mercy of their raiding corsairs. Not till the coming of the Normans in the latter half of the eleventh century were the Saracens driven back into Africa. Egypt, however, was not finally withdrawn from Abbasid authority until the Fatimid conquest in 969, when the revenues which had formerly drained into the coffers of Baghdad were diverted to provide for the adornment of Cairo, which became during the following centuries one of the most brilliant capitals of the Moslem world.

One by one the provinces in East and West assumed independence, and by the tenth century A.D. the Moslem Empire had ceased to be a political unity. But a unity of another sort, equally significant if less material, prevailed throughout its borders. Not for nothing was it that the same call to prayer sounded at the same hour from the minarets of Cordova, Kairawan, Cairo, Damascus, and Baghdad, that all eyes turned daily towards Mecca, and all hearts aspired to go thither on pilgrimage. And to this community of faith was added community of language, for Arabic was in every country the vehicle of religion and sound

learning. The prestige and splendour of Baghdad were mani-
fested by the widespread imitation of its government, customs,
and architecture; and the immense and unbroken flow of
commerce, extending by land and sea from farthest Asia to the
Atlantic, enclosed the varied peoples of Islam in the meshes of
an opulent and many-sided civilization.

In the earliest days of Islam, when Mahomet led his followers
from Medina to plunder the caravans, a simple division of spoils
was all that was needed in the way of financial organization. This
principle lasted well into the following stage; for the earlier
Umayyad Empire was, in effect, based on a system of plunder.
The conquering Arabs, lodged in great military camps, were
supported by the tribute exacted from the subject population;
the surplus revenues accrued to the central treasury at Medina,
out of which the Caliph dispensed bounty to his more important
followers.

It soon, however, became evident that this primitive plan was
insufficient for the needs of the Empire. As the faith of Islam
extended, so the revenue from taxation tended to diminish; for
only unbelievers were liable to tribute. The difficulty was met
at first by continuing to exact it from the new converts; but as
this class grew more influential, its grievances were bound to
cause trouble, and it proved ultimately one of the chief agents
in the downfall of the Umayyad house. Gradually the theory of
a dominant race, holding to ransom huge territories and peoples,
became untenable. One stage of the process is seen in the compromise by which all landowners, irrespective of creed, paid
ground-taxes to the treasury, while the poll-tax was reserved
for the unbelievers, an outward and visible sign of Moslem
superiority.

The breakdown of this exclusive system was only one of the
many changes which marked the advent of the Abbasid dynasty.
The dominions of Islam had been wrested from two ancient and
highly developed empires, Rome and Persia. Nothing in the previous experience of the desert nomads had prepared them for the
complicated administration made necessary by their new conditions. The Byzantine machinery of government, in consequence,

was taken over by the conquerors in Syria and Egypt, and the evidence of recently discovered papyri proves the continuance of the Roman fiscal and administrative system in these countries. When the capital was shifted to Baghdad, the influence of Persia, in its turn, made itself felt upon the central government. The new capital lay only thirty miles distant from Ctesiphon, the former centre of the Sasanid rulers; and the new dynasty at once endeavoured to secure a fusion of Arab and Persian, and to maintain an equal balance between them. The change is strikingly seen in the altered position of the Caliph. In the days of Abu Bakr, immediately after the Prophet's death, the authority emanating from Medina had been of a spiritual order: this authority had subsequently been transformed by the Umayyad statesmen of Damascus into an organized political domination, though traces of its Arabic origin still lingered in the patriarchal and nationalist character of Umayyad rule. The Abbasid Caliphate was, in one sense, a return to the original principles of Islam; the movement which brought it into being was largely of a religious nature, a reaction against the secular Umayyads, and in consequence the new rulers took care to buttress their authority with the theories of Medina theologians, theories constructed from the text of the Koran, eked out by oral tradition, and smelling somewhat of the lamp, since for over a century the theocrats of the Hedjaz had been alienated from the real practice of Moslem administration at Damascus. Mahomet had been absolute in all spheres, and so in theory was the Abbasid Caliph. This absolutism was, however, limited in several directions. The sovereignty exercised over the various emirates was, it has been shown, more apparent than real, and even in the capital itself the power of the Caliphate was often overshadowed by that of the Viziers. Weaker Caliphs were content to withdraw from the public gaze to the secluded pleasures of the harem, leaving to their officials the task of ruling the Empire, and to their Khorasanian bodyguard the defence of their persons. Leaders of the army also acquired political influence, and Caliphs were frequently made and unmade by the hands of the military.

Below the Viziers was a complex series of government departments, or Divans, which dealt with the affairs of the Treasury, the Chancery, the Army, the Imperial Household, and so forth. One of the most important of these was the Divan-al-Barid, or State Post, an interesting example of the manner in which the Caliphs inherited the traditions of both Rome and Persia. The name 'Barid' is derived from the Latin *veredus*, a post-horse, and like the *cursus publicus* it was a State institution, designed to secure centralized control and rapid movements of troops and officials. Other features are reminiscent of the old Achaemenid system of Persia, described by Herodotus; and like both its forebears, the purposes of the Abbasid postal organization included espionage, which was exercised on an extensive scale in all classes of society. The development of this espionage into one of the main instruments of government is typical of the Oriental methods of Baghdad. No official was trusted, and even the Caliph's own family was under strict surveillance. The police formed an important part of the intelligence service, and their duties included interference in the minutest details of daily life, while in every city a swarm of local officers, judges, tax-gatherers, and stewards of the Crown lands reduced still further the liberty of the subject.

The change from the nationalist, aristocratic government of Damascus to the cosmopolitan despotism of Baghdad only accelerated the amalgamation of conquerors and conquered. Henceforth all were slaves under one master; but the equalizing process had begun in Umayyad times. So long as the Arab, limited in numbers and still more in education, retained the monopoly of the True Faith, and lived in Spartan exclusiveness, fenced off from the common herd in his armed camp, drawing his livelihood from the Caliph's bounty, he was able to maintain his position of superiority. But these privileges were destined to be of short duration. On the one hand, material interest and religious indifference swelled the numbers of the non-Arab converts, and in consequence lessened the revenues from unbelievers; on the other, now that the wars of conquest were over, the Arab ceased to be a state pensioner, and became landowner, peasant, or small tradesman, subject to the economic laws and social distinctions of the country in which he found himself. Education and intellectual ability were needed, if he was to hold his own;

for the intricate civilization of Byzantine times continued with little change, demanding skilled administrators as before. Even in the early days Christians were appointed to positions of trust, particularly in matters of finance; and the toleration of non-Moslem faiths which was practised under the Umayyads left these communities free to prosper materially, provided they paid the necessary taxes, which were, on the whole, no heavier than those formerly exacted by the Byzantine government. A large measure of self-government was granted to the Christians, and churches and monasteries flourished; it is significant that these centuries were marked by a wave of missionary enterprise on the part of the Nestorians, which swept across Asia and even penetrated into China. Fanaticism, it is true, at certain periods gained the upper hand; Arab national pride, too, found expression in the ordinances forbidding Christians to keep Moslem slaves, denying them various legal privileges, and even insisting on a special dress. But the official attitude remained generally tolerant, and the dwindling of Christian communities was due to other causes than persecution. Among the educated classes, much common ground was discovered between the two religions, and the developments of Moslem theology in Syria and Egypt show the influence of Christian thought. Just as in these days attempts are made to harmonize modern science and religion, so the philosophic background of the ancient world, which had been to some extent reconciled with Christianity, had now to be invoked to explain the tenets of Islam, in order to secure the acceptance of thinking men. The unreflecting, meanwhile, saw the finger of God in the amazing successes of Arabian armies, and bowed before the *fait accompli*. Lastly, the splendour that radiated from the capitals of Islam, where a brilliant civilization was shaping itself under the impact of old and new forces, exercised a potent influence on the imagination. In Spain, for example, the barbarous Latin of the chroniclers and theologians could not hold its own against the attractions of Arabic poetry and literature; even among the Christians, a ninth-century writer bitterly complains, the beauties of the Arabic tongue are more esteemed than the writings of the Fathers.

The great expansion of trade which followed in the wake of

the Moslem Empire was one of the chief developments which impressed upon it that unity to which allusion has already been made. Besides the fact that the industries of Syria and Egypt—the richest provinces of the Byzantine Empire—continued as before to produce their glasswork, textiles, and other manufactured articles, special advantages were secured to commerce by the new régime. Once settled, the Arab tends naturally to engage in trade. The prosperity of the kingdom of Hira was based on its great fairs, just as that of Yemen, at the other extremity of the peninsula, was due to the Asiatic cargoes passing through its port, while the markets and caravans of Mecca constituted its staple industry. Mahomet himself had been a trader, and in the Koran an honourable position is assigned to the merchant. The conditions of Moslem social life were therefore more favourable to trading enterprise than those of the Graeco-Roman world with its contempt of the banausic. And the geography of the Arab dominions was specially advantageous for this purpose. The feuds of Rome and Persia, which had checked the flow of commerce between East and West, were now at an end, and a solid block of territory under one ruler stretched from the Atlantic coast to the steppes of Central Asia. The Red Sea and Persian Gulf were no longer rival, but alternative routes, and all the gold and ivory of Central Africa, the spices and perfumes of the Far East, reached Europe only after passing through Moslem hands. It is noticeable that the great cities of the Empire lie at the intersection of long travel routes. Damascus, situated at the point where the caravans from Central Asia approach the Mediterranean, received also the merchandise of Egypt, Syria, and the Red Sea traffic. Cairo was a mart for the raw products of Asia and Africa as well as a manufacturing centre, and from Egypt a series of prosperous trading towns along the coast led to the capitals of northern Africa and Spain. Basra, on the Euphrates, was built soon after the conquest of Persia, to control the Persian Gulf and its Eastern trade, but its importance was eventually eclipsed by Baghdad. A canal between Tigris and Euphrates united the latter city to the overland routes from Asia Minor, Syria, and Egypt, while caravans from Central Asia descended from the highlands of Persia and Bokhara at its gates.

More extensive still was the maritime trade. In the stories of Sinbad the Sailor, who is represented as having lived in the early ninth century under the Abbasid Caliph, Harun-al-Rashid, the voyages start always from Baghdad, and many of the incidents and places mentioned can be corroborated or identified from other sources. Arab itineraries describe the traders in Ceylon, Malabar, and the Indian coast towns, and Chinese records prove the existence of colonies of Arab traders under the T'ang dynasty. Some even penetrated as far as Korea. In the west, the ports of Egypt and North Africa showed great activity, and their shipping linked the cities of the southern Mediterranean shore as far as Spain. But little trade was done with France and Italy; the Moslems came to these shores as pirates, not merchants. Byzantium remained the centre of European commerce, and it was not until the tenth century that Moslem and Christian met together to exchange their wares, and Arabs trod the streets of Pisa and Amalfi.

The influence of Islamic trade, however, made itself felt far beyond the boundaries of the Empire. In the north, Trebizond was an important centre, not only for its fair, which attracted dealers from all over the Near East, but also because it formed the frontier between Greek and Moslem commerce. Textiles, metal-work, and other products found their way to Constantinople by this means, and their influence can be traced in Byzantine culture. A stream of traffic also passed up the Volga and other rivers, and reached Central Russia and Scandinavia through the Khazar Kingdom. A large number of Moslem coins, mostly from Khorasan and the Eastern parts, have been discovered as far afield as Germany and the Baltic regions, and their provenance and distribution point to a considerable volume of trade, reaching its height in the early years of the ninth century, between the Asiatic provinces and northern Europe.

Inside the territory of Islam, commerce was furthered by the pilgrimages which were enjoined by its religion, and promoted by the Caliphs. Communications were improved by the provision of wells and caravanserais, and great fairs were established at pilgrim centres. The Arab rulers, as they lost the ideals of their Prophet and the simpler manners of their ancestors, took over from the older empires which they had superseded the love of luxury and display, and surrounded themselves with splendid buildings and furniture, thus further increasing the demand for various skilled products and exotic wares.

Parallel with the material civilization of Islam went the development of its spiritual culture. Just as the Arab conquerors had found it necessary to adapt their primitive customs to the more highly developed systems of the subject races, so the theologians, faced with conflicting philosophies without and divergent tendencies within, began to elucidate the Koran, rearing upon this slender foundation a vast superstructure of commentary and exegesis. Inasmuch as they saw in the Koran the supreme source of religion, law, and ethics, it was essential to reconcile conflicting utterances, to classify and systematize various pronouncements, and by the aid of analogy and deduction to make the words of the Prophet apply to circumstances not envisaged by him. Hence the origin of a large part of the brilliant literary output of the Abbasid period can be traced to study of the Koran. Even Arabic grammar, according to tradition, was first scientifically studied for the purpose of safeguarding the text; and however this may be, the development of Arabic as a literary language is closely connected with the need for explanation felt by the adherents of the new religion. In order to show the sequence of the Prophet's teaching, research into his life and the traditions of his family was made, and this, combined with the study of the lives of early heroes of Islam, gave a stimulus to the writing of history, which in Moslem hands has always retained a strong biographical and anecdotal flavour. In the same way, a large legal literature grew up, based primarily on the Koran, as the fountain of all authority, but drawn largely from Greek and Jewish sources in the civil and religious spheres respectively. It was inevitable that this should be so, since the legal system had to be fitted into the framework of previously existing civilizations, of which Mahomet can have had little knowledge.

In dogmatic theology, the same problems soon began to exercise Moslem thinkers as had formerly troubled the peace of the Early Church. Under the influence of Greek philosophy, logical reasoning began to be applied to such subjects as the Unity and Attributes of God, and the question of Determination and Free Will. During the first half of the ninth century this challenge to the orthodox upholders of literal tradition came to a head in an organized attempt to reconcile reason with authority. The official scholasticism won the day, and henceforward the only escape from its aridities was by way of mysticism. Philosophy proper followed the same path. A definite attempt was made by Avicenna (d. 1037) to reconcile Aristotelean doctrines with Moslem thought, and his work was continued by the great school of Spanish thinkers which exercised so potent an influence upon medieval Europe. In the East, however, and especially in Persia, orthodox Moslem dogma held its own, and although Greek metaphysic and psychology played their part, the mystical element is predominant in the philosophic systems evolved in this region. Translations from the Greek were also responsible for the growth of works on medicine, and a great school of physicians developed under the Abbasid dynasty. Greek models stimulated the production of encyclopaedias, and the translations of Greek and Indian speculation in astronomy and mathematics led before long to original discoveries by the scholars and scientists of Islam. Meanwhile pure literature flourished at the Abbasid Court—a literature, it is true, rather of 'escape' than expression, but distinguished by great charm and technical virtuosity. Prose blossomed into conceits and subtleties, while poetry ranged from elegant love-songs and gay drinking staves to the brooding melancholy of mystical verse-writers.

Moslem Art is equally representative in character, for in its development may be seen with convenient clearness the many influences which combined to produce a great civilization. It is an epitome of the history of Islam in all its aspects. At first sight, owing to its rapid flowering, it gives the appearance of a new, original style, which from the ninth to the seventeenth centuries covered vast stretches of country—Spain, North Africa, Egypt, the Near East, Persia, Turkestan, northern India—with great cities, stately mosques, and glittering palaces, all strongly marked

a. MOSAIC: GREAT MOSQUE, DAMASCUS

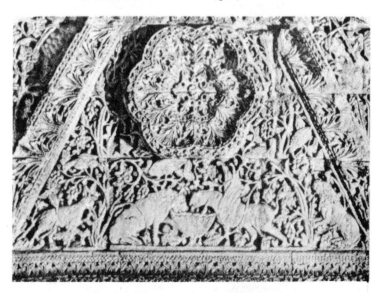

b. DETAIL OF RELIEF, MSCHATTA

VI

TYPES OF THE MINARET. *a.* MESOPOTAMIAN;
b. N. AFRICAN; *c.* EGYPTIAN; *d.* PERSIAN; *e.* INDIAN;
f. CONSTANTINOPLE

by homogeneity of structure and ornament, in spite of local variations. This appearance, however, is delusive. One must go back to the origins to discover that the style is a fusion of old elements, an eclecticism born of the peculiar conditions which enabled a conquering race to exploit the various techniques and traditions of some of the most artistic peoples that the world has seen. Apart from the riches and prosperity of the conquered lands, and the enormous revenues which the absolute power of the caliphs enabled them to spend in satisfaction of their personal caprice, the social and political developments of the Empire favoured the growth of Moslem art. The existence of a number of independent emirates produced a series of brilliant capitals, each one consciously rivalling the splendours of Baghdad, while dynastic changes and palace revolutions often resulted in the creation of new imperial cities. The Oriental character of the rulers is shown in their distaste for inherited buildings, their slackness in repair, their *ennui* ever counselling new places of residence. The Moslem inclination towards works of piety and public utility was responsible for the construction of schools, fountains, baths, hospitals, and caravanserais, as well as more strictly religious foundations, such as mosques, seminaries, and convents.

The expansion of Islam was marked from the first by great building activity. Five years after the death of the Prophet, Basra on the Lower Euphrates, and Kufa, south of Babylon, were founded, to serve as centres of Moslem influence in Mesopotamia. One of the first consequences of the conquest of Egypt was the building of the Mosque of 'Amr, named after the victorious general, while the so-called 'Mosque of Omar' at Jerusalem, and that of Sidi Okba at Kairawan, have a similar origin. The Great Mosque of Damascus was reconstructed to enhance the splendour of the Umayyads, and the centralizing of the government in that city was accompanied by a flowering of all the arts. The Abbasid ascendancy created the glories of Baghdad, and magnificent palaces arose during the eighth and ninth centuries, most of which were swept away by the Mongolian invasions. All the great periods of Moslem Art are linked in like manner to political events. The power of the Marinids at Fez, of the

Fatimites at Cairo, was shown by the adornment of their capitals; the dominance, in later centuries, of the Seljuk Turks in Armenia, of Timur at Samarkand, or of the Great Moguls in northern India is recorded by the buildings they have left behind them, a remarkable testimony to the unity and vitality of Moslem Art, in its mature stages, and its influence over Asiatic and uncivilized conquerors. In Spain, above all, the foundation of the Umayyad power ushers in an era of unequalled splendour, which reaches its height in the early part of the tenth century. The great university of Cordova is thronged with students from all parts of the Moslem Empire, while the city itself excites the wonder of visitors from Germany and France. The banks of the Guadal-quivir are covered with luxurious villas, and born of the ruler's caprice rises the famous Palace of the Flower, a fantastic city of delights. Little remains of the architecture of this period, which may well have rivalled, if not surpassed, the later triumphs of Alcazar and Alhambra, with which, some four centuries later, the Moorish potentates enriched Seville and Granada.

As the rise and fall of dynasties determine the flowering-times of Moslem Art, so the social conditions of the Empire, which have already been outlined, show themselves in its inner development. The Arabs of the pre-Islamic period possessed little architecture, and it was thus inevitable that the earlier Moslem structures should follow the tradition of the conquered territories. In Syria and Egypt Christian basilicas were taken over with little altera-tion, and even when new buildings were constructed, the pillars and capitals were looted from ruined churches. Byzantine mosaic and Coptic wood-carving were extensively used in the decoration of the mosques, and there is hardly a feature of structure or ornament which cannot be traced to earlier tradition. An interesting example of regional influence is the minaret in its various forms. In Mesopotamia, the minaret with helicoidal ramp, surmounted by a kiosk, is modelled on the ziggurats of ancient Babylon; the squat four-sided towers, with prismatic continuation, which form the minarets of Damascus, recall the funeral monuments of pagan and Christian times, and this type is found also in Spain and the Maghreb, carried to those regions by the religious and political influences of the Umayyad capital.

Egyptian minarets seem to owe their origin to the famous Pharos of Alexandria, with its retreating prisms and its crowning lantern; Persia, with its tradition of elegant and balanced shape, adopts the form of tall circular towers, while India, land of redundancies, masses its shafts in luxuriant designs. The Ottoman school, impressed perhaps by the triumphal columns of Constantinople, reared the high candles, ending in sharply pointed cones and girded by balconies at different heights, which dominate to this day the city of Stamboul.

Islamic Art, then, is not the sudden creation of a new style; like the other expressions of Moslem culture, it owes its origin to the long-matured achievements of ancient civilizations. It is the fusion of these borrowed elements which is new. Melted by the fires of Arab energy and conquest, they merge into one another and issue finally in a new substance. Transported from country to country, bands of architects and masons, armies of labourers and slaves transfer to a different medium their various techniques. Wood carving is applied to stone; the brilliant textiles of Persia are imitated in brick and marble, and effects of relief and design give way to those of contrasted material and colour. Above all, the inner spirit of Islam acts as a unifying force upon the fluid elements. The requirements of Mahometan ritual make themselves felt: the *mihrab*, or niche, facing towards Mecca, to which all eyes turn in prayer, receives architectural treatment commensurate with its importance; the courtyard and well impose a definite character upon the structure of the mosque. The injunction ascribed to Mahomet which forbade the representation of men or animals exercised a radical influence upon Moslem decoration. The Umayyads of Syria and the Persian rulers, faithful to the old figure-art of their countries, ignored the prohibition. But elsewhere, formal ornament alone is employed, and from the acanthus, the vine-tendril and other motives of classical and Asiatic art evolves the *arabesque*, the stylized running pattern of flowers and fruit, which accompanies so frequently the friezes of picturesque Arabic lettering. The process of abstraction goes yet further. Natural forms are distorted out of all semblance to their originals, and rhythm and symmetry are the main features of the magnificent designs of later Mahometan artists. Interlacing geometric systems, recti-linear or curvilinear, symbols of unity in diversity, satisfied the mystic appetites of the Arabian, presenting, it has been said, 'under the appearance of fancy and caprice the reality of a secret logic and a mathematical coherence'.

PART IV

THE AGE OF CHARLEMAGNE

XI

THE EUROPEAN BACKGROUND

I. THE ANGLO-SAXON INVASIONS

THERE is an almost complete absence of written records for the history of these islands between A.D. 400 and 550. Darkness hangs over them, and the mists of the Arthurian legend. In recent years the regional study of place-names, the excavation of dwellings, cemeteries, boundary and defensive earthworks, air-survey, and the efforts to establish reliable criteria for the dating of pottery, coins, and metal-work have accumulated material for a reconstruction of the course taken by various bands of invaders, the nature of their settlement, and the fate of the Romano-British population. A synthesis of such results may eventually enable some picture to be formed of these dim centuries. In the mean-time certain controlling factors may be noticed.

The coast-line of England has altered considerably since early medieval days.[1] The east and south coast, from the Firth of Forth to the Isle of Wight, presented at that time alternate stretches of cliffs and tidal marshes. The cliffs were easily defensible; only the gaps formed by river-mouths required to be guarded, and the remains of late Roman signal-stations and coast-fortresses show how this was effected. The marshy inlets, on the other hand, lay open to the boats of the invaders, with their shallow draught. The Humber estuary, stretching far inland, formed a huge waterlogged region, and similar conditions were repeated on a larger scale round the Wash, where the fen country extended as far as Stamford and Cambridge. 'For the plundering raider . . . the stagnant channels would float his vessel into the heart of the land, and on many an island in the swamps he could form camps in which to rest from fighting and collect his booty undisturbed.'[2]

[1] See the Ordnance Survey Maps of Roman Britain, and Britain in the Dark Ages.

[2] J. A. Williamson, *The Evolution of England* (Oxford, 1931), pp. 2 ff.

ANGLO-SAXON ENGLAND

Inland conditions show an even more striking picture. Drainage and deforestation have altered the face of the countryside, for in Roman and Saxon times a large part of England was covered by dense woodland, while the valleys were frequently an impenetrable morass. The history of the early settlements and of the formation of the Saxon kingdoms was thus largely determined by geography. The Humber estuary, continued by marshes, was joined on the west by the Forest of Elmet, which stretched to the slopes of the Pennine Hills; estuary, swamp, and forest forming in this way a barrier to communications between midlands and north. The Fen district cut off East Anglia from the midlands, just as the great forest belt, extending south-west from the Fens to Epping, isolated Essex and forbade westward expansion. The greatest forest of all, the Andredsweald, covered a broad tract reaching practically from Winchester to Hastings, leaving only a strip of a few miles in breadth where the South Downs run parallel to the sea. 'Even as late as the eighteenth century, when the Weald had been largely cleared, the Sussex coast was difficult of access from London during the greater part of the year.'[1] Farther west the forest belt, of which Cranborne Chase still remains, barred the way to West Dorset and South Somerset for the invaders proceeding northwards from Southampton Water. When this prevalence of swamp and forest is borne in mind, the significance of such earthworks as Bokerly Dyke, protecting the Romano-British settlements of Cranborne Chase, becomes apparent. Though now only a few miles of rampart set in open country, in those days it guarded the narrow entrance to a district elsewhere defended by natural obstacles.

The fortunes of the various kingdoms are explicable largely by their situation. Sussex, Kent, Essex, and East Anglia were doomed to political insignificance, since further expansion was denied them. Northumbria, Mercia, and Wessex, on the other hand, were able to extend their territory at the expense of the Romano-Britons, gaining not only in size but in variety of culture and population, and thus each successively emerged as the strongest units in England, during the seventh, eighth, and ninth centuries respectively. Wessex alone, whose hegemony lies beyond

---

[1] J. A. Williamson, loc. cit.

the borders of this book, achieved real political supremacy. Northumbria, though it included, at its full power, east Scotland below the Forth and northern England as far as the Ribble and Yorkshire Ouse, was torn internally by the struggles of Bernicia and Deira, and its Christian kings were more than once successfully challenged by the pagan leaders of Mercia. Its decline, which had set in strongly during the eighth century, was further hastened by the ravages of the Northmen. Mercia from the first was a mixed state, a conglomeration of war bands and adventurers of varied origin, occupying the large debatable territory of the western midlands, which must in the early years of the invasions have witnessed a fusion of Celt and Saxon, a compromise of two cultures. Controlled from the geographical centre of England, at Tamworth on the Watling Street, by ruthless and able chieftains, it bid fair at one period to establish a triple division of England for future ages, with Tamworth, possibly, and Lichfield as the Midland capital and archbishopric. Its sway extended at intervals over the Peak-dwellers in the north, the peoples of Cheshire and south Lancashire, and the Worcestershire Hwiccas in the south, while the long frontier which separated the Wrekin-dwellers from the Welsh kingdoms was perpetuated in Offa's Dyke, the work of Mercia's most famous ruler, the correspondent of Charlemagne, and the most important figure in England at the close of the eighth century.

The passing of Roman Britain still remains one of the great historical mysteries. Fuller knowledge, it may be conjectured, might tend to lessen the importance of actual dates, whether 407 or 440, for the cessation of Roman rule in this island. It is probable that Stilicho's reorganization of the coast defences towards the close of the fourth century represents the last serious effort made by the Empire to retain its outlying province; and parallel conditions in Gaul show that the transition to barbarian rule was not a single episode but a gradual process. The slow weakening of the central government, on the one hand, had resulted in widespread internal disorder and confusion, causing landowners and local officials to arm their retainers in self-defence, and the population to forsake the countryside and seek refuge in the walled towns, while, on the other, the first onslaughts of the barbarians were usually succeeded by a period of more or less peaceful infiltration. There is evidence of similar conditions in Britain. Since A.D. 250 the coasts had been exposed to ravages on east and west, from Saxon and Irish pirates, and the German invasions of the fifth century were only a culmination of such raids, followed subsequently by immigration of families. Signs, too, are not wanting of a certain slowing down of Roman civilization in this island, beginning as early as the third century. The technique of building deteriorates; even in the lowland, more fully Romanized districts, a growing sense of insecurity is shown by the fortification of towns, while the lofty stone castles of the Saxon Shore, with their strikingly medieval aspect, emphasize the dangers always present to the coast-dwellers. A deadly blow was struck at the fabric of Romano-British life by the great raid of 367, when a mixed force of Picts, Irish, and Saxons swept through the entire country, laying waste the manor-houses and inflicting irreparable damage on the agricultural system of Britain. A trail of burnt villas marks their path, and the permanent effects of the invasion are shown by the fact that coin-hoards discovered on isolated Roman sites show marked diminution in value after this time. The next hundred years must have witnessed a steady if intermittent decline in the civilization of the island. The villas are abandoned, though most of the fortified towns doubtless continued in some form well into the fifth century. In the country districts, the earthworks and hill-top camps of pre-Roman days once again form a refuge for the population. Under pressure of foreign raids and internal strife, local leaders arise, as in other parts of the Empire, and the barbarian invaders experience here and there a temporary set-back to their advance.

The analogy with continental conditions, however, cannot be pressed. The Anglo-Saxons were a people markedly different from the German tribes whose contact with Rome during four centuries, along the whole length of the Rhine and Danube frontiers, had deeply influenced their ideas and even their language. Nor could Britain, devastated and disorganized, present to the new-comers the impressive monuments, the indestructible texture of civilized life, which they encountered in southern France or north Italy. The Saxon leaders were incapable

of the admiration of an Alaric or a Theoderic for Roman institutions, the shrewd compromises of Clovis, or the city-life of the
Lombard dukes. Shreds of scattered evidence hint doubtfully
at their reactions to the ruined arches and columns of Roman
buildings. They suggest a mixture of superstitious fear and distaste, coupled with an uneasy humour; ghosts of dead men, or
powers even more mysterious, lurked there, as in the stone
chambers and earthen barrows of an older age, and the new
Saxon settlements habitually shunned Roman sites. The whole
impression is that of settlers entering a derelict and largely
depopulated country, and this is borne out by the evidence for
the eastern and southern counties of England, where Celtic
place-names, religion, and customs seem to have largely disappeared by the end of the sixth century. Enclaves of 'Welsh-
men', it is true, existed even here, in marsh or woodland, spared
or undiscovered by the conquerors, and in Mercia, Northumbria,
and Wessex the former inhabitants had gradually come to terms
with the westward-spreading invaders, although, as with Gallo-
Roman under Frankish rule, the *wergild* of the Briton was less
than that of the lowliest free Saxon. There is reason, moreover,
to think that the skill of the Romano-British craftsman, in Kent
and elsewhere, was not entirely lost during and after the turmoil
of invasion.

Continental parallels present themselves again when the subsequent evolution of the Anglo-Saxon kingdoms is considered.
Familiarity with Roman administrative methods had fostered
the growth of absolutism among the rulers of German tribes
settled within the Empire,[1] and encouraged the development of
written law. In this island Rome's office was performed by the
Church, whose influence in moulding Anglo-Saxon institutions
was more powerful than any other. A Kentish legal code, for
example, appears shortly after the arrival of Augustine, and the
authority of every successful Saxon king was buttressed by the
counsel and co-operation of his ecclesiastics, who realized that
a strong central government was essential to the interests of the
Church. Contact with the European mainland, and so with
the main stream of civilization, was maintained largely by

[1] See above, p. 41.

churchmen, trade and diplomacy at this date being of small importance, while in the growth of feudal elements, such as increased local jurisdiction and immunity from public burdens, the great monasteries, as landed beneficiaries of royal piety, played no inconsiderable part.

From a European point of view, undoubtedly the most striking aspect of the Anglo-Saxon conquest is the sudden rise of Northumbria to supremacy, brief but undoubted, in the world of Western culture. Britain under the Romans had always remained a frontier outpost of the Empire, a backward and unevenly civilized province in comparison with Gaul, Spain, and Africa. From 400 onwards connexion with the centre is lost, and the island gradually fades from the consciousness of Rome and Byzantium. Augustine's mission in 597 restored the links with the Continent, and the reunion of Celtic scholarship with the original tradition of Western learning produced the Northumbrian renaissance of art and letters. Never before or since has England occupied a similar position in the world's civilization. Even Rome was obliged to send for manuscripts to the northern kingdom, and Bede stands out, without possible rival, as the foremost scholar of the West, supreme in every branch of learning and in sheer intellectual force towering above the age in which he lived. The political decline of Northumbria in face of the growing Mercian power sapped the economic foundations of this brilliant culture, and the remnants of it perished during the Viking raids, when the great monasteries were sacked and burnt; but Alcuin and his fellows had already carried its inspiration to Aix and Tours, where it formed the basis of the Carolingian revival. The debt was repaid in part towards the end of the ninth century, after the Danish terror had passed, when continental influences helped to enrich the great Winchester school of painting and draftsmanship, in the capital of the flourishing kingdom of Wessex. Rhineland models seem also to have inspired the later Saxon architecture, though the unbroken insular tradition could challenge comparison with other varieties of Romanesque. The stately cathedrals of Durham and Winchester have vanished; the witness of a few village churches, eked out by meagre documentary evidence, is all that remains to us of the splendours of the later Anglo-Saxon achievement. It is sufficient, however, when taken in conjunction with the extant examples of Saxon sculpture and of the lesser arts practised in England at this time, to evoke some regret for the effacement of native methods before the magnificent, though often stereotyped, productions of the Norman builder.

2. THE SLAVONIC FLOOD

The last great racial movement in Europe which reached its climax before the end of the Dark Ages is the expansion of the Slavs —a process as momentous for the ethnic future of the Continent as any previously described, affecting, at its greatest extent, the whole land-mass east of a line drawn roughly from the head of the Adriatic to the mouth of the Elbe. It differs from the invasions and wanderings of other barbarians as an imperceptibly rising tide differs from a headlong cataract or from a winding river with alternating rapids and smooth reaches. The quiet entry of the Slavs on to the stage of European history is unnoticed by contemporary onlookers. It is not a brilliant raid led by outstanding personalities, like those of Goths or Vandals, or a swift rush from Asia, like that of the Huns. It is the steady expansion of a peasant race, forming at first the economic substratum of communities led by warrior rulers, Germanic or Asiatic, but increasing in numbers, absorbing its conquerors; without political cohesion or ambition, transplanted hither and thither, from Baltic to Adriatic, to serve the purpose of despotic khagans, a rising tide of population which flows in upon East Germany, down into Greece, and eastwards over the plains of South Russia when plundering nomads give it a brief respite.

The mist-hung depths of the Pripet marshes, where the majority of specialists are at present inclined to place the original Slav home, lay as far outside the vision of Greeks and Romans as the distant Asiatic steppes, where tiny mounted figures and their caravans could dimly be descried moving over a vast expanse of plain. The two pictures are indeed complementary, for the marsh-dwellers of Polesie, as this primitive Slav district was known in medieval times, can be regarded as one of those unhappy races, placed on the fringes of the steppe region, whose peaceful pursuits and sedentary life have made them the prey of fierce nomadic hordes.[1] Stray references in ancient authors show us a people formed by the silent expanses of reedy swamp and still meres, isolated families of fishers and husbandmen, occupying scattered clearings in bog-land and forest, a reddish-haired, primitive folk, shy traffickers in furs and honey, scantily clad and escaping from their pursuers into the water or neighbouring thicket; masters, too, of a missile and guerrilla warfare, and excellent soldiers when in foreign service.

They are a strangely anonymous nation. There is no tradition, no mythological genealogy of these original Slavs. The folk-lore of later times preserves memories chiefly of outside races who captured the Slav imagination. The terrible Avars figure as giants or monsters, while the Emperor Trajan, conqueror of Dacia (Transylvania and Rumania) in the second century A.D., becomes in Balkan legend the great Tsar Trojan, 'for whom burning gold and pure silver flow from seventy wells'. It is clear from this and other evidence that the Slavs had already begun to out-flow their primitive area before the first centuries A.D., percolating southward to the Danube by either extremity of the Carpathians, westward over the plains that lie between Elbe and Vistula, and eastward towards the Volga basin and the Sea of Azov. The central position of their old home—situated on the isthmus, as it were, of the European peninsula, formed by the great waterways of western Russia—exposed them to the two extreme cultural influences of the Baltic and the Black Sea, while racial admixture of Teutonic blood on one side and Asiatic stocks on the other helped to accentuate the differences which were later to divide and distinguish the various Slavonic nationalities.

Unnoticed by the annalists, the rising flood continued. Shortly before the reign of Justinian, Byzantium awoke to the existence of a Slav menace. All through the sixth century the Slav raids grew in intensity, devastating the districts of Thrace, Thessaly, and Macedonia, penetrating the elaborate lines of castles devised by Justinian to protect the Danube and the vital roads that joined the eastern and western parts of his empire. A cyclonic

[1] For a qualification of this view, see L. Niederle, *Revue des Études slaves*, vol. ii, pp. 19 ff.

storm-centre had established itself over Hungary in the shape of the Avars, lashing the waves of the Slavonic tide into furious currents, imparting to them a new and terrible driving force, and scattering them in spray far over Central Europe. From this time may be dated the Slavization of Greece, and the territorial sundering of Old and New Rome. Soon after 600, despite the valiant counter-attacks of Byzantine generals, the Danube frontier of the Empire ceased to have any practical existence. 'The Slavs took Greece from the Romans,' Isidore of Seville, a contemporary chronicler, notes tersely. The Roman- and Greek-speaking populace were driven to the Adriatic and Aegean fringes of the peninsula. The great trading city of Salonika, protected by her massive walls and siege-engines, and by the strong arm of S. Demetrius, her tutelary saint, withstood the assault, but the surrounding district of Macedonia was permanently occupied by the Slavs.[1] The flood poured down into the peninsula, and even reached the Aegean islands, but the coastal cities of southern Greece and the Peloponnese remained centres of Hellenic life and culture, ready to take part in the Byzantine reconquest three centuries later. Far on the west, the population of Roman Salona, capital of Dalmatia, streamed down the hill-side from their ravaged city and sought refuge within the walls of Diocletian's huge palace at Spalato. Others fled to the Adriatic islands and inlets, forming a fringe of Latinity which persisted until recent times. Only in 1898 died the last speaker of the 'mysterious language'—a debased descendant of the old Roman tongue.[2] Inland, communities of Latin speech seem to have survived in the former provinces both north and south of the Danube, and to their influence is due the origin of the Rumanian language.

Meanwhile the Avar tornado, from its centre in Hungary, whirled the Slav masses in all directions, dividing tribes and settling fragments of them on distant frontiers, westwards in Carinthia and the Tirol, northwards along the Elbe and Saale, using their man-power on the circumference of the Avar circle against the troops of Bavarians, Lombards, Saxons, and Franks.

---

[1] By the seventh century A.D. this region was so thickly populated by Slavs that it became known as 'Sclavinia'.

[2] Cf. L. Niederle, *Manuel de l'antiquité slave*, I. 68 (Paris, 1923).

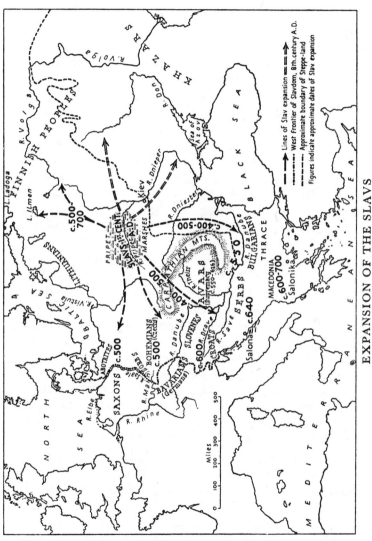

EXPANSION OF THE SLAVS

Lines of Slav expansion
West frontier of Slavdom, 8th century A.D.
Approximate boundary of Steppe-land
Figures indicate approximate dates of Slav expansion

The range of the nomad influence, which extended at one time or another from the Peloponnese to the Baltic, can be paralleled by that of Altaian empires in Asia, and it bears a close resemblance to that of their predecessors in Europe, the Huns. True to its steppe origin, the Avar rule was a plundering tyranny, dependent on brute force, maintained by terrorizing raids, and liable to sudden dissolution. Early in the seventh century the subject peoples rose in revolt. A Frankish merchant, called Samo, organized the Slavs of the Main valley against the Avars, and successfully maintained his kingdom against both them and the Franks. The Croats and the Serbs soon followed suit, and finally the Bulgarians on the Lower Danube formed an independent kingdom. Apart from the realm of Samo, however, the Avar masters in each district continued to dominate the Slav peasantry until they were merged in the surrounding population, and the medieval organization of these Balkan States shows clear traces of an Asiatic system.

A striking instance is Bulgaria, where a western offshoot of the Bulgars, a race akin to the Huns, who are first heard of as settled on the Don, had arrived on the north-western shores of the Black Sea, above the Danube estuary, towards the close of the fifth century. After freeing themselves from the Avar yoke about 640, they crossed the Danube, extending their territory southwards to within 150 miles of the walls of Byzantium, ruling, as a warrior caste, the Slav agricultural population, and drawing from them the necessary troops for the foundation of a mighty empire, which by the end of the ninth century stretched almost to the Adriatic on the west, and thrust its apex down to the Pindus mountains on the south. This First Bulgarian Empire decided the future history of the Balkans. Had it not been for the fierce Bulgar khagans and their militant boyars, the Slav immigrants of these parts would hardly have proved capable of offering permanent, organized resistance to the persistent efforts, century after century, of the Roman Empire, with its professional army and skilled tactics, to restore and retain the old frontier line of the Danube and the provinces which lay along its banks, and the glories of medieval Bulgaria, Croatia, and Serbia might never have been called into existence.

The weakening of the Avar power, which continued to decline until its final destruction by Charlemagne, produced repercussions on the whole series of Avaro-Slav States. The great westward tide of Slavdom had turned. In Upper Austria it receded, as the Germans of Bavaria pushed forward.[1] North of this, a line of more than thirty little Slav tribes stretched from the Danube to Mecklenburg, disunited, living in scattered settlements in swamp and forest. Bohemia, encircled by mountains, became a strong kingdom, but the Elbe Slavs were exterminated or Germanized, and Charlemagne's conquest of Saxony was only the prelude to a further advance of the Western power, a stubborn conquest pursued for many generations. On the Baltic shores, the vikings of Scandinavia, merchants and pirates, raided the Slav districts, and eventually established permanent strongholds. Gradually they gained possession of the great trade-route formed by the Russian network of waterways which links Lake Ladoga to the Euxine, and pushing southwards they established, soon after 800, the dominion of Kiev, the nucleus of the future Empire of Russia.

3. BYZANTIUM AND THE MEDITERRANEAN

The events of the seventh century completely transformed the position of Byzantium in contemporary Europe. The final triumph of Rome over Persia in 628, which had been the achievement of Heraclius, was followed almost immediately by the wave of Arab invasion, which shook the foundations of both these former world-empires. Heraclius had not been dead ten years before Egypt and Syria had been lost, and with the Moslem conquest of the African provinces, the Lombard advance in Italy, and the Slavization of the Balkans, the Roman Empire by the close of the century had shrunk to very small dimensions. The Italian revolt and the Frankish conquest of Italy lessened still further the influence of Byzantium in the West, and the course of Byzantine history can henceforth be considered apart from the development of the western European states, which, as Bury has remarked, were no longer deeply affected by what happened east of Italy or south of the Danube.

[1] Cf. p. 228.

The years which preceded the accession of Leo the Isaurian (717–41) represent one of the darkest hours in the long life of Byzantium. Her vitality seemed to be declining with the contraction of her frontiers. Art and letters decayed, the standard of education was debased, and superstition became grosser among all classes. The absolutism of the Imperial autocracy, which, owing to her precarious situation, was necessary to the very existence of Byzantium, had been seriously challenged by the aristocratic opposition, as is shown by the swift succession of emperors—no less than seven in twenty years—several of whom owed their elevation to the intrigues of the great landed nobility of the Empire.

The rise of the strong Isaurian house marks literally a new orientation of Byzantine affairs. Dynastic struggles, with their anarchical consequences, disappear, not to be seen again till the opening of the next century. The capital, menaced by the full might of the Umayyads in the great siege of 717–18, was superbly defended by Leo, a soldier by profession, at the very outset of his reign,[1] and the Empire thereafter held its own on the Islamic front until with the transference of the seat of power (c. 750) from Umayyad Damascus to Abbasid Baghdad the centre of disturbance receded into Asia. A thorough reform of the finances, encouragement to commerce, and a salutary development of military organization in the provinces, in the interests of threatened frontiers, must also be counted to the credit of the Isaurians. Such achievements can be paralleled by those of the Heraclians, the Macedonians, and other saviours of Byzantium in her hour of need. So far, then, the dynasty may be considered as being in the tradition. Here, however, the resemblance ends. The Isaurians are, in fact, the creators of a revolutionary policy, able innovators who deflected the course of Byzantine life during two centuries by the force of their alien, Asiatic idealism. That life was destined to flow once more in its customary channels. The *Weltanschauung* of a whole civilization is too strong a current to be changed by a few individuals, for it was nothing less than the Mediterranean inheritance which was challenged by the Isaurian rulers.

[1] See above, p. 157.

One of the chief elements in that inheritance was the Roman legal system, which governed so many aspects of Byzantine social life. The *Ecloga*—a popular handbook to the most important laws, issued under Leo III—shows a startling change in this system. No longer are the Roman jurists the sources of authority; jurisprudence is 'based on revelation', and legal doctrine is justified by texts quoted from the Scriptures. The notion of marriage as a civil contract, dissoluble by mutual consent, gives place to the sacramental view promulgated by the Church councils, and divorce is accordingly made more difficult to obtain. Ecclesiastical influence is also visible in other matters, for instance in the increased penalties for sexual offences and the substitution of mutilation for death as the supreme punishment, in order to leave the sinner opportunity for repentance. It is illuminating to find that this process of christianization was arrested towards the end of the ninth century, when a reaction to the principles of Justinianian law takes place. Byzantium, the holy city, defender of the orthodox faith, shows herself also, and more fundamentally, the heir and repository of the traditions of pagan Imperial Rome.

From this source comes also another deep-rooted conception in the Byzantine world, that of the indivisibility of Church and State.[1] The safety and prosperity of the Empire depended on spiritual no less than material resources, and the authority of the civil power was reinforced by religious sanctions. Emperors who, like the iconoclast Isaurians, interfered with the popular manifestations of religion—relics, icons, and reverence for monastic orders—betrayed the existence of a dualism, a possibility of conflict between secular and ecclesiastical authority, which was clearly contrary to Byzantine public policy, and therefore doomed eventually to fail. This tipping of the balance in favour of the State produced an opposite movement in the followers of Theodore, Abbot of Studium, (d. 826), who claimed complete self-government for the Church, and even supported the Pope against their own Emperor. Such ideas were equally alien to Byzantine thought, and both extremes finally disappeared, leaving the Emperor once more exercising supremacy over

[1] Cf. p. 93.

Church affairs, a supremacy, however, tempered by discretion in the handling of popular susceptibilities.

The final challenge to Byzantine standards was the Iconoclast movement itself. This, though in some aspects it formed part of the Imperial secular reforms, was essentially dictated by religious conviction,[1] and it is as a doctrinal question that the whole problem was viewed by contemporaries. To deny the possibility of representing Christ by a visible image, claimed the adversaries of Iconoclasm, was to deny the reality of the Incarnation, and therewith the basis of the Christian faith. The intense bitterness of the struggle can be fully appreciated only if this central contention is constantly borne in mind.[2] The Iconoclastic controversy, however, was a dispute which gathered into itself religious, political, philosophic, aesthetic, and perhaps racial differences, many of which had their origins in a long-distant past. No modern formula can recapture and recreate for us the complicated issues involved. The war was waged on all levels, and opinions ranged from the two extremes through every form of compromise. It is easy to discover absurdities on either side—Emperors, on the one hand, who carry on the campaign by canonizing Judas Iscariot and removing the 'Saint' from place-names; a magical cult of images, on the other, which at its most degraded belongs properly to the pathology of fetichism. The philosophic difference, however, was real and important, though it may be doubted whether, through the clouds of misrepresentation and heated feelings, most of the combatants viewed clearly the shapes against which they tilted. The difficulties inherent in the relation of images to what they represented were an old story in pagan times, and the argument had been carried on through all the centuries of Christianity. Both sides had therefore a copious store of precedent on which to draw, apart from the passages which were torn from their original context in scriptural or patristic literature and moulded to serve as ammunition in verbal warfare.

---

[1] Religion and politics, as we have just seen, cannot be wholly separated, and no doubt in the eyes of the iconoclast rulers—who were not so sternly rational as they have sometimes been painted—the safety of the State from earthquake, pestilence, and invasion depended to a considerable degree on the prevalence of what they considered correct dogma.   [2] See Appendix B.

The Iconoclast party was recruited largely from Asia Minor, the home of the Isaurian emperors, the greater part of their troops, and many of their officials. In this region flourished several puritan sects, and not only these, but the doctrines of their Islamic neighbours may have had their effect in producing antipathy to 'idolatry'. But the emperors themselves were not heretical; they could appeal, equally with their opponents, to the orthodox tradition of the Church. Nor must too much stress be laid on the antithesis of an Asiatic, abstract symbolism to the 'representative' Graeco-Roman art. The Mediterranean had for many centuries been exposed to Oriental influences,[1] and Byzantine art had already lost many of its classical characteristics. The mosques and palaces of the Asiatic caliphs exerted at this time, as was natural, the powerful attraction which a wealthy and magnificent art never fails to inspire; but it is probable that the iconoclastic struggle did not fundamentally affect the evolution of the Byzantine style, the main principles of which had already established themselves under Justinian.

In 725 Leo began his campaign for the destruction of images. Soldiers mounted on ladders and removed the great figure of Christ over the Palace gate in the main square of Constantinople. An angry crowd gathered, rioting followed, and a soldier was done to death by the mob. A series of disorders in the capital, Greece, and the Cyclades resulted from the Imperial decrees; a rival emperor was even put forward, but the conspiracy was crushed, and Leo's policy finally prevailed, supported on the whole by the educated classes. Under Constantine V the struggle became yet more bitter, and the political activities of the monks —a danger to the State which Leo had already foreseen—crystallized into a demand for Church autonomy. Constantine, equal in military genius and superior in statecraft to his father, met his opponents on their own ground, and Iconoclasm was upheld by all the resources at his command. In 787 Irene, taking advantage of a popular outburst, restored the images, but Iconoclasm returned on the wave of another reaction, in 815. Gradually, however, its power dwindled; the army lost influence at Court, and the monks of Studium gained the ascendancy. In 843 the

[1] See p. 87.

Empress Theodora, acting as regent for her son Michael, was able to combine the fulfilment of her own wishes with the demands of policy by giving back to the populace the image-worship that they had never ceased to desire.

The repercussions in the West of the Iconoclast controversy can be over-estimated. Intense feeling was aroused, for images and relics played a vital part in popular devotion, but the philosophic issues involved were not understood. Hatred of Byzantine officials and Byzantine taxes, local patriotism and politics were more potent causes of the Italian revolt, and it was Byzantine military weakness which produced the Frankish intervention. The quarrel was only one episode in the growing estrangement between Papal Rome and Imperial Constantinople. The return of image-worship did not mend matters, for the fundamental differences were not really doctrinal. The periods of schism between the two churches, which had become longer and more frequent, culminated in the final rupture of 1054, but even after that date agreement on dogma could have been reached. It was not the 'Filioque clause', but the papal claims to supremacy and the calculations of the Eastern and Western Emperors which prevented a reconciliation. At the same time, the barrier of speech and custom grew continually higher. Leo the Isaurian, as a counter-stroke to the Pope's defiance, had attached Sicily, South Italy, and Dalmatia to the Byzantine patriarchate, and an influx of Greek refugee monks into Italy during the reign of his successor popularized many elements of Eastern worship there. But the conquest of Sicily by the Moslems in the following century weakened the hold of Byzantium upon the West, while the heathen Slav nations of the Balkans formed an additional obstacle to direct intercourse. Bulgaria, converted to Christianity from Byzantium in the ninth century, after dallying with the alternative of allegiance to Rome[1] finally remained Orthodox, and her western boundaries (which then included much of modern Serbia) marked the frontier of Byzantine religious and cultural influence. A new line of division was thus added to the innumerable causes of Balkan discord, the consequences of which remain to the present day.

[1] Cf. S. Runciman, *A History of the First Bulgarian Empire*, pp. 99 ff. (London, 1930).

XII

THE FRANKS

AT the death of Clovis, in 511, his kingdom was divided among his four sons, 'as if it had been a private estate'. This Frankish custom of inheritance is a cardinal fact in Merovingian history; to it is due much of the incoherence and confusion of the period. Following the death of successive rulers, continual partitions are made, often based on purely personal considerations. The east of France, for instance, was combined on this occasion with the Auvergne, and no account was taken of races or nationalities. But in spite of this division, the kingdom was still regarded as a unity, as its contemporary title, *Regnum Francorum*, implies, and the four sons of Clovis recognized their common duty to complete the conquest begun by their father. The four capitals, moreover, Rheims, Orleans, Paris, and Soissons, were situated at the extremities of each domain, in close proximity to each other, thus forming a centre of German influence.

The dynastic story of the next half-century is a long series of murders, annexations, revolts, and repartitions. Unity was temporarily restored in 558, when, out of all the descendants of Clovis, only Chlotar remained. In spite of civil wars, the consolidation and extension of the conquests of Clovis had steadily proceeded. Burgundy had been finally subdued in 534[1] and now formed part of the Frankish dominions, though its hundred years of independent existence had given it a certain unity of culture which was never completely lost. Provence, which had once belonged to Theoderic, the Ostrogoth ruler of Italy, was relinquished by his successors about the same time. Septimania, the district lying between the Rhône and the Pyrenees, still remained in Visigoth hands, and Brittany acknowledged no more than a nominal overlordship on the part of the Franks. Roughly speaking, however, Gaul had been conquered up to its natural boundaries. Outside these limits, Frankish arms were not so successful. Expeditions into North Italy and Spain led to no permanent result, though the weakness of Ostrogoths and Visigoths

[1] Cf. p. 76.

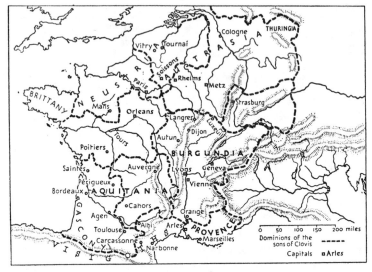

A.D. 511–561

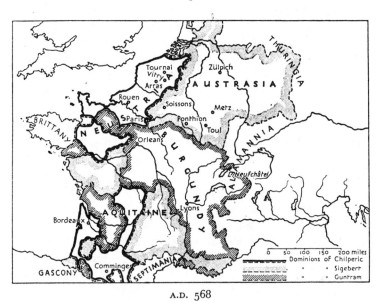

A.D. 568

MEROVINGIAN FRANCE

prevented any possibility of reprisals. Theudibert, the most enter-
prising son of Clovis, had planned at one time to join the Gepids
and Lombards in a concerted raid upon Thrace, and is even
said to have contemplated an attack upon Byzantium itself. But
too much must not be made of this. Theudibert was neither a
Charlemagne nor an Otto, and there is no evidence to indicate that any real political insight lay behind these grandiose
schemes.

The real advance during this period was in the eastward direction. The Franconian conquests of Clovis were rounded off.
Bavaria yielded allegiance; Thuringia was subdued. The Saxon
tribes of the great plains of Central Germany proved more
recalcitrant, and drove back the invaders with heavy loss. A
beginning, however, had been made of the process which Charlemagne was to bring to fulfilment, and the way was being prepared for the Christian missionaries who were later to undertake
the conversion of Germany.

A great contrast is presented by the character of the next half-
century. Conquest now gives place to civil war. Expeditions
into North Italy continued, as before, but no permanent annexation followed. Efforts were made to wrest Septimania from the
Visigoths, and the walls of Carcassonne and Nîmes witnessed the
clash of arms; but the district remained subject to the rulers of
Spain, and passed later under the Moslem yoke. Bretons and
Basques still maintained their independence, and the Avar raids
on Thuringia which took place at this time forbade any further
expansion on the eastern frontier.

The wave of conquest had spent itself, and within the Frankish
realm the forces of dissolution were in full play. The pages of
Gregory of Tours hold for us the story of this time. They chronicle
pestilence and famine, murder, and sudden death. Beggars and
highwaymen infest the roads, and even the churches are not
safe from rapine. The Meroving princes, in their internecine
feuds, call to their aid the nobles of their kingdoms; the result is
seen in the growth of feudal independence and lawlessness, and
in the antagonism of Austrasia and Neustria, Burgundy and
Aquitaine, which appear destined to form separate principalities.

Chlotar, the last surviving son of Clovis, died in 561, leaving four sons. Of these, Charibert, king of Paris, lived only till 567. Sigebert, king of Metz, and Chilperic, king of Soissons, carried on a bitter contest for supremacy, while the fourth brother, Guntram, king of Orleans and Burgundy, endeavoured to hold the balance between them. The enmity between Sigebert and Chilperic became even more deadly when both married royal sisters, Brunhilda and Galswintha, from the luxurious and civilized Visigoth court. Chilperic's wife, Galswintha, was found strangled in suspicious circumstances, and Chilperic returned to his former mistress, Fredegund. Shortly afterwards Sigebert, in the hour of victory over Chilperic, was brought down by the poisoned daggers of Fredegund's agents. Brunhilda was made prisoner, but managed to escape to her son's kingdom, where she planned revenge for the double murder. The period is dominated henceforth by the figure of Brunhilda, queen and regent of Austrasia—that is, the Eastern Franks—and by her struggle against Neustria, the domain of Chilperic in north and west (*niust* .. 'newest', i.e. the latest conquests). Chilperic is a type of the Merovingian despot; his two ruling passions are the increase of his wealth and the extension of his borders. In pursuance of these aims he sells bishoprics, levies oppressive taxes, and fines his wealthy subjects, while no treachery is too mean, no cruelty too savage, in his schemes against rival princes of the Meroving house. To Gregory of Tours, he is the Nero and Herod of his age. Such qualities are common form among his contemporaries; but Chilperic has claims to originality. Despising the Germanic tongue, he composed Latin hymns and poems; four letters were added to the alphabet by his decree. The Three Persons of the Trinity were condemned as anthropomorphic follies, and his free-thinking even challenged the Salic Law, that bulwark of Frankish custom, in an attempt to allow the inheritance of women in certain cases. Brunhilda, his principal opponent, presents an even more remarkable personality. For more than thirty years she controlled the destinies of Austrasia, holding her own against the attacks of Chilperic, the arrogance of nobles, and the insubordination of her sons and grandsons. From 575 to 596 she ruled as regent for her son. By the help of loyal vassals and of a timely coalition with Burgundy, she hunted down her treacherous nobles. One perished in the flames of a burning castle, another was killed by tiles hurled through the roof of the bishop's chapel at Verdun. Her two grandsons were set on the thrones of Burgundy and Austrasia; but Brunhilda still held the reins of power. When the Austrasian prince revolted against her tyranny, she turned his brother against him, and he was defeated and put to death. But the end of her long career was in sight. In 613 the Burgundian ruler died, and Brunhilda's efforts to combine Austrasia and Burgundy under her great-grandson were unsuccessful. The nobles of Austrasia, led by Arnulf, bishop of Metz, and Pipin, mayor of the Palace, the founders of the Caroling fortunes, called in the Neustrian king to their aid, and Brunhilda was taken prisoner on the shore of Lake Neufchâtel. She was tortured for three days, and finally her body was tied to the tail of a vicious horse, which was set loose and lashed into fury.

Brunhilda had known how to control the forces of her realm. She had treated the Church with great firmness, at the same time making many gifts to bishoprics and monasteries. The correspondence carried on with her by Pope Gregory the Great shows that he realized her power in Church and State, and the importance of her influence in France. Under Chlotar II, who now succeeded to the throne of the whole kingdom, the nobles seemed to have won the day. In Austrasia, especially, their co-operation had been decisive in gaining the victory, and the price they extorted was seen in the Edict of 614. The Church asserted its independence, and demanded freedom of episcopal elections and extended powers for the ecclesiastical courts, while the landed aristocracy secured a triumph over the Court officials, since the Counts[1] were henceforward to be chosen from the districts they were to administer, local and hereditary influence thus having full- -play. Considerable autonomy was granted to Austrasia and Burgundy; each of the kingdoms now had its distinct character and separate administration, headed by the mayors of the Palace, who were as much the representatives of the interests of the local nobility as they were of the king. Already

[1] Cf. p. 203.

the kingdoms themselves were being parcelled out into seignories, carrying the disintegration farther still.

At this point, however, the process was arrested for a brief space, and the reign of Dagobert (629–39), the last great Meroving, witnesses a final burst of vigour on the part of the central power. For ten years he ruled the whole of France, virtually relegating his brother to the position of Warden of the Basque Marches. The arts flourished at his brilliant and scandalous court, the goldsmith's activities being specially favoured. Abbeys were founded, and there was considerable missionary enterprise. Bretons and Basques were made to swear allegiance, and Frankish influence was felt in the affairs of Italy and Spain. Dagobert even concluded an alliance with Heraclius, to provide for concerted action against the Slavs and Bulgars of Central Europe, who threatened alternately the Rhine and Danube frontiers of France and Byzantium.

On the death of Dagobert, the kingdom was divided into two, and the decentralizing process resumed its course. Even during his lifetime, Austrasia had demanded a separate ruler in the person of the king's son, and the separatist tendencies of the three parts of France now showed themselves more openly. The history of the following century is the story of the rival ambitions of the mayors. Meroving princes are born and die, short-lived phantoms worn out by premature debauchery, *rois fainéants*, exhibiting at best a weak piety or a pliant amiability. But the real power lies in the hands of the great officers of state, whose struggles for personal ascendancy decide the issues of the kingdom. The position of the mayors was a contradictory one in certain respects. They were at the same time, as we have already noticed, the representatives of the king, and the heads of the local nobility. When these rival interests clashed, some of the mayors took one side, some the other. Grimoald, mayor of Austrasia, had the hardihood to declare himself against both. In 656 he banished the Meroving prince to Ireland, and set his own son on the throne. But the time was not yet ripe for such an adventure; he was overpowered by the nobles, and delivered over to the king of Neustria, who put him to death. A hundred years were to elapse before his descendants, the Carolings, found themselves strong enough to exercise the regal power in their own name. Meanwhile the civil wars went on, each mayor striving to exalt his own province, either to satisfy the king whom he served, or to placate the land-grabbing instincts of his fellow nobles.

Under the fierce energy of its mayor, Ebroin, the Neustrian kingdom gained the upper hand in 657, but Austrasia demanded its own mayor and king, and Burgundy, led by the bishop of Autun, afterwards canonized as St. Leger, likewise asserted its independence. Leger was captured and put to death with cruel tortures, which won for him in later times the crown of martyrdom, and Neustria once more resumed its hegemony. The supremacy of Ebroin was maintained until his death (681), but already a new star had risen above the horizon. Pipin II, leader of the Austrasian nobles, had suffered defeat at the hands of Ebroin, but a few years later, taking advantage of the dissension which prevailed among the Neustrians, he marched into the rival kingdom and on the field of Tertry, near Péronne, overcame all resistance, and established himself as the real ruler of France (687). The Battle of Tertry was not a victory of the Germans of the East over the Romans of the West; for Pipin had gained the support of a large Neustrian faction. It was in appearance a victory of the nobles over the royal authority which had been championed by Grimoald and his successor; but in reality it was the personal triumph of Pipin. From henceforward he was master of France, bestowing mayorships on members of his family, and ruling as a king in all but name. It is thus virtually the end of the Merovings, and the beginning of the Caroling dynasty.

From 687 to 714 Pipin had controlled the country, and his strong hand had restored it to a prominent place in the politics of Western Europe. At his death, the fortunes of his family and the unity of France hung once more in the balance. His two legitimate sons had died before him, and his grandsons were not yet of age. Burgundy and Neustria split asunder, and the general disorder spread to all parts. In the north-east, the Frisians devastated the country about Cologne; the Saxons, farther south, had followed suit, while Aquitaine seized the opportunity once again to proclaim its independence. But the Caroling house had found its champion as well as its name-giver. Charles Martel, third son of Pipin, triumphed successively over all obstacles. Using, like his father, the Austrasian power, he quelled the Neustrian dissidents, reduced the Aquitanians to submission, restored the eastern frontiers in a series of successful campaigns, and in 732 routed the Arab forces on the field of Poitiers,[1] following up his victory, five years later, by an expedition into Provence. Aquitanian independence, however, proved to have been only scotched, not killed; and the Arabs still retained possession of Narbonne, from whose walled shelter they sallied forth upon the cities of the Rhône valley.

It was Pipin, son of Charles, who finally accomplished the reduction of Aquitaine. His conquest was deliberate, successful, and permanent. More statesmanlike than his father, he took care to conciliate the Church by studied favours, and to form a loyal party among the Aquitanians themselves. His careful policy had shown itself earlier, in a notable event. In 751, having obtained from the Pope a favourable response to his project, Pipin assumed the crown of France, the last of the Merovings being tonsured and relegated to the monastic life. Three years later Pipin was formally crowned at St. Denis by Pope Stephen II, who had crossed the Alps to seek Frankish aid against the Lombards. Coronation was a novel rite for the Franks; it set the seal upon Pipin's election to the kingdom which had already been approved by the assembly of the people. The theory of Divine Right vested in a single family was to assume a greater significance in subsequent French history; but even at this period the sacred unction of the Church, with its scriptural precedents, was felt to be necessary in that it counterbalanced the sacrilege done to the Merovings, descendants of the legendary Sea-God, who retained even in their decline the mysterious sanctity of far-off pagan times.

The alliance of Pope and Caroling, which was to alter the whole course of European history, was no casual event. It is true that the form which it took was due to the policy of certain

[1] Cf. p. 156.

outstanding personalities; but the converging influences which made that policy desirable were the outcome of slow-moving developments. Clovis, it will be remembered, had created what amounted to a national church. This independence was continued under his descendants, and even Gregory the Great, in spite of his legate at Arles, could not enforce his claims to authority, but was obliged to limit himself to the employment of indirect influence through such a medium as Brunhilda. The confusion caused by the civil wars was reflected in the state of the Church; in the divided realm no general councils could be held, and the bishops were embroiled in the political discord. Temporal and ecclesiastical powers were intermingled, and the voice of the Papacy could not make itself heard amid the din of arms. When order was restored under the Carolings, it was found necessary to complete the political union of France by more strictly organizing the administration of the Church. Charles Martel had only increased the disorder, for he had rewarded his followers with gifts of bishoprics and abbeys; but Pipin and his brother Carloman, who afterwards retired to a monastery, were favourable to the projects of reform set before them by Boniface, and a series of decrees followed, regulating the hierarchy and morals of the Church in France. Boniface, an English missionary, had already performed notable services in Germany, where he had converted vast numbers of the heathen. His remarkable achievements will be referred to again, but the significance of his work in the present connexion lies in his close relations with the Papacy. Boniface was a loyal servant of the Pope; from every bishop under his jurisdiction he demanded an oath of submission to the Church of Rome, St. Peter, and his Vicar. Pipin and Carloman, while maintaining sovereign rights over the Church, frequently had occasion to consult the Pope, and the bond between the two great powers of the West became gradually closer. Already Charles Martel had received an appeal for succour from the Papacy, hard pressed in its struggle with the Lombards. He had not responded, for his position was not sufficiently secure to allow him to embark on foreign and hazardous campaigns; the Lombards, moreover, were the natural allies of the Franks, and had joined him in his warfare against the Saracens. There was also the position of the rulers of Byzantium to be considered, who still, as Roman Emperors, laid claim to the overlordship of Italy. But events were moving rapidly to a conclusion. In 751 the Lombard king hurled his forces upon Ravenna; the Exarch fled, and the Byzantine domains in North Italy were lost for ever. In the same year, with papal encouragement, Pipin assumed the crown, displacing the last Merovings. The Lombard menace to the Papacy now became an instant peril; absolute submission was demanded, and the fall of Rome appeared inevitable. Pipin still hesitated, and two years later the Pope himself crossed the Alps on his memorable mission, which was destined to bring the Frankish forces into Italy, and to perpetuate the union of Pope and Caroling in the Holy Roman Empire.

Much has been made of the survival of the Imperial idea during the centuries which elapsed between the fall of Rome and the coronation of Charlemagne. It is true that the Western Empire had its roots in the far distant past, and drew naturally upon ancient precedent; moreover, its foundation did not revolutionize the political situation in the West; it merely gave formal expression to a state of affairs already in existence. But the curious circumstances of its origin, and the very considerable differences which separated it from its prototype, the old Roman Empire, were due in no small measure to the remarkable amalgam of German and Latin cultures which characterized the inhabitants of the Frankish dominions. Of this, only the most fleeting impression can be given here. A complex process of three centuries, varying in each district and each period, and insufficiently known to us from fragmentary records, precludes the possibility of confident generalization.

In appearance, it might seem that the political and administrative organization of France was little different from that of Roman Gaul. Methods and terminology had been borrowed from Rome, and Latin was actually the official tongue. It is noticeable in this connexion that only 10 per cent. of the words in modern French are of Germanic origin. As far as their relative legal status was concerned, only the *wergild* distinguished the Franks from the rest of the population, while the ranks of the

higher clergy, as well as the financial offices, were filled largely
by Gallo-Romans. But if the forms remained unchanged, the
spirit of these institutions was profoundly altered, not only by
direct Germanic influences, but also by the new conditions
brought about by the invasions. The Roman Empire had re-
posed on the abstract idea of the State, of laws and government
equal for all, and independent of those who represented them.
One was a citizen of the Empire, rather than a subject of the
Emperor. The Frankish kingdom, on the other hand, depended
for its existence on the personal relation of man to man. The
power of the monarch was personal; it varied with the character
of its holder. His subjects were bound to him by an oath of fidelity,
a personal tie, constraining them to follow him in war. A new
order of nobility developed, dependent at first on the monarchy,
and later gaining strength from hereditary local influence, and
from the immunities bestowed on it. In the legal sphere, the
personal element was equally apparent. A man was tried by the
laws of the race to which he belonged, whether Gallo-Roman,
Salian, Ripuarian, or Burgundian. The old German principle
of the blood-feud was not yet extinguished, and the pages of
Gregory of Tours teem with stories of revenge. The highly
specialized bureaucracy of Roman Gaul no longer existed; more
primitive conditions rendered it useless. Chamberlain, Seneschal
and Constable surround the King, and special missions are performed by courtiers chosen without system. The districts are
ruled by Counts, selected by the monarch from all classes of the
population, and the frontier marches are given into the hands of
military Dukes, who often become, as in the case of Bavaria or
Thuringia, practically independent national rulers. Toll-gates
and ferries still paid their dues, though these had in many cases
been usurped by individuals, but the elaborate system of taxation which had characterized the Roman administration was
allowed to fall into disuse; there was no place for it in the scheme
of a ruler who had no public services to keep up, and who
regarded money as something which formed part of a 'hoard', to
be transformed, when possible, into gold plate or jewelled trin-
kets. Even the army is not a public charge; the 'host' is gathered
afresh for each campaign. It is the personal following of the king,

and serves at its own costs. The only permanent forces are the *antrustions*, or royal bodyguard, and a few frontier detachments.

The 'hierarchy of the *wergild*'[1] ranges society at first into conquerors and conquered, placing the Gallo-Roman beneath the lowliest Frank. This does not last long. Personal distinctions assert themselves, and while the senatorial class continues to supply bishops and officers of state, the richer Franks acquire a veneer of Roman culture. The two classes merge into one another, and the slaves, freedmen and *coloni* of both races follow their example. Here, too, the loyalty of individual to individual is the binding force. Bishop or abbot, court official or local governor are the king's *leuds*, his 'men', attached to him by a special tie, and placed under his protection. The same principle is found in each *pagus*; the counts range themselves under the dukes, and lesser men seek the protection of the count. Already the feudal chain is forming, though still unrecognized by law, and the word *leud* is beginning to be superseded by the significant term *vassus*. This personal dependence, moreover, is reinforced and materialized by the growth of large estates. As in the later centuries of Roman rule, the smaller landowner hastens to place himself under the protection of a powerful patron, surrendering his freehold for the promise of security. Abbeys and bishoprics add field to field, for Church property, once acquired, is inalienable, and over a third of France has fallen into ecclesiastical hands. The weakness of the central power shows itself also in the misdoings of its subordinates, and in order to save themselves from the exactions of these officials, the greater landowners obtain 'immunities'. Henceforth the royal officers are excluded from such lands, and the rights and profits of taxation and jurisdiction devolve upon the owners. Ownership and sovereignty are in fact becoming identified, and the shadowy monarchy has thus divested itself of its few remaining powers. The transition from the central government and wide horizon of Roman days to the local grouping and restricted outlook of the Middle Ages is nearing completion.

The old city life is gone. Temples and amphitheatres lie in ruins, and inside the walled towns the empty spaces are occupied

[1] Cf. p. 66.

by gardens. The rural population clusters round the dwelling of the big landowner, with its church, its mill, its forge, bakeries and stables, and all the apparatus of a self-contained existence. Sometimes the cottages of the dependents are in outlying parts of the estate, but more often they stand in streets, the ancestors of most of the villages of modern France. The houses of the rich have still their porticoes and columns, their baths and fountains. Churches are rising everywhere, some of basilican type, others cruciform, with central tower and lantern, others again constructed of wood, after the Teutonic fashion. The interiors are . bright with coloured marble and rich with silken broideries; but the marble has been torn from some classical edifice, and the silken hangings are of Byzantine origin. Sculpture is barbaric, and the great tradition of the Arlesian sarcophagi has finally died out. Only the craft of the metal-worker flourishes. It enjoys special favour at the Meroving Court, and the goldsmiths' quarter is already established under the shadow of Notre Dame at Paris.

The spoken tongue is changing rapidly. Little difference is to be found between the literary and the vulgar language, and under the pressure of phonetic laws the various dialects are already in process of formation. *Flumina de sanguine* is used for 'rivers of blood', and *promissum habemus* for 'we have promised'. Many German loan-words have been adopted, and the German tongue holds its own in the eastern districts. Apart from the history of Gregory of Tours, literature is practically confined to the Lives of Saints, which repeat, for the most part with wearisome similarity, the miraculous exploits of their heroes. Stock phrases and clumsy sentences succeed one another; no writer is master of his words. Knowledge of the Classics is to all intents and purposes non-existent, and even theological dogma has become a sealed book to most of the Gallic clergy. Popular religion is permeated by pagan customs, and paganism itself is by no means extinct. The Celtic deities of lake and stream have still their secret worshippers, and Odin his dwelling-place in the deep forests of the Ardennes. The preaching of the Church, reinforced by the terrors of the secular arm, will deprive the old gods of their authority, but the Black Huntsman, the Witches'

Sabbath, and all the rout of fairies, dwarfs, and monsters will remain to haunt the imagination of the Middle Ages. Already the Devil ('the Enemy', as he is beginning to be called—a word of fear and mystery) has become prominent in popular beliefs, and religion takes on a more sombre cast. The vengeance of God or the malice of the Evil One can be averted only by ritual observance. Saints appear in the fields, miracles and portents are affairs of everyday experience. Dreams and omens exercise men's minds, and sanctuaries and relics acquire talismanic powers to heal or hurt.

What more natural, in such a world, than that the Emperor Constantine, miraculously cured of his leprosy, should have turned to Christianity, bringing with him the whole of the Roman Empire; that he should straightway have bestowed on Pope Sylvester the Imperial government of the West, himself retiring humbly to Byzantium? Or that St. Peter, in person, should be reported to be summoning the Frankish forces to the defence of his holy city? And how, in such a welter of forms and institutions, could the terms *patricius, imperator, respublica*, with their long and complicated history, hold any accurate constitutional significance for the statesman of that time?

XIII

THE PAPACY

THE two centuries which followed the death of Gregory the Great witnessed the development, slow, uncertain, and obscure even to its authors, of papal influence in Western Europe. The personal character and prestige of Gregory had raised the See of Peter to an eminence which his successors were unable to maintain. Once his commanding authority was removed, the instability of his claims became manifest. Some of the problems presented by the barbarian kingdoms had been solved, but new and greater difficulties were making themselves felt. Arianism was a dying force. The Lombards had turned to the Catholic faith, and Spain followed their example when Reccared (586–601) adopted Catholicism as the national religion. The danger was now a different and more serious one. The Germanic rulers, each engaged in building up a strong central power, could not afford to dispense with any element of sovereignty. A series of national churches, owing lip-service only to the Papacy, would have been a blow at the very heart of Rome. Already there were ominous signs of such a thing. Clovis and his successors had brooked no interference with their ecclesiastical control, and the Papal Legacy at Arles remained an honorary position, not a vice-gerency of the Roman pontiffs. The conversion of the Lombards had not put a stop to their aggression. The Papacy, *inter gladios Lombardorum*, might well dread the advent of a Germanic kingdom of Italy. In Spain, Gregory's activities had been more fruitful. A close connexion was established between Rome and the Spanish bishops, and the final century of Visigoth rule was marked by the growth of episcopal influence, which extended even to secular affairs, overshadowing the power of the monarchy. Papal rulings were irksome to the independent spirit of the Spanish Church, but a more serious blow to Catholic authority was dealt by the onset of the Islamic host.

The balance, however, was to be redressed from another

quarter. The remnants of British Christianity had retreated before the advance of the Saxons into the Western regions. They had carried the Faith into Ireland, and a new centre of civilization had arisen, attracting saints and scholars from other parts of Western Europe. In this strange backwater of antiquity, untouched by the Germanic invaders, the tradition of the old classical culture lingered on, attenuated and barbarized, in the great monasteries. The peculiar atmosphere of this exotic world is shown by its Latin poems, in which Celtic rhythms and assonance are already perceptible, and by its exquisite manuscripts, of which the Book of Kells, with its outlandish ornaments and capitals, is an outstanding example.[1] But the Irish Church was not content to remain in isolation. Columba spread the Gospel in Scotland and the Western Isles, and Iona became a famous centre of Christianity. Columban crossed to France, and founded his ascetic monasteries in the Vosges. Gall in Switzerland and Kilian in Bavaria extended the influence of Hibernian ideals.

There were dangers to the power of Rome in this evangelizing activity. Apart from minor, though controversial, differences, such as the date of Easter and the method of tonsure, the Celtic Church, both in Ireland and in western Britain, retained many primitive usages, and was disinclined to recognize the value of the organized hierarchy which had developed in more civilized regions, modelled on the administration of the Roman Empire. Diocese and parish, bishop and metropolitan, councils and canons, and above all the central authority at Rome—a logical system of this kind aroused no enthusiasm among the tribal monastic communities of Ireland. And though visionary enthusiasts from the Isle of Saints might boldly rebuke kings, and even brave the wrath, on occasion, of the terrible Brunhilda, statesmanlike popes such as Gregory realized that the permanent influence of the Church upon lay society was only to be secured by the use of more secular weapons, and by the creation of a disciplined force. The monkish orders were to be an invaluable aid in the realization of this ideal; they could be trusted to uphold the papal authority in the face of unruly bishops, who were, all too often, only powerful nobles who had extorted their office

[1] Cf. p. 88.

from a yielding monarch. But it was not the individualist Irish monks, bidding defiance to king and bishop, and even to the Pope himself, but the Benedictines, sinking their personality in submission to their spiritual superiors, who were to be made use of in this way.

Gregory's dispatch of Augustine on his English mission was the turning-point in this process, little as it may have appeared at the time. The gradual conversion of England, which occupied the greater part of the seventh century, was a series of advances and setbacks, caused partly by the varying fortunes of the kingdoms, and partly by the antagonism between the Roman and Celtic Churches. Canterbury remained a stronghold of Roman influence, but Mercia was a pagan realm, and Northumbria wavered between allegiance to her Kentish ally and loyalty to the Celtic preaching of Iona and Lindisfarne. The Synod of Whitby, in 664, which assured the triumph of the Roman system, gave the signal for what may be called the organization of an Anglo-Latin Church. The country was parcelled into bishoprics, and the minster became the effective centre of each diocese. Stone churches replaced the wooden structures of former times, and the parish system, after a time, came into existence. Regular synods were instituted, and monks and priests alike were subjected to the rule of their superiors. Britain was gradually becoming a loyal province of Rome's spiritual empire. Education flourished in the great schools, and church music and ornaments were imported from overseas to enhance the splendour of Hexham and Wearmouth. Religious enthusiasm invaded the ruling class. Royal ladies entered the cloister, and kings inquired diligently for relics, or donned the pilgrim's habit, and set forth to end their days in Rome.

Wilfrid of York began the series of Anglo-Saxon missionaries in Germany and the Low Countries, a series culminating in the great name of Boniface. The political consequences of the work of Boniface can hardly be over-estimated. The scene of his labours, for the most part, was a country which had lain outside the Roman Empire, and the conversion of its uncivilized inhabitants would have been impossible without the support of Charles Martel, whose conquests, in turn, owed much to the co-operation of Boniface and his followers. In 732 the Pope conferred upon Boniface the dignity of archbishop, and the Church of Germany was organized, under his leadership, as a faithful member of the Roman obedience. Bavarians and Alamans, previously converted by Irish monks, were persuaded, with the help of Frankish influence, to admit the papal superiority. The work of Boniface did not end here. At the invitation of Pipin and his brother he proceeded to reform the Frankish Church. Abuses were put down, regular councils were arranged, and the authority of the Pope expressly recognized by the bishops.

Boniface had introduced Christianity and civilization into Central Germany; he had facilitated the advance of Charles Martel in that region, which foreshadowed the later annexation of Charlemagne; he had helped to lay the foundations of Caroling supremacy. He had secured to the papal allegiance the two great Churches of Germany and France, and had cemented the alliance between Pope and Frankish ruler which was destined to decide the history of Western Europe. The political forces whose coalescence resulted in the creation of the Holy Roman Empire, the extension, that is, of papal influence, and the consolidation of Caroling power, owed no less a debt to Anglo-Saxon Christianity than did the subsequent revival of art and learning which the tradition of Benedict Biscop and the Venerable Bede, developed by Alcuin and his followers, engendered at the Court of Charlemagne.

2. THE ITALIAN BALANCE OF POWER

The conditions of Lombard settlement within the Empire were wholly different from those which had accompanied the entry of most other Germanic races. The latter had been received as *foederati*—theoretical defenders of the Roman State—and formed, as it were, the fighting part of the population. The Lombards, on the other hand, occupied Italian territory as avowed enemies and conquerors. Roman landowners were not permitted to share their property with the barbarian 'guests'.[1] They were summarily exiled and deprived—at least in the early stages of the invasion—of all legal personality. There was thus

[1] Cf. p. 65.

no possibility of a dual organization such as had characterized the kingdom of Theoderic,[1] and the attitude of the victorious Lombards seemed calculated to preserve their racial unity and customs intact, free from dilution by Roman ideas and institutions.

Romanization, however, was destined to be brought about by other means, and by the period of Frankish intervention two centuries of settled residence in a country permeated with the influences, spiritual and material, of over a thousand years of Mediterranean civilization had wrought great changes in the manner of life of the invaders. Stone-built cities were regarded no longer as fresh places to sack; they had become the seats of Lombard kings or nobles, military and administrative centres of the territory which provided the ruling classes with their means of subsistence. The monarch took up his residence in the old Romano-Gothic *palatium* at Pavia; and the quick appreciation of the barbarian for the luxuries of civilized existence soon rendered indispensable the services of a host of Roman artificers and tradesfolk—architects, masons, jewellers, armourers, and purveyors of every variety of requisites for city life. The change is well seen in the pages of Paul the Deacon, a Lombard who composed the history of his people during the latter half of the eighth century. The dress and manners of his ancestors at their first appearance in Italy are already a historical curiosity, known to him only from the scenes from Lombard story which Queen Theodelinda, about A.D. 600, caused to be executed for her palace at Monza. The pictures, he remarks,[2] show clearly the general appearance of the Lombards of that time, and their fashions in clothes and hair-cutting. The back of the head was shaved clean, but the hair in front was long, parted in the middle, and hanging down over the cheeks. They wore, he continues, loose clothes, mostly of linen, like those of the Anglo-Saxons, with broad stripes of various colours, and boots open almost to the toes, laced crosswise. Later on they took to wearing hose, with rough woollen coverings over them when they went riding; but this, he adds, was a custom which they took over from the Romans.

Roman influence was not confined to fashions in clothing or

[1] Cf. p. 69.   [2] Paul. Diac. iv. 22.

weapons. Though few, probably, could speak Latin at their first entry into North Italy, altered conditions and greater complexity in the demands of everyday life favoured the more civilized speech, and eventually the use of Lombard words came to be considered vulgar by the nobles. Inter-marriage, as well as constant intercourse, with a population far outnumbering its conquerors completed this process, and Italian, as a result, has remained to this day the purest of the Romance languages. Nor must the cultural influence of the Church, with educational centres, such as the great monastery of Bobbio, in Lombard territory, be overlooked. Contracts, moreover, and other legal documents were invariably Roman in form, and although the Lombardic law was Germanic, here, too, Roman ideas had crept in, and—as invariably happened with Teutonic tribes in contact with Imperial methods—the absolutism of the ruler received a powerful impetus, though the position of the 'dukes' wavered between that of subordinate officials and practically independent kinglets, according to the personal strength and character displayed by the monarch. Benevento and Spoleto increased their liberties as the eighth century took its course, but the duchies of North Italy gradually submitted themselves to the central authority.

It is, however, significant that the Lombard ruler continued to call himself *Rex Gentis Lombardorum*. His people were, and remained, distinct in status from the Roman inhabitants of Italy, and the instruments of the culture which has been noticed above were largely in the hands of Roman traders, artists, and workmen. The sailors whose craft plied busily along the Po, the armourers of Lucca and Cremona, the growers of fruit and vegetables for the courts of Lombard nobles—such men were Roman for the most part, as were also, perhaps, the famous *maestri Comacini*, that shadowy guild of artists—survivors, possibly, of the collegiate system[1] of Late Roman times—whose name is invoked so frequently in discussions of the origins of Italian Art. There is, in fact, no real evidence on which claims can be based for the existence at this period of a specifically 'Lombardic' style either in architecture or decorative *motifs*.

[1] Cf. p. 27.

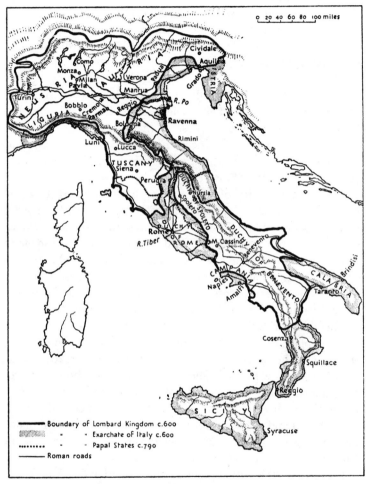

ITALY
7TH–8TH CENTURIES

The history of Italy from A.D. 600 to 800 can be summarized
as a struggle between five powers, with aims mutually incompatible. Two of these powers—the Lombard Kingdom and the
Byzantine Empire—lose their decisive influence upon Italian
politics at the end of this period. The third—that of the Frankish
host—intervenes fitfully and at intervals, but during the last
half-century plays a predominant role, culminating in the
supremacy of Charlemagne. The fourth—the Papacy—grows
steadily in influence, an influence none the less real because
obscured by its physical helplessness. The fifth—the Duchies of
Benevento and Spoleto—represents the pair of knights on the
Italian chessboard, insignificant in themselves, but holding
interior lines, and often deciding a major issue by their incal-
culable moves and unexpected attack.[1]

The constant policy of a strong Lombard king was the complete subjection of Italy.[2] Such an aim, dictated no less by the
need of rewarding his followers with land than by that of personal
security and prestige, was naturally opposed by the other four
powers. But Byzantine exarchs at Ravenna did not hesitate to
employ the Lombard forces against rebellious Popes, while the
Papacy on more than one occasion appealed to the Lombard
ruler to suppress the activities of Benevento and Spoleto.

The object of Byzantium was to keep her hold on the maritime
districts of Italy, to maintain her officials against the growing
strength of the landed nobility, and that of the greatest landowner of all, the Papacy, and, finally, to exact the tribute required for the defence of those eastern territories where her real
interests now lay. Only in so far as his support contributed to
the political and religious unity of the Empire was the influence
of the Pope anything but an inconvenience to the Roman
Emperor.

Meanwhile, the settled purpose of the Roman See was simply
to keep in being. The policy is kaleidoscopic; but the ultimate
end is constant and unvarying. Time, and the growth of the

[1] It should be noted that these two Lombard vassal states did not act in concert.
[2] This finds expression in the legend which represents Authari (584) as riding
into the sea at the southern extremity of Italy, and touching with his spear a solitary
column projecting from the waves as he cried, 'This shall be the boundary of the
Lombard realm!'

Western nations, were on the side of the Papacy. It is not likely that this was apparent to the Papal Chancery, but it was, at all events, clearly felt that the Pope must not be degraded, on the one hand, to the status of a Lombard bishop, or, on the other, to that of a Byzantine official. The suzerainty of the Emperor is therefore punctiliously acknowledged up to the last moment; but far-sighted Popes, whose gaze could penetrate beyond the Alpine passes to the plains of France, can hardly have been blind to the ultimate consequences of their delicate manoeuvring in regard to Byzantium.

The aims of Spoleto and Benevento were simple and immediate —local independence, and increase of territory at the expense of their neighbours, while Frankish policy, before the conquest, was determined by three principal motives, internal weakness and traditional Lombard friendship counselling non-intervention in the affairs of Italy, until the fine threads of papal diplomacy drew the invading forces of the Carolings to the gates of Rome.

Compromise, and a precarious balance of power, the consequence of internal difficulties or weak rulers, had reconciled for a time these warring elements. The successors of Gregory the Great had fallen far short of his commanding stature in character and statecraft; the Roman Emperors who followed Heraclius had been preoccupied with the menace of Islam; the Lombard kingdom was troubled by succession quarrels and unruly vassals, while France was still torn asunder by the struggles of the rival mayors. The decisive period in Italy coincides with the appearance of strong personalities at the head of affairs— Popes Gregory II (715–31) and Gregory III (731–41), Leo the Isaurian (717–41), the Iconoclast Emperor, and Liutprand (712–44), greatest of the Lombard kings. The thunderous impact of these individual embodiments of conflicting policy lights up the stormy landscape of Italy with a revealing flash which shows the real transformations that are taking place.

By about A.D. 700 the Byzantine position was already undermined. Although the higher functionaries were still controlled by the Imperial authority, the actual power was in the hands of the feudal families of *tribuni*, whose competence in their districts was not only military, but embraced jurisdiction and taxation as well. A new organization had arisen, and an Italian revolt would be no longer, as in the past, that of a rebellious Exarch, but of these local, and far more dangerous, officials. A symptom of the true state of things appeared in 692, when the Emperor Justinian II, pursuing the traditional Imperial policy, summoned the Trullan Council, or Quinisextum (completion of the 5th and 6th Oecumenical Councils), to standardize belief and practice in East and West alike. The Pope refused his assent to its decisions, and an important Byzantine officer, the Protospatharius, was dispatched to Rome with instructions to arrest the unruly pontiff. But the days of Vigilius' humiliation at the hands of Justinian I[1] were long past. The Italian militia flocked into Rome, and to escape their fury the Protospatharius was compelled to take refuge underneath the Pope's bed.

Twenty-five years later the crisis was repeated, when the Emperor Leo, having successfully defended Byzantium in the famous siege of 717–18, ventured to impose new taxation in the West. Revolution flamed out in Italy, and the Exarch, allied with Liutprand, the Lombard king—a novel combination—marched against Rome, who had rallied to her aid the Duchies of Spoleto and Benevento. The political and economic struggle was suffused by a religious glow when the Emperor, in 725, proclaimed his Iconoclastic policy.[2] Dogma was a sealed book to the Italian populace, but images formed a vital element in its devotion, and the controversy became a powerful weapon in the hands of the Pope. Leo was soon represented as Antichrist himself. Gregory II, says a contemporary, 'armed himself as against an enemy', and addressed the Emperor in language hitherto unprecedented in one of his subjects. Nevertheless, the Italian revolt was finally put down, though not until one Exarch had been killed, and another dispatched from Byzantium to enforce order.

A further stage was now reached in the severance of East and West. The dioceses of Sicily and South Italy, as well as those on the eastern shore of the Adriatic, were removed by the Emperor from the jurisdiction of the Bishop of Rome to that of the Patriarch of Constantinople. This momentous step determined the medieval history of southern Italy, which became, during the

[1] See p. 116.   [2] Cf. p. 191.

following centuries, increasingly Hellenized in culture, sympathies, and even population, owing to a considerable inflow of Orthodox refugees during the Iconoclast disputes. At the same time it reduced the Pope's influence, so far as territory within the Empire was concerned, to that of a provincial bishop, controlling the two themes (now separate and independently organized) of Ravenna and Rome.

The Imperial connexion, however, was still essential to the independent existence of the Papacy. Charles Martel had declined the invitation to take part in Italian politics, and the Lombard kingdom, stronger than ever under the leadership of Liutprand, could not be left without a counterpoise. Once more the Pope intervened on behalf of his Imperial master, and Ravenna, the centre of Byzantine administration in North Italy, was saved from imminent capture at the hands of the Lombard forces.

The death of Liutprand was followed by internal disturbances, but when Ratchis, his pious successor, was superseded by Aistulf, a strong central power resumed its traditional purpose of the complete subjugation of Italy. Rapid developments followed. In 751—the year in which Pipin, at papal suggestion, had assumed the crown—Ravenna fell before the Lombard assault, and Byzantine rule in the Exarchate was finally extinguished. The next year found Aistulf gathering his resources for an attack on Rome. In 753 Pope Stephen crossed the Alps to seek the assistance of the Frankish ruler. Seven months later Pipin declared war on the Lombard kingdom, and invaded Italy. Routed near Susa, Aistulf's army took refuge behind the walls of Pavia. Restitution of Ravenna and papal territory was exacted from the vanquished, and Pipin returned home, only to be summoned more urgently, in 756, by tidings of renewed aggression. Once more Pavia was besieged, and in return for peace Pipin was acknowledged as overlord of the Lombard kingdom, while the Exarchate was given into the hands of St. Peter and his successors in the See of Rome.

Aistulf died that year, leaving the situation in Italy formally unaltered. Pipin's suzerainty over his dominions was accepted, but he had not yet conquered them territorially. The Pope had become the supreme authority not only in Rome but also in the Exarchate, yet both were still nominally a part of the Empire. Frankish intervention continued to be an uncertain quantity, and meanwhile the Lombard danger to the Papacy appeared likely to revive.

Desiderius succeeded Aistulf, and the Pope's fears were redoubled when Charles, son of Pipin, was married to the daughter of the Lombard king. For a few years after the death of Pipin, in 768, a German *bloc* of Franks, Bavarians, and Lombards seemed on the point of materializing under the influence of the Dowager Queen Bertrada. But Charles's repudiation of his Lombard wife in 772 changed the situation abruptly. Two years later, at the summons of Pope Hadrian, Charles invaded Italy. Pavia surrendered, after a long siege, Desiderius and his family were carried into captivity, and by the end of 774 the independent Lombard kingdom had ceased to exist.

Such, in barest outline, are the facts of the Frankish intervention in Italy. Behind them lies a dark, half-realized background of tortuous diplomacy, private ambition, and the interplay of two civilizations—the Roman, with its long history of legal and constitutional concepts, its language redolent of centuries of settled government and philosophical distinctions, and the German, with its personal loyalties, its tribal memories, and its incomprehension of abstract terminology. It is impossible, in this strange world of legend and superstition, of ancient, half-understood Imperial formulae, to piece together from credulous papal biographers and illiterate monkish chronicles a satisfactory account of the long-drawn process by which the bishops of Rome severed their connexion with the old Roman Empire, and placed themselves under the protection of the dominant Western power. The significance of each symbol can be endlessly disputed. What was the nature of the *dicio*, the authority which the Popes claimed to exercise, on behalf of the Emperor, over Italian territory? What was the extent of the 'Patrimony of St. Peter', the districts whose ownership transformed the Papacy about this time into a temporal power? Or what meaning was to be attached to the successive 'donations' of Pipin and Charlemagne?

Each gesture was now elevated to constitutional significance, and subsequent medieval arguments as to the relation of Empire and Papacy were based on the sending of keys and banner to the Frankish king, the title of 'patrician', or even the holding of a bridle-rein. Pictures and legends assumed documentary force. The famous story of the Emperor Constantine and the Pope Sylvester,[1] which throughout the medieval period formed one of the principal arguments for the papal claims, seems to have emerged into full daylight at this period, and may perhaps be regarded less as a conscious forgery than as a 'rationalization', a translation into the terms of current thought, or current piety, of the political relation of the Popes to the Emperor at Byzantium. Constantine the Great, it was asserted, had not only resigned his Lateran palace to the Pope, and given him the *dicio*, or dominion, over the West; he had also offered him the diadem and purple, in accordance with his future position, while his clergy, who were henceforth to replace the Senate at Rome, just as his subordinate bishops occupied the posts of the provincial governors, were privileged to use white horse-trappings and to adorn themselves with the coveted Senatorial boots. In this extraordinary perversion of history can plainly be seen the reflection of contemporary conditions and disputes, the rivalry between the Papal Curia and the Byzantine officials in Italy, the contested validity of the Frankish 'donations', and the problem of Lombard claims to conquered territory.

Most significant of all, however, is the survival of the Imperial idea, as the very substance of this dream-world of Roman theocracy. For over twenty-five years the Iconoclast emperors had been, in Italian eyes, not only hated tax-gatherers and tyrants, but impious schismatics as well. Yet nowhere is there word breathed of a possible independent existence for the Papacy outside the Imperial domains. Nothing can indicate more clearly the fact that to the mind of the eighth century the world-empire of Rome, whose head was the Emperor at Constantinople, was still the sole conceivable pattern of the terrestrial order. Only by transferring the emphasis from the person of the Emperor to the immemorial (and, from a Roman point of view,

[1] Cf. p. 206.

the only true) seat of Empire, namely Rome herself, was it possible to justify theoretically the coronation of a Western Emperor, whose *raison d'être*, from the papal standpoint, was the armed protection of the Church's interests in Western Europe, and, above all, of the ancient capital of Augustus and Constantine, the holy and oecumenical see of St. Peter and his successors.

Meanwhile, though shadowy premonitions of such possibilities may be discerned, the immediate situation remained obscure, and the next thirty years in fact witnessed a steady lowering of the papal hopes which had been pitched so high at the downfall of the Lombard kingdom. The balance of power in Italy had been upset. Pipin had crossed the Alps on two crusading missions to win salvation by his response to the Petrine summons. Charles, on the other hand, was now established on Italian soil, a permanent and secular overlord. Spoleto and Benevento, in their strivings for independence, had been invaluable, if uncertain, allies of the Pope. Now they were vassals of the Frankish ruler, and their recalcitrance could bring no profit to the papal interests. Henceforward, were Pope and Caroling to fall out, there was no possible defender to whom the Church could turn for assistance. Nor was this all. Each new and brilliant conquest swelled the proportions of Charles's empire, dwarfing into insignificance the puny dimensions of the papal State. The union of Western Europe under one master brought international relations into prominence. Papal claims to Istria and South Italy must be subordinated to the diplomatic exchanges of Aix and Byzantium. The bitterest of papal complaints concerning the intransigence of the Archbishop of Ravenna or the aggression of the Duke of Spoleto went unheeded while Charles was campaigning on the Saxon frontier. Even as head of Western Christendom, the Pope was assigned a more passive role than that of the armed champion of the Faith, who, with *Christiana Religio* inscribed on his coinage, his weapons sanctified by the prayers of the Church, went forth to exterminate the heathen of Central Germany and plant new bishoprics beyond Bavaria. Rumours even were abroad in the North, voiced by Offa of Mercia, that Charles intended to depose the Pope in favour of a Frankish prelate. Even the realm of dogma was not secure from the new Western autocracy. At the Synod of Frankfort, summoned by Charles in answer to the recent Council of Nicaea in the East, the youthful Frankish theology found its voice, in shrill, confident accents condemning equally iconoclast and iconodule, branding the Emperor and Empress as heretics, and even accusing the Greeks of a want of critical spirit in regard to the Sylvester legend. The Pope, who had approved the decisions of the Nicene Council, could make no effective protest. He was even prepared, if Charles wished, to declare the orthodox Emperor heretical, should the latter persist in withholding the Greek dioceses and the South Italian patrimonies which the Pope claimed as his own. The subordination of doctrinal issues to the temporal interests of the papal State is not less remarkable than the Pope's subservience to Charles's momentary anti-Byzantine aims. Not since the days of Justinian had the Papacy sunk so low. Even in Rome itself, the pontifical authority was not unchallenged. Papal elections were constantly accompanied by the fierce street-fighting, conducted from fortified palaces, which forms such a familiar feature of medieval Italian cities, and the rivalries of feudal nobles and Church officials frequently found satisfaction in the bloody conflicts of Pope and anti-Pope.

XIV

CHARLEMAGNE

On Christmas Day, 800, as Charlemagne, during the celebration of the Mass, rose from his knees before the shrine of
St. Peter at Rome, the Pope placed a crown upon his head, and
the Roman people saluted him with tumultuous cries: 'To
Charles Augustus crowned of God, great and pacific Emperor
of the Romans, long life and victory!' The scene has kindled
the imagination of historians. In the ancient basilica, glowing
with candlelight and jewelled vestments, the foremost warrior
of Europe, conqueror of Saracens, Avars, and Saxons, whose
realm stretched from the Baltic to the Adriatic shore, from
Northern Spain to the Middle Danube, seals his protective
mandate over Western Christianity by the solemn ritual of
Imperial Rome, and 'in the union of the Roman and the Teuton,
of the memories and the civilization of the South with the fresh
energy of the North . . . modern history begins'.[1]

It was, unquestionably, one of the most picturesque moments
in the history of the Papacy, comparable only, perhaps, for
dramatic effect, with that other wintry scene in the snowy, wind-
swept courtyard of Canossa, where a suppliant Emperor waited
for three days to obtain forgiveness of the Pope. Yet its significance, like that of Hildebrand's triumph, does not lie on the
surface. The ceremony in St. Peter's was not a constitutional
solution of the difficulties inherent in Charles's relation to the
Papacy. It changed nothing in the actual situation and settled
nothing for the future.[2] But it is, nevertheless, as Bryce showed,
the beginning of a new age, in that it determined the lines of the
unending struggle between Papacy and Empire which constitutes the background of medieval European politics.

Since the days of Theodosius, when Christianity had become
the official religion of the Roman Empire, no permanent reconciliation had been possible between the claims of Church and

---

[1] J. Bryce, *The Holy Roman Empire*, p. 49 (8th ed. London, 1892).
[2] For recent views concerning the significance of Charlemagne's coronation, see
K. Heldmann, *Das Kaisertum Karls des Grossen* (Weimar, 1928).

State. Stability could only have been achieved by the complete subordination of one to the other. Still less possible was it now to demarcate spheres of interest, when the temporal influence of the Church was more highly organized than ever before. The papal claims can be seen in the legend of the Donation of Constantine. Charles's position, on the other hand, may be expressed in Alcuin's words: 'May the ruler of the Church be rightly ruled by thee, O King, and mayest thou be ruled by the right hand of the Almighty.' Even Justinian would have approved such phraseology, apart from the suggested dualism of Church and State. Only a temporary compromise, then, or the overwhelming preponderance of one side, could stay the conflict of the spiritual and temporal empires. So long as Charles lived, his supremacy was not in dispute. Only when his Empire was in process of dissolution under the weak rule of his son and grandsons could writers like Jonas, bishop of Orleans, and Hincmar, archbishop of Rheims, venture to sympathize with theories which set the *auctoritas sacra pontificum* above that of the Emperor. Succeeding centuries elaborated with a wealth of precedent this problem of the relations between Church and State. Enshrined within a general philosophy, it inspired the controversial writings of jurists and theologians, and moulded the theme of the greatest poem of the Middle Ages. Yet although the more politic Popes and Emperors might hesitate to pursue it to its logical conclusion, the conflict of two absolute autocracies remained, to be settled in practice by arguments of *force majeure*.

Such antitheses, however, were not yet clearly formulated, and it is even doubtful whether Charles had fully considered the constitutional question in regard to Byzantium. There were some in the West who affected to consider the Imperial throne vacant, since Irene had blinded and imprisoned her son, the Emperor, and now reigned alone—a woman on the throne of the Caesars. Charles's protracted negotiations with Byzantium, which ended finally in his recognition as 'Basileus', or Emperor, in 812, in return for the cession of his Dalmatian conquests, indicate that he did not share this view. Doubtless the theory remained of one single Imperium Romanum, governed in East and West by two co-ordinate Emperors, but the changed circumstances of Europe had divested it of any relation to the facts. Differences in law and administration, in religion, culture, and language, in economic and political interests, had sundered the Eastern and Western parts, divided even geographically, at this date, by the Slav kingdoms of the Balkan region. Practically speaking, the relations of the Western Empire, as it may now be called, with that of Byzantium were those of two foreign states, concerned for the jealous maintenance of their frontiers and the peaceful settlement of disputes, but owning no longer a common outlook towards the barbarian.

Charles's predominant position in Western Europe, which was formalized by the Imperial Coronation of 800, had been reached by a remarkable and incessant activity not only in internal government but in external conquests. During the forty-six years of his long reign, no less than sixty military expeditions took place, half of which were directed by the Frankish ruler in person. Each year, after the general assembly at the Field of May, levies of those districts nearest the frontier in question were led forth upon merciless campaigns into the enemy's country. 'The king', writes Alcuin simply, on one occasion, 'has gone with his army to lay Saxony waste.'

Many of these expeditions were undertaken in defence of the frontiers; Pipin's reduction of Aquitaine led to Charlemagne's crossing of the Pyrenees to establish a Spanish 'march', and the transformation of Bavaria from a semi-independent duchy to an integral part of the Empire involved the destruction of the aggressive Avar kingdom on the Theiss. But the greatest conquest of all, that of central and northern Germany, though it may have originated in reprisals for Saxon raids upon monasteries in the Rhine district, went far beyond its primary purpose. By the end of Charles's reign, the frontier had been advanced from Rhine to Elbe; the vast territory that lay between them had been added to the Empire, and the civil and ecclesiastical organization of medieval Germany had received its framework.

Not much light is thrown on the military aspect of this astonishing achievement by contemporary records, which are often of the nature of official *communiqués*. The country presented great

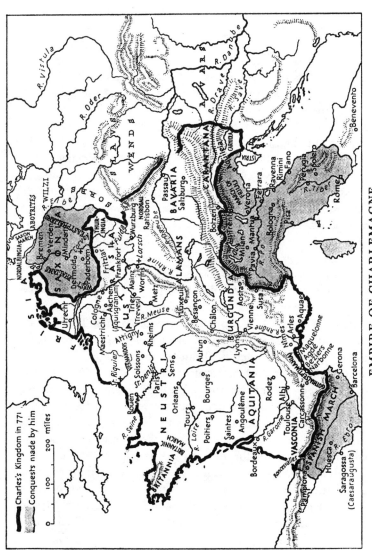

EMPIRE OF CHARLEMAGNE

physical difficulties, large tracts being covered by forests or swamps. Beginning a few leagues from the right bank of the Rhine, the Saxon territory extended to the Elbe across the wooded plains of Central Germany, the land successively of Westphalians, Angrarii, and Eastphalians. On the north, more inaccessible still, lay the marshy coastal district between the estuaries of Weser and Elbe, and beyond it, at the base of the Danish peninsula, was the home of the Nordalbingians, the last defenders of Saxon independence. Although punitive raids were carried out almost every summer between 772 and 780, the Elbe being reached in the latter year, no thought of systematic conquest seems to have existed as yet, apart from the formation of a frontier march in the Ruhr district, secured by a triangle of fortresses at Heresburg, Syburg, and Carlsburg. The co-operation of missionary effort, however, which had already been seen in the alliance of Boniface and Charles Martel,[1] was continued, and the combination of terrorist marches and Christian propaganda seems to have been Charles's regular policy for the cultural education of Saxony. An ill-advised policy, whose evil consequences were soon manifest. Secret rebellion was stirring in the German forests. A Westphalian leader, Widukind, arose, and found adherents in other parts. Abbeys were burnt, priests put to flight, and a considerable Frankish force, marching eastward against the Slavs, was cut to pieces on the Weser. Charles now decided upon definite conquest. Widukind sought refuge among the Danes, and 4,500 Saxon prisoners were slaughtered at Verden in cold blood. Strenuous summer expeditions reduced Eastphalia to apparent submission, and in 784 Charles actually wintered in Germany, preparing for the final campaign. By the end of 785, the whole of Saxony had been subjugated, except for the marshy coastland on the north, and the territory beyond the Elbe.

The victory, however, was not so complete as Charles's triumphant letters to the Pope would indicate. Nor were the measures now taken of a sort calculated to consolidate his gains. The *Saxon Capitulary*, probably issued on the morrow of the conquest, is a remarkable study in coercion. The country was parcelled into districts, ruled by counts, who alone, apart from the Royal *missi*,

[1] Cf. p. 210.

might convoke any public assembly. But the effective engine of Frankish tyranny was the Church. 'Let the priests see to it', concludes the *Capitulary*, 'that these orders are not disobeyed.' By a stroke of the pen, paganism was to be exterminated, and the whole manner of Saxon life, from the cradle to the grave, utterly transformed. Refusal to accept baptism was punishable with death. Eating of flesh during Lent incurred the same penalty. Crippling fines were imposed for failure to have a child baptized before the year was out, while the funeral cremation of a corpse, after the Saxon and Norse custom, was a capital offence. The primitive and savage nature of Saxon religion is shown by the ordinances forbidding, on pain of death, such practices as ritual cannibalism and human sacrifice, and it is all the more surprising that it should have been thought possible to apply, in this difficult and untamed country, a régime in which the alien parish priest, maintained by forced services and tithes from his congregation, should wield the confessional[1] as a political weapon to ensure submission and loyalty to 'the king and the Christian people'— that is, the Franks.

Alcuin had seen the danger, and his disapproval of the measures had found utterance in pungent aphorisms. 'It is the tithes, men say, that have undermined the faith of the Saxons.' 'One ought, moreover, to recognize that faith comes of free-will, not of compulsion. How can a man be compelled to believe what he does not believe? You may force a man to the font, but not to the faith.' His warnings were unheeded. For some years all seemed to go well, and Saxons were even employed in the frontier wars against Slavs and Avars. Under the surface, however, sullen resentment smouldered, and at last flared into revolt, the flames of which spread rapidly throughout Germany. Churches were burnt and plundered, bishops and priests slaughtered, and the whole Frankish organization in Saxony threatened with destruction. Charles, taken unprepared, was unable to concentrate his forces immediately, but during the years that followed Saxon resistance was finally broken by a series of converging marches, and in 797 even the northern coastland, that refuge of escaped rebels, was reduced. At Aix,

[1] *Saxon Capitulary*, Article XIV.

that autumn, a new constitution for Saxony was promulgated, after deliberations at which not only Frankish counts and bishops, but delegates from German territory were present. The brutal laws of the conqueror were repealed; henceforward Saxony was to be governed by a system analogous to that which prevailed in the other Frankish dominions. The final stage was the taming of intractable Nordalbingia, but this was only achieved in 804, when the last regular campaign of Charles's reign took place, by the forcible removal of the population to another part of the Frankish realm, its lands being bestowed on the Abodrites, a neighbouring Slav people who had proved their loyalty as allies.

This frontier district of 'Dania', as it came afterwards to be called, was the northern outpost of a system of military 'marches', controlled by carefully selected governors, who were subsequently known as margraves, or counts (*grafs*) of the frontier (*mark*). Although a loose sovereignty was exercised over the Slav peoples on the east, the Elbe and Saale constituted the real limits of the Frankish dominion. Farther south, Bavaria was incorporated in the Empire, beyond which, in Hungary, lay the realm of the Avars. Holding, like their nomad predecessors, the Huns, a key-position in Central Europe, at the western extremity of the great Asiatic steppe-belt, the Avar horsemen had for two centuries terrorized the peoples from the Baltic to the Peloponnese, and had more than once threatened Byzantium itself. At this period, however, their power had dwindled, and many of the Slav tribes, on whose labour they depended, had thrown off the Avar yoke. But they were still strong enough to menace the eastern frontier, and when Saxon affairs allowed a brief respite, the armies of Charles proceeded to take the offensive. Advancing over the Danube, Eric, Duke of Friuli, stormed the great Ring, a circular earthwork which formed the principal Avar stronghold, and captured immense treasures of gold, precious stuffs, and vessels, the spoils of generations, plundered probably, for the most part, from the cities, monasteries, and churches of the Byzantine Empire. Subsequent campaigns completed the destruction of the Avars. Austria now formed part of the Empire, and this region, together with western Hungary,

began to be populated by Germanic settlers from Bavaria.[1] Even
the eastern Hungarian parts were henceforth reckoned as belonging to the Franks, and thus the old Roman frontier-line of Pannonia was restored after many centuries.

The huge land-mass of Western Europe, save only Spain and
South Italy, was once more under a single master, controlling a
ruling class of Frankish, Bavarian, Aquitanian, Alamannic, or
Lombard nobles, and with incredible swiftness manœuvring
armies from one end of his territories to the other, to push back
the frontiers of hostile paganism. It was this unifying ideal of the
militant Christian Empire which gave its prevailing colour to
medieval civilization in the West, which survived the disintegration of the Carolingian realm into a multitude of warring principalities, and which still, perhaps, continues to operate as a
certain community of feeling within the European concert of
nations.

Nowhere is it seen more clearly than in the magical halo of
romance which surrounds the memories of the tragic day of
Roncesvalles. Charles had entered Spain, at the invitation of his
Moslem ally, the Arab governor of Barcelona, who was attempting to shake off the authority of the Umayyad Caliph at Cordova.
Charles's alliance with the infidel is significant, as is the fact that
the first Frankish success was the capture of Pampeluna, a city
belonging to the Christian kingdom of the Asturias. The expedition failed to take Saragossa, and as the retreating columns
wound slowly through the narrow Pyrenean passes, its rearguard
was attacked by the Basques, members of a Christian but hostile
race, and utterly annihilated. It was not possible to avenge the
disaster, but subsequent campaigns in this difficult country
finally established a Spanish March in the district immediately
south of the Pyrenees. Legend, making free with the historical
facts, transformed the unsuccessful foray of 778 into a glorious
crusade. The unlucky rearguard action became a battle in
which paynim hosts such as no land on earth had seen before
overwhelmed the Imperial paladins, who fell as martyrs in
defence of the Faith. Three centuries later the popular story,
enshrining not literal truth but the widespread ideal of Christian

[1] Cf. p. 187.

chivalry, was elevated into the magnificent epic of the *Chanson de Roland*, and became part of the imaginative heritage of Europe.

The machinery by which Charlemagne controlled the affairs of his huge empire was, like that of the Merovings, predominantly Germanic. Most of the old institutions survived—the local government by counts and their subordinate officials, the racial law-system and the annual assemblies. Above all, the personal and fluid character of Frankish rule, which has already been contrasted with the fixed, abstract nature of Roman administration,[1] maintained itself even under Imperial conditions. The Emperor was still, in a sense, the Teutonic war-chief, surrounded by his trusted companions in arms, whose services to him were constantly interchangeable. Counts of the Palace might command armies on the frontier, a seneschal direct the kitchen, or a butler be sent on a diplomatic mission to Bavaria.

Financial administration was equally primitive. The elaborate Roman system of public services had died out under the Merovings, and taxation had been reduced to its simplest forms— ferries, tolls, and charges on certain individual tenures. Upkeep of roads, bridges, and fortifications was demanded in certain cases, and lodging and provision for imperial agents. But the copious and detailed regulations, found in the capitularies issued by Charles, for the ordering of trade and control of prices must not blind us to the fact that the principle of State finance, here as with other Germanic rulers, was still that of the king's 'hoard'. The basis of revenue was the produce of the royal estates, supplemented by fines, confiscations, war booty, and obligatory 'presents'. Thus the Teutonic war-chief rewarded his followers with grants of land, or local privileges of jurisdiction and taxation, out of what he considered his own private property. The complex conditions created by the fusion of two cultures, and the exercise of German rule over countries to which Rome had given an advanced civilization, render such statements liable to endless distinctions and qualifications. Yet the broad contrast remains, between the Byzantine Empire, the direct continuation of Rome, with its civil service, its intricate and ordered system of

[1] Cf. p. 203.

taxation, its standing army and fleet; and the Romano-German countries of Western Europe, in which the central power, buttressed by no permanent financial resources or administrative organization, rested solely on obligations of personal service and personal allegiance due directly to the ruler from each individual subject. The growth of intermediate authority, caused by the appearance, already visible at this period, of the elements of feudalism, was bound to prove ruinous to a monarchy of this nature which could not, in effect, delegate any portion of its control without losing it altogether.

The process is well seen in the Carolingian army. Military service was probably the heaviest burden imposed on its subjects by the State, and the expense of equipment pressed heavily on the poorer freeman, who was still, according to the German custom, liable to the duty of bearing arms. Measures were taken to alleviate his distress; only the richer classes of a district were called up for service if the campaign was to take place on a distant frontier, and often two or three smallholders were permitted to join together to send one man to the 'host', and provide his equipment. But this did not suffice. The conditions which had rendered possible, in more primitive times, an armed assembly of all the free members of a tribe, roughly equal in economic position, had long ceased to exist. Inequalities of wealth had increased, and warfare was slowly becoming the exclusive business of the *seigneurs*, and of those who possessed horse and armour. To the latter class belonged those who had received a 'benefice', or through 'commendation' had entered into a relation of vassality to their 'senior' which carried with it the obligation of military service.[1] The change by which the army, originally a band of freemen bound only by loyalty to the war-chief, became a body of seignorial contingents, in which the king, as the supreme *seigneur*, commanded only through his subordinate nobles, belongs properly to the centuries which followed. But already Charlemagne had recognized the official status of the overlords when he ordered the levies to proceed to their rendezvous either under the count, the Imperial governor of the district, or under the command of their local *seigneur*. The

[1] Cf. p. 204.

time was not far distant when vassality would become hereditary, when the allegiance of the vassals would be due only to their immediate lord, and when, under a weak and unpopular monarchy, the nobles would lead their forces to the destruction of the royal authority.

For the moment, however, the strong personality and unwearying vigour of Charlemagne maintained strict unity of control throughout his wide borders. His counts, ruling each a district of the Empire, were authorized to check the proceedings not only of their own subordinates but also of the officials of ecclesiastical and secular lords. Further, to complete the chain which connected the ruler with every one of his subjects, the peculiar institution of the *missi dominici*, the king's envoys, was developed. The whole Empire was divided into groups of several counties (*missatica*) through which the *missi*, usually in pairs, an ecclesiastic and a layman, would travel each year 'to do justice'. Their duties covered a wide field. Not only had they to administer the oath of fidelity sworn to the Emperor by his subjects, and see to it that the revenues from crown forests and domains were duly forthcoming, that the capitularies—the royal edicts—were both understood and enforced, crime punished, justice rendered, and military service properly discharged; they were also commanded to inspect churches and monasteries, 'to assure themselves that the priests observe their discipline, the monks follow faithfully the rule of St. Benedict, that the Imperial regulations for chanting the services are carried out, the canonical books are purged of errors, the buildings kept in good condition; that the congregation attends Mass on Sundays, knows its Credo and Pater Noster, and has not been led away by old superstitions'.[1]

A remarkable picture of the progress of these *missi* has been drawn for us by Theodulf, bishop of Orleans, the most accomplished poet of the Carolingian Renaissance, who was himself one of their number. His photographic delineation of detail, his broad humanity and sly humour, his ripe and sophisticated outlook, totally different from the monastic innocence or fanaticism of so many contemporaries, inspire confidence in his account, which sets vividly before us the conditions in southern France at

---

[1] Lavisse, *Histoire de France*, vol. ii, p. 319 (Paris, 1903).

the close of the eighth century, depicting a further stage in the process of transition already recorded by Ausonius, Sidonius Apollinaris, and Gregory of Tours.[1] Personal reminiscence is clearly visible in his 'Exhortation to Judges', the fruit of experience gained on the southern circuit. The contrasts of Provençal scenery are sketched in a few touches—steep, rocky hills and rushing torrents, airless and stifling gorges, the deadly, malodorous marshes of the coast district, the broad sweep of the Rhône, and the noble cities with their high walls—Arles, Avignon, Nîmes, Orange, Marseilles, and many others find mention in the poem. Next we are taken to the court-house at Narbonne, doubtless some Roman *curia* which still adorned the former provincial capital. Round the lofty entrance has gathered a crowd of clamorous litigants. The judge, after attending Mass, enters the court, accompanied by his clerk, and the porter, after admitting all those entitled to be present, shuts the doors on a throng of curious sightseers. Seating himself on the curule chair, surrounded by the city notables, the judge then selects his assessors, and the business of the day begins. Theodulf pauses at this point to deliver advice on procedure. The magistrate should not speak too fast or too slow; he must direct the pleaders and help them to explain their case, encourage the timid, browbeat the insolent, silence the loquacious, and dominate the hubbub of shouts by the use of his powerful voice. He should, however, keep his seat, and refrain from employing a stick on head and shoulders, as some impatient justices have been known to do.

The author, himself of Visigoth descent, and accustomed to Roman legal traditions, emphasizes the drawbacks of the Germanic method of statement and rebuttal by means of oaths. The whole machinery of oath-helpers and sworn accusations, filling the court with noisy cries of 'yea' and 'nay', seems to him barbarous and inefficient, and he prefers to proceed by 'inquisition', carried out through witnesses of proved qualifications, separately examined by the judge. Nor can he approve the Germanic principle whereby property is held more important than life. He is shocked that theft should be punished by crucifixion, or the loss of hand or eye, while murder can be compounded for by

[1] See above pp. 31, 68, 194.

payment of the requisite *wergild*. Worst of all abuses, however, is the universal practice of bribery to obtain a favourable verdict. Every one is corrupt—the porter, the assessors; even the judge's wife has been suborned by an interested party, and hangs round her husband's neck, beseeching him, while her nurse and impudent little waiting-maid reproach the master for his unkindness to her.

Theodulf, it is plain, has handled many of the objects thrust at him, like so many siege-engines, to batter the ramparts of his integrity. Oriental glassware and jewels, fine gold coins bearing Arabic characters, figured brocades with oxen and geometric patterns of Asiatic design, armour, horses, and—greatest treasure of all—a massive silver vessel, survival of Roman Imperial times, with the Labours of Hercules moulded in relief on the outside. Suitors of humbler station are no less insistent with offers of Cordova leather, bleached or scarlet-dyed, linen and woollen stuffs, shoes, hats, gloves, and even face-towels, while one crafty fellow, aware, probably, of the literary tastes of the bishop, produces triumphantly a roll of purple vellum. All these the honest judge will refuse; but lest feelings may be hurt, trivial, friendly gifts may be accepted—garden and orchard produce, bread, eggs, and goats-milk cheese, tender pullets, and small birds, 'diminutive in body but good eating'.

It is a varied and coloured pageant of mingled races that passes before us in the Provençal sunshine. Much of the old Roman life has survived; despite Frankish influence, the general procedure of the court, with its presiding judge and aristocratic atmosphere, its impressive ceremony and complicated case-list of contractual and testamentary disputes, is far indeed from the primitive German assemblies of free warriors. Yet behind the visible world stand already, in full muster, the dark terrors of medieval imagination. In a powerful and sombre series of antitheses Theodulf contrasts the gold and silken raiment, the furs, perfumes, and delicate food and wine, the spacious dwellings, numerous possessions, and thronging clients of the rich man in this life with the squalor and confinement, the poverty and utter solitude, the horrible dissolution of the grave. His description of the Last Day, with its thunder and clanging trumpets, though more conventional in treatment, might well serve as text to innumerable sculptured reliefs on the portals of later Romanesque or Gothic cathedrals.

The legendary figure of Charlemagne, a majestic giant with beard reaching to the waist, is probably without foundation in fact. He appears to have been tall, but not abnormally so, with a short neck, prominent stomach, round head, large, expressive eyes, a rather long nose, abundant hair; he was clean-shaven, except for the customary Frankish moustache. His manner was friendly and simple; he could wander among a crowd of his subjects at the annual gatherings, and say the right word to each, gaining their confidence and gleaning shrewd comments on local conditions. Straightforward and sincere, a man of forceful and sensuous character, of boundless energy and untiring devotion to detail, he impressed his contemporaries as much by the strength and sweetness of his personality as by the magnificence of his achievements.

A rich store of incident and anecdote has come down to us concerning Charles and his Court, for the meagre annals of monastic chroniclers are suddenly reinforced by a gallant company of poets, striving to depict the scenes among which they lived in conscientious imitations of Ovid and Virgil. Even more valuable is Einhard's celebrated biographical sketch, which, though doubtless open to criticism in detail,[1] carries conviction by its mastery of the Latin instrument, which has made possible a vivid and personal style, rivalled, perhaps, only by Bede during the past three centuries in the West. Charles himself was responsible for this remarkable outburst of intellectual energy, whose productions bear witness to careful and sound training in grammar and rhetoric. He had summoned the foremost scholars of Western Europe to his court, from England, Ireland, and Lombardy. Peter of Pisa, Paul the Deacon, and their compatriots brought the riches of Italian learning to France, and the 'Scots', or wandering scholars from Irish monasteries, continued the work of their missionary predecessors as educational influences

[1] Its Suetonian echoes have aroused suspicion; and it is clear that the author, writing after Charlemagne's death, had not been in a position to secure first-hand knowledge of certain aspects of his policy.

in the Frankish Empire. The most important organizing figure, however, in the Carolingian Renaissance was undoubtedly Alcuin, under whose teaching the ideals and methods of Northumbrian culture dominated the revival of learning at the court of Charlemagne. The north-east corner of England had witnessed, during the eighth century, the brilliant and surprising achievements of Anglian civilization. It was the age of the Lindisfarne Gospels, with their exquisite script and illumination, of the great abbeys and seats of learning at Hexham, Jarrow, and York; the age of Bede, the most celebrated writer of Western Europe, and of the great Bewcastle and Ruthwell crosses, whose hieratic sculptured scenes, superior in plastic feeling to any contemporary continental work, bear witness to possibilities which will not be found hereafter in the linear, story-telling designs of later English artists. It was an eclectic culture of rapid growth, caused by the convergence of different influences on a vigorous kingdom of semi-barbarians. Celtic inspiration may perhaps be seen in its decorative motives and the range of its classical studies. Benedict Biscop's importation of manuscripts and church ornaments from France and Italy to embellish his foundations at Jarrow and Monkswearmouth introduced Byzantine characteristics, prevalent at that time throughout the Continent. Alcuin's efficiency in organizing schools and *curricula* suggests the survival of Graeco-Roman methods of instruction, passing, it may be, from the papal nominees at Canterbury, Hadrian and Theodore, to the educational centre at York, while the strange, unearthly poetry of the Germanic invaders, with its heroes and monsters, its grim humour and cryptic dialogue, was still cherished by the Northumbrian monks, and passed into Carolingian school-books in the shape of riddles and epigrammatic questionnaires, which must have delighted the heart of Charles, devoted as he was to the saga literature of his Frankish ancestors. With the declining fortunes of the Northumbrian kingdom, and the subsequent supremacy, first of Mercia, then of Wessex, this culture languished and finally disappeared, trodden out under the heel of the Viking raider; but already, transplanted to Gallic soil while yet in full bloom, it had become the dominant strain in the Carolingian reflowering of Western civilization.

BEWCASTLE CROSS. DETAIL FROM E. FACE

The study of letters, ever since Christian apologists had found it necessary to state their position with regard to classical learning, had been regarded as subservient to a higher end, namely, the comprehension of theology. Charlemagne expressly recognized this ideal, but political considerations also urged him in the same direction, for a higher moral and intellectual standard among administrators, both clerical and lay, and a closer organization both of Church and State furthered the interests of both, combined as they were in the indissoluble unity of his Christian Empire. Thus the palace school at Aix became a centre of cultural activity, attended by the royal family and the sons of Frankish nobles. Its pupils were frequently placed at the head of great monasteries, in the Rhineland and elsewhere, which subsequently became homes of art and learning for their districts, with libraries, schools, choirmasters, ivory-workers, jewellers, and copiers of manuscripts. Theodulf of Orleans organized local instruction in his diocese, and in Italy certain cities were already beginning to be known for their educational facilities.

Their newly discovered medium of expression was applied by the court writers not only to rhetorical themes but also to the description of their actual surroundings. It is a scene of bright colours that they display, of fresh, rather crude beginnings. The new palace of Aix stands in the midst of a rich, wooded landscape, dotted with herds of deer, and intersected with streams, the haunts of various waterfowl. We hear the creak of waggons bringing the white blocks, and the noise of stone being sawed, as the great church rises, whose gilded dome will presently tower above the low, spreading buildings occupied by the king and his numerous family, dominating the courtyard, with its equestrian statue of Theoderic, greatest of previous Romano-German rulers, which has been transported from Ravenna, and the open-air swimming-baths, with marble steps surrounding them, where Charlemagne and a hundred companions can bathe at once. There is profusion of gold—massive gold vessels in the church and at the Imperial table on feast-days, gold chains and rings, gold on baldrics and sword-hilts; the pale golden hair of the princesses when they ride out at dawn to the hunting, and the palace gates open as the cavalcade streams through, with neighing of horses, deep baying of hounds, and shouts that re-echo in the surrounding forest. Dresses are gay and brilliant, long white and blue cloaks, or short woollen mantles coloured in stripes and checks. Silks and fine linen are worn indoors, and ceremonial robes and vestments are richly embroidered and edged with seed-pearls.

Envoys of every nation throng the palace, representatives of Mercian or Northumbrian kings, Danish or Slav chieftains, papal messengers, Byzantine officials, or Moslems from Spain and Africa. Even Harun-al-Rashid sends presents from far-off Baghdad, and Charlemagne's influence with the Caliph secures privileges for the Christian pilgrims to Jerusalem. Exotic wares of distant countries are named with precision by writers of this time; Asiatic spices—pepper, cloves, cinnamon and the like— are used freely to disguise the flavours of food and wine, or to act as aids to the digestion. But the needs of the Imperial household are mainly satisfied by the produce of the enormous royal estates; fish, game, cheese, butter, mustard, vinegar, honey, wax, soap, and wine are all provided from this source, while cucumbers, melons, artichokes, peas, carrots and onions, leeks and radishes are also mentioned in the *Capitulare de villis*, which contains regulations for the ordering of the royal manors. It is probable that Roman methods of cultivation lingered on these lands, some of which may well have formed part of the *patrimonium* of Roman emperors.

It is a strange mixture of vigorous, barbaric life and faded classical culture. Einhard and his companions study Vitruvius as well as Virgil, and columns and marbles plundered from Ravenna are inserted in the new buildings, just as Ovidian and Suetonian tags figure prominently in the compositions of the time. Yet there are signs of activity and experiment in contemporary architecture, as in the exceptional design of Theodulf's church at Germigny-des-Prés, the noble pile of St. Riquier, or the abbey of St. Wandrille, with its massive tower, crowned by a squat, gilded spire, and its spacious refectory, whose walls are decorated with scenes of martyrdom and sacred story. Contrasts are no less striking in the atmosphere of the Court itself. Pilgrims and merchants, soldiers and monks, nobles, scholars, gay ladies and handsome pages mingle, not without occasional discord, in its precincts. Charlemagne himself goes to school, and curious points of etymology or science are eagerly discussed by him and his friends. Yet this is but one outlet for his immense physical and intellectual energy. Behind all the gaiety and magnificence of Aix, the hunting and swimming parties, the intrigues and scandals, the serious work of administration goes on, and every summer the Frankish horsemen ride out to do battle beyond the frontiers of Christendom.

Conditions in France as a whole must not be inferred from this picture of Court life. Charlemagne's strong government maintained order in the country, and trade prospered accordingly, especially in the Provençal cities and the Rhine district; but it was a trade mainly in luxuries. There was no sudden change in the economic system of Western Europe. The clearing of forests continued, with consequent increase of arable land; large estates gained at the expense of small, and the position of the petty freeholder became steadily more precarious. As before, the life of the population centred round the manors of lay or ecclesiastical magnates; mill, forge and church, local market and court of justice bounded the horizon of the inhabitants.

Charles died at Aix, on January 28, 814, and with the removal of his outstanding personality the great Frankish Empire which he had brought to completion fell speedily into disruption and anarchy. Einhard, writing in the reign of Louis the Pious, his successor, looks back already on the days of Charlemagne as on an almost mythical Golden Age. The glittering splendour of Charles's court, which dazzled the eyes of his contemporaries, blinded them to the unstable and evanescent character of his Empire, just as the personal dignity and charm, the shrewdness and administrative ability of Charles himself concealed from them his lack of far-seeing statesmanship. Viewed by the light of subsequent events, Charlemagne appears, not as the first Western Roman Emperor, descendant of Augustus and Constantine, but as the final representative of that long line of heroes and leaders of the barbarian wanderings which is headed by Alaric and Ataulf. Like them, he respected, and, to some extent, entered into the achievements of Graeco-Roman civilization; but it is significant that he shared with Theoderic the Great the inability to do more than write his own signature. His limitations, like theirs, were those of a conqueror, vigorous in execution, but far less successful in consolidating his gains. Charles had extended his frontiers to the Elbe and the Danube; his power reached over the Pyrenees, and to the district south of Rome. Yet of these frontiers not one, with the possible exception of Saxony, had been effectively secured. The lack of a standing fleet and army placed the coast-line of France and Italy at the mercy of Northern and Saracen raiders, and the same circumstance led in course of time to the practical independence of many of his 'marches', some of which became the nuclei of future European states such as Austria and Prussia. The lack of a considered Mediterranean policy, equal in calibre to the mature statecraft of Byzantium, prevented Charles from bringing all his forces to bear on Benevento—which retained its independence throughout his reign—and thus settling the question of South Italy, which was to prove for succeeding ages the thorniest problem in the peninsula. The lack of Roman administrative methods, with their legions and colonists, their impersonal and interlocked bureaucratic machinery, rendered inevitable the disruption of the Empire when once the strong hand of its ruler was removed. In Italy, where feudal tendencies had already made their appearance under Lombard rule, the results are plainly seen in the strengthening of local powers of jurisdiction and taxation at the expense of the central authority. Even the bishops who acted as royal *missi* began to claim these rights as hereditary privileges attached to their sees, while the counts were no longer Imperial officials, revocable at will, but vassals, holding their possessions as *beneficia*, not as temporary perquisites of office. The Frankish and Bavarian nobles settled in Italy became territorial magnates, and three great families emerged supreme in the districts of Friuli, Tuscany and Spoleto.[1] Similar disruptive influences were

---

[1] All three may be regarded as frontier regions, threatened respectively by Slavs, Saracen pirates, and Beneventan raids. The Margrave Eberhard, of Suabian origin, 'The Shield of Italy', is succeeded by son and grandson in Friuli; the Bavarian Counts of Lucca control Corsica, and exercise influence over Luni, Pistoia, Volterra, Florence; Spoleto, divided into counties by Charles, regains its unity and independence under the noble Frankish dynasty of the Lambertini.

at work in other parts of the Empire; Aquitaine and Bavaria increased their independence, and in Germany tribal divisions, headed by dukes, were destined to form one of the principal barriers to the later Ottonian revival of Imperial ideals.

The Germanic cast of Charlemagne's political thought is made evident by his arrangements for the succession. In the Partition of 806 there is no vestige of an idea that the Empire is to continue after his death. The territories are divided between his three sons, exactly after the manner of Clovis and his successors.[1] Two of these sons predeceased him, and it was thus a mere chance that at Charlemagne's death in 814 the whole of the Frankish conquests remained under one lord. Louis, surnamed the Pious, had been invested by his father with the Imperial title in the previous year; but one of his first actions was to re-divide the Empire among his three sons. The eldest, it is true, became the associate and heir of his father's authority, and his two brothers were made subordinate to him; but these latter controlled, in practice, the military resources of their kingdoms, and were not slow to use them, so that the remainder of Louis's reign was filled with their rebellious struggles and the consequent repartition of territory.

A further stage in the dissolution of the Empire was marked by the Treaty of Verdun in 843, by which Charlemagne's grandsons, after fierce civil war, agreed to the creation of three kingdoms, consisting of three long strips of territory running from north to south. The eastern strip contained all Frankish possessions east of the Rhine; the middle strip, long and narrow, stretched from the Low Countries, through Austrasia, Burgundy, Provence, to North and Central Italy. The western strip consisted of the remainder of France together with the Spanish frontier march. The artificial character of this division needs no emphasis, and it was soon illustrated by the dismemberment of the middle kingdom at the death of its ruler. By the end of the ninth century, the Empire of Charlemagne had dissolved into five separate and antagonistic states—France, Germany, Italy, and Upper and Lower Burgundy.

[1] Cf. p. 193.

EUROPE IN TRANSITION

An attempt may now be made to present some picture of the changes wrought by four centuries of darkness and confusion. Viewed from a height, as if from an imaginary aeroplane travelling swiftly over time and space, the Eurasiatic land-mass appears to be undergoing an intensified phase of those continuous movements of population which form the substructure of world-history.[1] Urged on by primal needs, its peoples surge to and fro in sudden waves of invasion or slower tides of penetration, controlled, like flood-waters, only by unconscious forces and geographical obstacles, or by the unequal capacity of different areas for supporting human life. A nearer view discloses man's handiwork in the creation of artificial barriers. At one extremity, the Great Wall of China stands as the symbol of a settled Empire, a notable victory in the eternal conflict between the Steppe and the Sown Land. At the other, the Roman *limes*, flanked by the frontiers of the Persian Sasanids, obstructs the western movement of the Germanic tribes. Between them lie the immense plains of Central Asia, breeding-grounds for the nomad hordes which sweep out of the desert on to the fertile countries which border it, bringing destruction though often, also, an infusion of fresh vigour. Storm over Asia is the danger-signal for old civilizations. Mongols and Manchus breach the Great Wall, and age-long Chinese dynasties are overthrown. Huns and Avars roll through the steppe corridor of southern Russia, and the successive shocks of their impact drive the Germanic hosts before them to end Rome's dominion in the West,[2] and—two centuries later—to hurl the Slav masses with centrifugal force against the mid-

---

[1] Cf. A. and E. Kulischer, *Kriegs- und Wanderzüge*, pp. 1–46 (Berlin, 1932).

[2] Rome's Rhine frontier had held up the Germanic migration for four centuries, thus becoming a pressure-area for the westward-surging peoples. This pressure had been relieved partly by the peaceful penetration of many Germans, both individually and tribally, into the Empire, partly by the migration of great eastern Germanic tribes from the Baltic region to the Dnieper and Black Sea. These latter, however, were the first to feel the Hun impact, which drove them against the Danube frontier.

continental peoples. Close upon this comes the tide of Arab invasion, submerging Syria and Egypt, flowing on over North Africa and Spain, and advancing at the same time north-eastwards beyond Persia, till it meets the vanguard of the Turkish hordes, awaiting their cue for Asia's final entry on the stage of Europe.

Coming closer to earth, we notice the network of Roman roads still covering the face of the countryside, but no longer, in A.D. 800, dotted with the busy long-distance traffic of merchants or officials, or threaded with the stone-built inns and posting-stations which a Chinese observer, in the first century after Christ, marked as characteristic features of the Roman Empire.[1] Trade is by no means extinct, and it is clear that much of the economic structure of Imperial times remains in large districts of France and Italy. Even the town, in many instances, retains its former importance as a local centre of commerce. Boats pass up the Po, Rhine, and Rhône, and the ferries and bridges of Roman Gaul and Italy still continue to pay their tribute to the Franks and Lombards, though this does not necessarily indicate more than local traffic. Numberless examples of such commercial activity could be given, but a broad contrast nevertheless remains between classical and early medieval economic conditions in Europe, and the researches of Dopsch and other scholars have served only to qualify, not to destroy it. During the first and second centuries A.D., under the aegis of the *Pax Romana*, the mass-productions of the provinces were freely and systematically exchanged by land- and sea-borne traffic from Britain to Syria, furnishing the inhabitants or the armies with the ordinary necessities of life, corn, wine and oil, metals, lumber, clothes, and pottery. The gentleman farmer of Boscoreale, who lived at this time on the hills above the Bay of Naples, with his large-scale, specialized production of wine for export, to the exclusion of all other household produce, his frescoes and bronzes, fashionable inlaid furniture and magnificent silver, even his bricks and pottery, his hoes and pruning-hooks, his clothes and food-stuffs, all bought from the neighbouring city or from overseas, is an organic member of a world-wide interdependent commercial

[1] Cf. F. Hirth, *China and the Roman Orient*, pp. 6, 38 (Munich, 1885).

system, a typical unit of the Roman civilization.[1] Outside the Mediterranean area, that civilization doubtless thinned to a surface polish, yet the ubiquitous pottery and metal-work of continental origin found on Romano-British sites show its importance in everyday life even in this island.

Very different is the situation round about A.D. 800. Making all allowances for variety, one may justly term the prevailing system in Western Europe a 'closed house-economy' (*geschlossene Hauswirtschaft*), in which the needs of life were supplied by the labour of self-sufficient communities, and 'exchange of goods takes a subordinate place to production'.[2] Long-distance trade, broadly speaking, is confined to luxuries for Court and Church —spices, jewels, ivories, incense, works of art. Even in France, where most favourable conditions existed for a rebuilding of society, the vast, well-organized estates of the royal house or of the powerful abbeys (e.g. St. Germain-des-Prés) were in no sense factories, as is sometimes implied, producing for outside markets wholesale supplies of agricultural and industrial commodities, but simply overgrown farms, supplying necessaries for the royal or ecclesiastical house and table, just as its Italian patrimonies had done for the Roman Church in the time of Gregory the Great.[3] This system of 'local horizons' was directly due to the breakdown of Roman government, communications, and trade, and the turning-point may perhaps be placed not in the fifth century but rather during the fifty years of anarchy and invasion, 235-85, which virtually destroyed the intricate economic fabric of the Empire. Diocletian and Constantine restored political order; they stabilized the currency, fixed the price-level of commodities, and harnessed industry to the chariot-wheels of the army and civil service. But they could not replace the delicate strands of commercial venture, and the two centuries' respite which they gave to the West saw no revival of inter-provincial trade, but rather a recession to more primitive conditions of isolated self-sufficiency, especially in lands such as Britain and

[1] See Tenney Frank, *An Economic History of Rome* (2nd ed., London, 1927), ch. xiv, esp. p. 266.

[2] Cf. E. Kulischer, *Allgemeine Wirtschaftsgeschichte*, pp. 3, 299 (Berlin, 1928-9).

[3] See above, p. 132, and cf. *Greg. Epp., passim*, and E. Spearing, *The Patrimony of the Roman Church in the time of Gregory the Great* (Cambridge, 1918).

Northern France, where Celtic organization still survived, in contrast with the town-centred districts of the Mediterranean.[1]

So far as Western trade and industry, then, are concerned, the Late Roman and the Early Medieval periods show no definite break. Mediterranean shipping, or what remained of it by the fifth century, was crippled by the Vandal pirates, and no Carolingian revival was possible after the rise of Islamic sea-power.[2] The overland route to the east was equally blocked by the troops of westward-marching invaders, by the subsequent occupation of Hungary by Huns and Avars, and by the immigration of Slavs. Certain local products, it is true, maintain or create their markets—Toledo weapons, Cordova leather, Frisian cloths. Northern towns such as Etaples, Utrecht, London, Slesvig, and Birka in Sweden find mention as trading centres. Annual fairs, as at Troyes and St. Denis, attract pedlars from all countries, kings legislate concerning trade, and big towns have their regular merchant quarters. The great frontier marts of the Rhine district under Roman rule[3] are paralleled by Charlemagne's row of licensed trading stations on the Slav boundary. Certain long-distance routes, like the Baltic–Black Sea waterway, show increased activity in the eighth century, while Arabs, Jews, and Syrians, purveyors of eastern curiosities, are not unknown in the Frankish cities. Yet the fact remains that the early medieval period shows no regular commercial activity in the West which can be called indispensable to the maintenance of society. Conditions in the Byzantine Empire were quite otherwise, for here the Roman economic structure had remained intact, with its currency and credit, its markets and commercial legislation, and maritime trade connexions with the Far East, severed since the second century, had even been restored.

Agriculture presents a somewhat different picture, though here, too, the barbarian invasions produced no real break; the

[1] Cf. P. Vinogradoff, *The Growth of the Manor*, p. 66 (London, 1905).

[2] Pirenne's view, that regular traffic from end to end of the Mediterranean continued until the eighth century, has been criticized by N. H. Baynes, *Journal of Roman Studies*, xix (1929), pp. 230 ff.. For further bibliography of this question see *Byzantion*, vii (1932), pp. 495–509, and cf. also E. Patzelt, *Die fränkische Kultur und der Islam* (Vienna, 1932).   [3] Cf. Tac. *Germ.* c. 41 and *Hist.* iv. 64.

early Middle Ages in Western Europe are a continuation of a steady progress, dating from the time of Caesar, in which skilled methods of tilling the soil spread outwards from the circle of the Roman Empire into the heart of the Continent. From the Rhineland and north-eastern France, Roman instruments and technique crossed the frontier into Germany,[1] and with the settling-down of the barbarian tribes, a pastoral and hunting existence was replaced by stable agricultural occupations over an ever-increasing part of Europe. Behind this zone lay the dim world of marsh, forest, and steppe, of nomad peoples and food-gatherers. The boundaries of this world were continually receding, but large portions of it lingered behind—immense virgin forests in France and Germany, shepherd-peoples roaming the Balkan uplands. Further diversity was introduced into the agricultural map of Europe by peculiarities of soil and climate, and by tribal and local custom. Thus North German methods can readily be distinguished from those prevalent in South Germany, while in England the heavy Saxon ploughshare, turning up the deep clay of the unfenced strip-fields surrounding the settlements of the invaders, ousted completely the Romano-Celtic cultivation, with its small square fields situated on chalky or gravel soil, and ushered in the first of the three great transformations of our countryside.[2]

But the main line of cleavage in the West is one still visible to-day, between the Mediterranean intensive culture, on the one hand, with its individually owned patches of corn, vines, and olives, its short furrows, and light plough, and, on the other, the extensive husbandry of more northern latitudes, where a rough climate, a sparse population, and large districts of forest or morass produced systems of cultivation in which grazing plays a large and often a predominant part, human labour is scarce and unskilful, and the heavy plough with its eight oxen traces long furrows down the open field-strips.

---

[1] Orchards and gardens also became known to the Germans by Roman agency, as is shown by the Latin-derived names for fruit, flowers, and vegetables. The great monasteries continued to impart this knowledge.

[2] The enclosures of later medieval times, culminating in the eighteenth century, are responsible for the second, and the Industrial Revolution, completed in our days by mechanized farming, for the third.

The real importance of these contrasted conditions is psychological. The clear-cut Mediterranean system, which prevailed in Italy, southern Gaul, Spain, and North Africa under Roman rule, with its strong individualism, its self-sufficient, absolute ownership of land, lent itself admirably to purposes of taxation and definition of status, though even here the rotundities of Roman legal phraseology have concealed the rough edges of various anomalies. Natural conditions in the North, however, produced a co-operative mentality, a world of thought in which rights of private ownership were dim and vaguely formulated. Rotation of crops, intermingling of strips, common use of wood and water, shared pasturage—habits of life arising from customs such as these created a rural economy more flexible, more irregular than that of the Mediterranean area. Its characteristic elements persisted in Celtic Gaul and Britain even after the Roman conquest (though the centralized villa-system made headway in both countries where it found a suitable locality). They may be seen at every stage of Germanic agriculture, from the temporary occupation of land during the migration period to the full-fledged developments in Anglo-Saxon England. They have left their traces upon village life and the local, self-governing institutions of medieval days, and they form an essential component in the growth of the Manor, delaying, and in many cases permanently preventing, the complete symmetry which feudal influences would otherwise have imposed.

It is, however, a false simplification to extend this contrast to the social evolution of Western Europe during the early Middle Ages, and to represent the issue as the submergence of German personal freedom and democratic institutions beneath the weight of Roman juristic conceptions, founded on centuries of organized oppression of the lower classes, and a Mediterranean view of the cheapness of human life and labour. It is true that this period is marked by a widespread 'debasement and breaking-up of the class of common free men'.[1] Only in the far north, in Norway and Sweden, does the *bonde*, the small peasant, remain independent, able to stand on his rights. In Denmark and England he becomes not only a 'husbandman' but a 'bondman'. The

[1] *The Cambridge Medieval History*, vol. ii, p. 652 (Cambridge, 1913).

Frankish *villanus*, member of the *villa*, is transformed into the medieval *villein*, a man of low origin and condition. In the kingdoms of Kent and Wessex the intermediate ranks of society disappear, leaving a gulf between nobility and churldom. The same process is at work elsewhere. Yet it is clear that converging tendencies on both sides, Roman and Germanic, prepared the way for this 'aristocratic transformation of society'. The breakdown of Roman government placed power, actual though not wholly constitutional, in the hands of the local magnates, who became petty sovereigns over their *coloni*, judging and taxing their tenants. The economic depression of the Empire, however, while it converted small freeholders into dependants of the landowner, and restricted their freedom of movement, rendered them indispensable to him owing to scarcity of labour, and thus gave them a bargaining advantage; and meanwhile the improved status of the slave, due to humanitarian, and, later, Christian ideas and legislation, brought him nearer to the *colonus* and thus contributed to the formation of a large 'half-free' class, the *laborantes*, who, together with the *orantes* (the Church) and the *bellantes* (the nobility) formed the constituent elements of West-European society.[1]

The Teutonic side of the picture, on the other hand, is by no means one of ideal primitive freedom and democracy, as enthusiastic historians of the nineteenth century sometimes proclaimed. 'The armed free tribesman', Professor Vinogradoff points out, 'was undoubtedly endowed with a rough average of rights, though the recognition of his social status had nothing to do with modern democratic theories'. The warriors of a primitive community, as in early Greece or Rome, were valuable to the State, and had therefore to be conciliated; they might even be given a certain share in policy. Yet even in the days of Tacitus there were inequalities of rank among the Germans; when the migrating tribes settled permanently, these inequalities were perpetuated by land-grants. A hereditary nobility might be replaced by a nobility of service, as the kings gained power; but this new nobility soon became hereditary, and from the earliest days of the settlement, side by side with the free villages, we find a steady

---

[1] See Appendix B.

growth in the estates of nobles and abbatial landlords. The anarchy of Merovingian days produces a similar effect to that of the Roman collapse; free men 'commend' themselves to gain the protection of a powerful landowner, while the central power is constantly found bartering or giving away its control. Yet the process which was to culminate in the feudal system is slow. In the days of Charlemagne, the extent of the lands in possession of smallholders and free communities largely exceeded that of the great domains, and even the latter show clearly the co-existence of manorial authority and older popular units and institutions.

Developed political theories, which arise always from contemporary conditions, are naturally not to be looked for in centuries of turmoil, when the *de facto* maintenance of any authority at all is vastly more important than the *de jure* claims of him who exercises it. Yet two main changes may be noticed in men's ideas of the State, produced by the break-down of the Roman Empire in Western Europe, which were fated to influence the whole medieval period. The first is the altered relation of the secular and ecclesiastical authorities, which becomes fully apparent only after the dissolution of the Carolingian Empire. The second is the prevalence of habits of thought derived from barbarian tribal conditions.[1] The mixed populations, of varying degrees of culture, in the Romano-German kingdoms provided difficult problems of administration, which were solved by adopting the curious principle of the 'personality of law'.[2] Each man lived by the law of his people, Roman, Burgundian, Visigoth, Bavarian, Salian or Ripuarian Frank. 'Of five men sitting or walking together', Agobard of Lyons exclaims, pleading for a unified legal system in the Frankish Empire, 'none will have the same law as his fellow'.[3] The process of fusion between these systems is a mirror of the larger cultural development of Western Europe. Personality, as a principle, gives place eventually to territoriality, but not before it has served its purpose in ensuring the survival, during a critical transition period, of legal customary variants. 'Custom', in fact, comes to be regarded as the ultimate sanction, and in this we may recognize the triumph of 'the ancient

[1] C. H. McIlwain, *The Growth of Political Thought in Europe*, pp. 171 ff. (London, 1932).   [2] Cf. p. 66, above.   [3] *M. G. H. Legg*, iii. 504.

Germanic idea of a tribal law, immemorial in character, and binding upon king and people alike'.[1] Closely connected with this notion of the supremacy of law is that of the kingship 'based primarily on service to the nation'.[2] This principle of responsible sovereignty, which contests with its Asian rival—the principle of the monarch ruling by divine right, mystic, sacerdotal, *solutus legibus*, vice-gerent of God—for the future of European government, is essentially Germanic, though by no means a new-comer to the West. For it is inherent also in Republican Rome,[3] whose delegation of the supreme power to elective officials survived far into the Empire under the form of the *lex de imperio* and the ceremonies of acclamation by army and people which legitimized a new emperor. Even in later Byzantine times, when the Hellenistic and Hebraic conceptions of monarchy appeared to have finally proved victorious, Roman ideas lingered on still in Imperial titles and traditional duties and virtues associated with the ruler. In the West, the Church Fathers had spoken with divided voice, according as they inclined towards Old Testament theocracy or the Ciceronian view of the State,[4] and the assertion of Germanic influence at a critical period was thus necessary for the continued union of power and responsibility which made possible the subsequent Western constitutional developments.

All the more necessary, perhaps, in view of the momentous change which Constantine introduced, when by his identification of the interests and unity of Christianity and Empire he took the Church, as it were, into partnership, and intensified the hieratic cast of governmental authority. By the grant of jurisdiction to the Church, it became henceforth an organ of administration, and the gaps left by the gradual ousting of Imperial control in Italy were steadily filled up by the developing Papal organization. The barbarian rulers, despite their independent and sometimes threatening attitude towards the papal claims, likewise made use of the Church to serve their national ends, for only in

[1] Cf. Tac. *Germ.* c. 7. 'Nec regibus infinita aut libera potestas.'
[2] McIlwain, op. cit., p. 175.
[3] Isidore of Seville, in the seventh century, notes the old Roman nursery rhyme, 'Rex eris si recte facies, si non facies, non eris'. For an earlier version cf. Hor. *Ep.* i.1. 59. 'At pueri ludentes "rex eris" aiunt, "Si recte facies"'.
[4] Cf. A. J. and R. W. Carlyle, *History of Medieval Political Theory in the West*, vol. i, ch. xviii (London, 1903).

its ranks did they find sufficient knowledge of Roman methods to cope with the complex problems of a civilized community. The turning-point in this process is reached in the remarkable 'change of heart' in regard to the 'barbarians' which Gregory the Great introduced into papal policy. To the minds of Leo I, Augustine, and Jerome, the mission of the Church might be universal in theory, but in practice it was limited by the boundaries of the Roman Empire.[1] Even to Salvian, that eulogizer of primitive German virtue, the invaders were a scourge of God, a people whose clothes and smell put them outside the pale of civilized society. Gregory's great missionizing and diplomatic activities in Western Europe ended all this, and prepared the way for new and undreamed-of possibilities, and with the growth of papal influence in the new kingdoms eventual severance from Byzantium, the Imperial world-centre, gradually became a conceivable thing. In Spain, the Visigoth realm was controlled, during the last years of its existence, by episcopal councils. In England, the Anglo-Saxon rulers relied on their spiritual advisers for assistance in policy and law-making. In France, ecclesiastics soon entered the Frankish service. From Clovis to Charles Martel, conquest was made possible by their co-operation. Charlemagne, continuing the Merovingian tradition, maintained the position of the Church as an essential instrument of government, though subordinate at all points to the royal authority. Ecclesiastical abuses were to be removed, so that the Church might fulfil her chief function in christianizing the manners and outlook of the Frankish subjects. Education, administration, even repression (as in Saxony) were placed largely in the hands of ecclesiastics. The theocratic character of Charlemagne's system is as strongly marked as that of Justinian and his successors. Alike in Eastern and Western Europe, the ninth-century Emperors govern their dependants by divine mandate, and the life of the common man is overshadowed by the rules and observances of the State religion, to an extent that would probably have astonished a Roman citizen of the pre-Constantinian era.

The character of the cultural transformation produced during

[1] Cf. E. Caspar, *Geschichte des Papsttums*, vol. i, p. 558 (Tübingen, 1930).

these centuries by the collapse of Roman government in the West may perhaps be described as a crumbling and disintegration of the topmost layer of civilization. Fragments of this layer survived, in some places almost intact, but no longer as constituent parts of the universal pattern. Older, regional traditions, obscured for centuries by the standardized design created and superimposed by the Roman Imperial machine, emerged once more on the surface. New and revolutionary ferments, long working underground, became apparent in their effects.

Economically, the world-wide nexus of trade dissolves, and is replaced by a system of local self-sufficiency. Politically, the Western provinces fall asunder, into Germano-Roman kingdoms. United for a brief space under Charlemagne, they split again into a number of antagonistic States. Educationally, the disappearance of Roman administration removes the incentive to a rhetorical training; schools and universities are extinguished, together with the political and economic system which supported them, while the leisured classes, whose exchanges of elegant and allusive correspondence had preserved the social status of literature, cease to exist as a European intelligentsia. Many, no doubt, perished in the invasions, or sank to a peasant level. A large number of noble families migrated to Byzantium. Others, isolated in their fortified manors, occupied themselves with the chase, or entered the profession of arms, the only lucrative calling at such a time. Monasteries offered a refuge to the few, but neither the monastic life nor the service of the Church provided opportunities for secular learning.

Artistically, the official Empire style, seen at its worst in the mass-productions exported to outlying provinces ('Samian' ware and the like) declines in company with the causes of its creation and distribution, and local, non-Roman traditions resume their sway in certain districts—flexible Celtic patterns, massive Teutonic jewellery, and the fanciful designs of the Scandinavian craftsman in wood and metal. In Rome itself, the change from ancient to medieval may be seen by a comparison of the Trajanic reliefs (c. A.D. 101), formerly part of the orator's rostrum in the Forum, with those, similar in subject, on the Arch of Constantine (c. A.D. 315), in which typical 'Byzantine' characteristics are

VIII

a. TRAJANIC RELIEF FROM FORUM

b. RELIEF FROM ARCH OF CONSTANTINE

already apparent.[1] In the former, the Emperor Trajan and his attendants are depicted with all the representational skill, the delicate handling of drapery, the subtle recession of successive planes, which are associated with the classical Graeco-Roman style. In the latter, Constantine presides, a stiff hierarchical figure, over the dwarfed and lumpish rows of his senators and subjects. The contrast is striking. Coarseness and crudity of technique are visible, formal and over-symmetrical composition, a lack of plastic sense, and a tendency to 'sketch with the chisel', details being left to be supplied by the addition of colour—a turning, in fact, from sculptural methods to those of the painter. But it is a mistake to regard this either as 'decadence'[2] or, on the other hand, as an inherent development on purely artistic lines of evolution, conditioned by technical problems to be solved.[3] The true 'decadence' of ancient art is to be found in those photographically realistic statues of rheumatic fishermen, emaciated crones and brutal pugilists which satisfied Roman aesthetic demands in the third century.[4] A decline both in skill and in public taste may be inferred, certainly, from the Constantine reliefs, but the change lies deeper than this. It is a change of spirit, of outlook, pervading every aspect of life, which here seeks expression, hesitatingly at first, but evolving later into the triumphant certainties of Byzantine and Romanesque. The predominant character of this change is Oriental. In religion, it appears in the prevalence of mystery-cults, and in the final victory of the greatest of these, Christianity. In thought can be traced a concomitant development of Eastern symbolism. In art, the Christian and mystical outlook transforms from within the products of classical tradition and is reinforced from without by the material influence of Asiatic styles and techniques.[5] With the Empire centred at Byzantium, this influence becomes

---

[1] Cf. H. Lietzmann, 'Das Problem der Spätantike', *Sitz. d. preuss. Akad. d. Wiss.*, 1927, pp. 342 ff.

[2] Cf. L. von Sybel, *Christliche Antike*, p. 10 (Marburg, 1906).

[3] Cf. A. Riegl, *Spätrömische Kunstindustrie* vol. i, pp. 45 ff. (Vienna, 1901).

[4] See A. W. Lawrence, *Classical Sculpture*, p. 370 (London, 1929).

[5] Symbolism is, of course, by no means incompatible with the most uncompromising realism. This is seen especially in the Antioch school. The influence of Semite art on Christian iconography is already visible in the Dura frescoes of the third century A.D.

steadier and more powerful, and the cultural and economic supremacy of the capital results in the dispersion of its artistic output over the whole of barbarized Europe, to serve as models or correctives in the development of medieval art.

Similar tendencies—the emergence of old popular forms, the action of new ferments—can be seen at work in the transformation of literature and language. The aristocracy of Greek metres, with their delicate music of quantitative syllables, had maintained a precarious hold over Latin verse, the natural roots of which were fixed deep in the stressed peasant rhythms of threshing-floor, spinning-wheel and country dance, the gnomic saws of the rustic oracle, and the heavy tramp of the marching legionary. Fragmentary snatches of this folk poetry can be caught underneath the swelling chorus of Imperial singers—a children's rhyme, a ribald catch of Caesar's veterans, an amatory line scrawled on the street-wall of Pompeii. During the second century this accentual verse was adopted by a group of literary innovators, and from this movement blossomed the exquisite *Pervigilium Veneris*. The weakening of cultural standards encouraged such developments, and the new spirit discovered a congenial vehicle of self-expression in the broad emotional effects of strongly stressed rhythms. Spain and Africa were fruitful soil for this metrical evolution. The crude anti-Donatist songs of Augustine, written for massed community-singing, with their rough scansion and shouting choruses, are significant of the changed conditions, while the stately processional hymns of Prudentius, for all their mastery of quantitative subtlety, cannot disguise the growing insistence, beneath wavering melodies and shifting harmony, of the regular beat, the clockwork rhythm of the popular trochaic. Rhyme and assonance, features already familiar to folk-poetry,[1] become prominent at the same time, and the creation of medieval hymnodic forms is thus practically complete.

Prose followed the same course, though the absence of fixed scansion prevents us from following its successive stages. The stressed accent and the enfeeblement of quantity, however, are seen in the *clausulae*, or formal cadences at the end of sentences

---

[1] Cf. E. Norden, *Die antike Kunstprosa*, p. 811 (Leipzig, 1898).

and paragraphs, used by the later fourth-century writers, and the transition from metrical to rhythmical prose is accomplished by the time of Gregory the Great.[1]

The spoken language itself undergoes a parallel transformation. Here, once more, the basis of the change is psychological. Caution is necessary in dealing with a medium so fluid and evanescent, but certain persistent tendencies are observable. Vulgar Latin, fundamentally speaking, is to be distinguished from high literary Latin by the quality of the thought which it expresses. Though not uninfluenced by the Hellenic discipline, noticed above, which pervaded educated speech and writing,[2] its spirit remained impervious to the external impress of Greek antiquity, and it thus continued to be the property of the common folk, which survived the political and economic *débâcle* of the West, and was subsequently differentiated into the various Romance languages. 'Hellenized Latin', on the other hand, 'thanks to its literary mummification, could neither live nor die after the downfall of the Roman state. As "Middle Latin" it led a supernatural existence in the Church, the school, on paper, on the tongues and in the ears of scholars.'[3] Goliardic songs brought it nearer to earth, but it remained poised in mid-air, above the currents of everyday talk which are the effective forces in the development of language.

Meanwhile popular speech, freed from the constant pressure of alien modes of thought, lay open to the twin influences of this time—a revival of local tradition, and the action of new stimuli. Changes in vocabulary and syntax reflect the corresponding change of mentality. With the disappearance of the aristocratic, personal, Stoic attitude to life, there goes also the variable word-order and studied emphasis, together with the inflexions which made them possible. In their place come the impersonal style, aiming at communication rather than self-expression, the over-statement characteristic of uneducated speech, and the altered meaning of the future, which is no longer accepted with resignation or determined resolve, but becomes the object of passionate

[1] Cf. A. C. Clark, *The Cursus in Medieval and Vulgar Latin*, p. 13 (Oxford, 1910).
[2] The *sermo urbanus*, as opposed to the *sermo plebeius* or *vulgaris*. Cf. F. F. Abbott, *Classical Philology*, 1907, pp. 444–60.
[3] Cf. K. Vossler, *The Spirit of Language in Civilization*, pp. 57–75 (London, 1932).

hopes and fears. The contrast is seen fully in the gulf that divides the individual, monumental style of the great classical writers from the subtle variations on a common idiom which distinguish their present-day French or Italian successors. 'Compared to a page from Livy, Tacitus, or Virgil, all modern Romance . . . seems like a pamphlet compared to a bronze tablet.'[1]

Greek development in literature and language brings out even more clearly the tendencies already outlined. Studied utterance had always been regarded as a work of art, and the substitution, for certain purposes, of prose for poetry only gave scope for completer artistry. The great age of Athens created a brilliant prose style which dominated Greek writing for 1,500 years, resisting successfully the Oriental influences which entered with the rule of the Diadochi, surviving the Roman conquest, and—with comparatively little change—adopted by the long line of medieval Byzantine authors.[2] The spoken word, however, was not equally immune from the effects of political and economic developments, and changes can be traced here parallel to those which took place in Latin. A common speech, consisting largely of debased Attic, submerged the local dialects, and served as a medium of intercourse throughout the Hellenized East. With this dilution of Greek culture among non-Greek races came a more serious danger for the language; pronunciation began to alter, the sonorous vowels of the Periclean age thinned to the 'e-sounds' of later Greek, a process which affected even the consonants, and finally, with the entrance of an alien stress-accent, the distinction between long and short syllables was obscured.[3]

These changes in the spoken language removed the very foundations of classical Greek poetry and prose, which were based on quantity and on musical pitch. Henceforth the breach widens between popular speech and the 'learned' arts of versification and rhetoric, where century after century, in the sheltered, conservative circles of university and official life—the tradition was never broken as it was in the West—the prosody and intonation of earlier days were carefully studied and appreciatively

[1] K. Vossler, op. cit.   [2] Cf. E. Norden, op. cit., pp. 367 ff.
[3] For an admirable sketch of these developments cf. H. Lietzmann, op. cit.

admired. It may be surmised that the crowded and fashionable congregations which Chrysostom and Basil drew to their churches in the fourth century A.D. were attracted not only by the brilliant delineation of contemporary manners and the fragments of Greek botany and zoology which these preachers used as the vehicle for moral instruction and scriptural exegesis, but also by the skilled employment of the whole orchestral resources of classical oratory. Yet even the *clausulae* of Basil's periods show signs of the new stress-cadence, and by the end of the century it had become the prevailing form.

Poetry in the old metres, with its numbered syllables and strict rules of quantity, remained impervious to the 'dynamic' or stress accent, though its artificial character is clear from the occasional slips made by practitioners after the fourth century; but the spirit of Christian mysticism found an outlet in the creation of new rhythms, inspired by Syrian models, which pervade the hymns of this period, with their Oriental refrains and ecstatic fervour, reaching their highest development in the magnificent liturgical chants of Romanus, which echoed under the great dome of St. Sophia.

The rich heritage of Hebraic thought and worship which had been taken over by the Church during her earlier centuries of existence profoundly influenced the formation of the Christian liturgy. But this heritage is itself only one manifestation of a religious consciousness, an approach to the mystery of the Unseen shared by the dwellers in the Near East, whose origins must be sought far back in the immemorial traditions of Egypt and Babylonia.[1] The passive, brooding contemplation of the Divine essence, the eager abandonment of individuality which distinguish Oriental religiosity from the active, concrete, humanistic conceptions of Hellenic thought demanded for their expression new emotional rhythms, a new vocabulary, and even a new structure of the sentence. In the poetry and prayer-ritual of the Christian Church can be traced features common to the Old Testament, the Koran, and the magical papyri, and just as in the artistic sphere the revolutionary content transfigured the Graeco-Roman form which conveyed it, so here the negative,

---

[1] Cf. E. Norden, *Agnostos Thèos*, p. 222 (Berlin, 1913).

non-rational attributes of Deity, the preoccupation of the worshipper, not with the activities, but with the nature and being of God, found utterance in participial and relative constructions, in strange invocations and free-moving rhapsodies which finally, in the case of the liturgy, resulted in the creation of a new form of Greek poetical prose.

Oriental influence upon the art, religion, and literature of the Mediterranean world exercised a constant pressure, varying only in intensity, which stretches back far into prehistoric times. Mystery cults, ultimately of Eastern origin, entwined themselves early into the structure of Greek religion, and the emotional, esoteric rituals of Egypt, Asia Minor, and Syria, introduced, as a result of Roman conquests, by legionaries, slaves, and merchants, spread rapidly throughout the West, and captured the imagination of the populace.[1] Yet though Roman belief succumbed so completely to Asiatic modes of worship, the religious psychology of the West retained its distinct character, and more than one aspect of the dogmatic controversies of the early Christian centuries can be explained by the contrast, not only between the legalistic, concrete attitude of Latin theology and the speculative, metaphysical proclivities of Greek writers, but between the emphasis laid by the West on the personality and saving activities of Christ, and the passionate absorption of Eastern thought in the supra-temporal essence of the Divine nature.

Similar differences are displayed by the West in its use of symbolism and allegory, which may, broadly speaking, be taken as the characteristic mental processes of this period. The naïve, often grotesque interpretations of scriptural passages to which Gregory the Great lent his authority bear somewhat the same relation to the subtle and poetic images of Origen that the riotous fantasy, the literal picturesqueness of Romanesque sculpture and miniatures bear to the more delicate, abstract, and restrained treatment of symbols in Byzantine art, where, for various reasons, the repertory of the craftsman was more strictly limited both in subject and style. To look behind language, behind the visible world apprehended by mind and senses, to another, secret

---

[1] The writings of Firmicus Maternus present a striking picture of the real character of popular paganism in the fourth century A.D.

language, a secret world known only to the initiate, is the privilege of the poet and mystic in all ages. Plato had used the myth, conscious of its limitations, to shadow forth the ineffable; others before him had sought to conserve the hallowed expression of outworn beliefs by allegorizing its grossness or absurdity. The subjective method, however, is a dangerous one; lacking objective controls, the individual lies open to all the hidden currents of his time. Primitive animism—the conviction of the *mana* residing in words, actions, and inanimate objects—now recrudescent in a revival of sorcery and divination entered into Neoplatonism when its poetic powers of organization weakened, and the distinction between the symbol and that which it represented was disastrously obscured.[1] Magic, which is fundamentally materialistic, destroyed the spiritual basis of allegory, and the decay of intellectual and imaginative energy ruined the appositeness of the symbol.[2] Philo, the Hellenized Jew, endeavoured to reconcile the Septuagint with the conceptions of his time by an essentially prosaic perversion of the literal meaning; the ewers, basins, and other furniture of Solomon's temple, for example, signified various virtues and ornaments of the devout soul. His methods were eagerly copied by Christian commentators, and Augustine himself, seriously arguing against a Manichee who had questioned the ethics of the story of David and Bathsheba, can assert that David is Christ, Uriah is the Devil, and Bathsheba, taking her bath on the roof-top, represents the Church, soon to become the heavenly bride, washing herself free from the stains of the world below. The legitimate use of symbolism, however, was not forgotten. Origen, a true poet and possibly the greatest of early Christian thinkers, harmonizes the discrepancies between Old and New Testaments, between the Synoptists, between the writings of Paul and of his colleagues, by the musical metaphor of a symphonic composition;[3] discordant notes can be reconciled

[1] Cf. A. von Harnack, *History of Dogma*, vol. ii, p. 144 (Edinburgh, 1907). 'What we now understand by "symbol" is a thing which is not that which it represents; at that time [second century A.D.] "symbol" denoted a thing which, in some kind of way, is that which it signifies.'

[2] Cf. the perversion of Platonic thought in Ecclesiasticus xxxiii. 15, 'Look upon all the works of the Most High; and there are two and two, one against another'. xlii. 24, 'All things are double, one against another.'

[3] See his remarkable orchestral image in *Philokalia*, vi. 2. (P.G. xiii, col. 832).

by the exercise of what amounts to poetic imagination, and such primitive conceptions as the literal Six Days of Creation made acceptable by a mythical interpretation. The method gave scope for the intelligence, and, in the hands of equally brilliant successors, promise of future development: but this was not to be, and the growth of anathema, the stiffening of dogma, and the adoption of non-rational formulae combined to make dangerous the path of an independent reasoner.[1] With the break-down of general culture, the sense of the word, unchecked by reason, gradually retreated into fantasy, and on this the Middle Ages reared its structure of thought. Jerome's scholarly collation of Septuagint manuscripts still maintains the importance of the historical fact, as distinct from its interpretation, but to the followers of Alcuin, mindful of the precepts, rather than the practice, of their teacher, not even the text of the Bible itself is sacred: in their passionate anxiety to strip off the material husk and extract from the Scriptures their spiritual meaning,[2] they are prepared to alter and interpolate in accordance with the views of Patristic commentators.[3] Pagan authors fared no better, their contents being recklessly allegorized for purposes of edification. Even to the opening words of the *Aeneid*, 'Arma virumque cano', a moral twist was imparted. 'Arms' signified virtue, it was held by some, and 'man' wisdom.[4] Such methods were actually a mistaken short cut to the distant goal which the Church had set before herself—the arduous remoulding and gigantic synthesis of all extant knowledge in a universal and self-consistent scheme of Christian philosophy. The process had been begun by the great thinkers of the early centuries, but—owing in considerable measure to the waywardness of symbolic fancy—no general advance was subsequently made for some 600 years, at which period the movement started (not without inspiration from Moslem Spain, where Arabic translations had preserved certain aspects of Greek thought) which culminated in the *Summa* of

See Appendix B.

Cf. Bede, 'retecto cortice litterae, altius aliud et sacratius in medulla sensus spiritualis invenire'.

[3] Cf. H. H. Glunz, *History of the Vulgate in England from Alcuin to Roger Bacon* (Cambridge, 1933).

[4] Radbertus (*M.G.H. Epist.* vi. 6–16, 143) is not content even with this, but desires to expunge Virgil from the list of authors to be studied.

Thomas Aquinas, and in the supreme imaginative expression of medieval Christianity which is the *Divina Commedia*.

During the ages of transition, the Western Church as a whole definitely feared and distrusted the pagan learning; there were notable exceptions to this attitude, but the uncompromising tradition of Tertullian proved stronger, and finally prevailed with the influence of Gregory. In a natural reaction from earlier depreciation of the 'Dark Ages', stress has recently been laid on the 'humanism' of the medieval Church; but it is not difficult to overstate this view, for it is certain that the sole purpose of education at this time in the West was to train ecclesiastics for the performance of their duties.[1] The knowledge required for an understanding of the Latin services, and—in the case of more advanced pupils—for the study of Christian controversial and expository literature, the computation of Easter and other festivals, the legal and administrative system of the Church, provided in many cases an admirable curriculum, and the organized life of the monastery, with its regular hours, its library, and its economic security, gave opportunities for the preservation of culture in dangerous times which no other institution could have afforded. But the extraordinary achievements of scholars like Bede and Aldhelm, and, judged by contemporary standards, the high intellectual level of Canterbury, York, Wearmouth, and Jarrow in seventh-century England, and even of lesser centres, Malmesbury, Nursling, and Bishops Waltham, must not blind us to the fact that our gratitude for the preservation of classical literature would have incurred the censure of the most orthodox ecclesiastical authorities,[2] nor cause us to minimize the great gulf which divides the learning of this age from that of Jerome, and still more that of Origen, when all the resources of ancient civilization were still available. For several centuries these resources had been declining; and the Church further reduced and diluted the supply. Creative thought had long ceased; the taste of the time had turned to epitomes, anthologies, grammars, and works of reference. Genuine mastery of the Greek language

---

[1] Cf. M. Roger, *L'Enseignement des lettres classiques en France d'Ausone à Alcuin*, pp. 437 ff. (Paris, 1905).

[2] i.e. Gregory the Great and his influential school. Cf. Appendix B.

disappeared wholly from the West; after Boethius there was no real assimilation of Hellenic philosophy. Decorative Greek characters, isolated passages, and words from glossaries are found in Irish manuscripts, and Bede, exceptionally, shows some acquaintance with the Septuagint,[1] but of a creative use of Greek there is no indication. Passive encyclopaedists, like Isidore of Seville and Raban Maur, are the characteristic product of the early Middle Ages—an indication of the stern necessity for the preservation of extant knowledge in face of the barbarism which threatened to engulf it.

The close of the sixth century witnessed a definite break-down of culture in France and, to a lesser extent, in Italy also. Gregory of Tours, the foremost writer in Gaul, was not employing a figure of rhetoric when he bewailed his lack of grammar and education,[2] and the generations which followed him were plunged into yet deeper abysses of barbarism.[3] Literary Latin, the medium of thought, degenerated into a strange jargon, as may be seen in the scanty documents of this period, and the most polished poets of the Carolingian revival composed their Latin verses in a tongue nearly as foreign to them as it is to a French schoolboy at the present day. At the same time many popular beliefs and superstitions found their way into the official teaching of the Western Church, sponsored by the immense authority enjoyed by Gregory the Great.[4] Augustine, though aware of its dangers, had already sanctioned the cult of relics in its extremest form,[5] and with the break-down of communications, uncertain conditions of life, and confusion of standards and cultures, a powerful impetus was given to rumour and credulity, belief in marvels and demons and in the efficacy of magical objects.

It is not to be supposed that any more rational attitude had previously prevailed among the unlettered. There had always been more gods than men in the ancient world; State religions

---

[1] For knowledge of Greek at this time, see M. L. W. Laistner, *Thought and Letters in Western Europe*, A.D. 500–900, pp. 125 ff., 19 ff. (London, 1931).

[2] It is noteworthy that we do not possess a single classical manuscript which can be shown to have been copied in Gaul during this century. Cf. S. J. Crawford, *Anglo-Saxon Influence on Western Christendom*, 600–800, p. 81 (Oxford, 1933).

[3] Cf. M. Bonnet, *Le Latin de Grégoire de Tours*, p. 86 (Paris, 1890).

[4] A. von Harnack, *Dogmengeschichte*, iii, pp. 257 ff. (6th ed. Tübingen, 1922).

[5] Cf. J. Zellinger, *Augustin und die Volksfrömmigkeit*, pp. 54 ff. (Berlin, 1932).

and educated syncretism had not destroyed the immemorial worships of the countryside. Even the philosophers moved in an atmosphere where old customs and ways of thought haunted every household, hovering, perhaps, on the verge of folk-lore and picturesque fancy—half-believed, if no more. Nor did such tendencies vanish at the close of the Middle Ages; sorcery reached perhaps its highest development in the sixteenth, and witch-hunting in the seventeenth, centuries. Christianity, however, did not succeed in altering the situation in this respect, and just as the Roman State had finally given much of her organization to the victorious Church, so dying paganism also bequeathed its heritage to the medieval mind. Europe, moreover, during these centuries was only imperfectly Christianized. Rome and many of its senatorial families long remained a stronghold of the ancient cults.[1] Upper Italy, Austria, and southern France still celebrated the worship of the deities of classical times. Down to 650, paganism, with its temples and statues, still flourished openly in all parts of Gaul, and even after this time it continued its activities north of the Seine and in the Rhineland districts as late as the eighth or ninth century. In the Mediterranean area, Greek gods assumed the thinnest disguise. The healing virtues and ritual of local deities and sacred springs were transferred almost without change to the appropriate saint, and the *heroon*, the tomb of the pagan demi-god, became in many instances the *martyreion*, the pilgrimage-centre containing the operative relics of the Christian martyr.[2] Much of this process was deliberate—a concession made by the Church to the strength of popular feeling, and to the desperate need for some visible source of consolation and refuge. Thus Augustine explains that the changing of seasonal hero-cults into festivals of saints is a necessary yielding to heathen weakness; *sortes Biblicae* in Gaul replace

---

[1] Cf. F. Schneider, *Rom und Romgedanke im Mittelalter* (Munich, 1926). A striking example of the continuance of pagan customs at Rome is the *Cornomania*. From 876 to the time of Gregory VII, on the Saturday next after Easter, the Prior of the Schola Cantorum performed in public a grotesque dance on the Lateran Square, wearing a wreath with horns on his head, and swinging in his hand a rattle with bells. He would then scatter laurel leaves, with the cry 'Iaritan, iaritan, iariariasti; raphayn, iercoin, iariariasti'.

[2] For the salutary need of caution in tracing such pagan survivals, see H. Delehaye, *Les légendes hagiographiques*, pp. 140 ff. (3rd ed. Brussels, 1927).

pagan divination; the Frankish trial by ordeal is given the validity of a decision of God, while in England Mellitus, bishop of London, is instructed by Pope Gregory not to suppress the sacrifice of oxen 'to the devils', but to order his people, in celebration of the festival oi the martyr whose relics were locally honoured, to make bowers about their churches, and, feasting together, to 'kill cattle unto the praise of God'.[1] Often, however, the adoption of such practices and ways of thought was an unconscious tendency, due to the pagan surroundings of Christianity in earlier centuries, the deficiency of knowledge among church officials, even the highest, and the adoption of half-understood Christian doctrines into lives governed by earlier social systems.

Certain diversions were consistently opposed by the Church. Dancing, closely connected with primitive ritual, threatened at one time to invade the Christian liturgy in Egypt, and successive councils and preachers in the West, from 589 to 1617, banned the morrises and mummers, with their men-women, maypoles, antlered heads, carnivals, and carols.[2] Traditional love-songs were also condemned; the glorification of romantic passion and of the fierce joys of battle celebrated in Celtic legend and Norse saga was forbidden to the Christian,[3] and the German tongue itself, the vehicle of pagan ideas, was denounced as the devil's language.

Yet paganism lived on throughout the Middle Ages, a tortuous underworld of mingled beliefs originating from various periods and racial strata, of vegetation-spirits from Italy, Celtic water-sprites, Teutonic ogres and fairies, Scandinavian monsters, and the diminished forms of gracious Greek divinities. Beneath all changes of name and ceremonial, the peasant observed his ancient seasonal festivals, and paid his homage to the fertile spirits of seed-time and harvest. Tristan, Beowulf, and the heroes of the *Nibelungenlied* remained on the lips of men,[4] and even the exploits of Alexander and the old tale of Troy were not

---

[1] Bede, *Hist. Eccl.* i. 30.

[2] Cf. Dom Gougaud, 'La Danse dans les Églises', *Rev. d'hist. eccl.* xv, 1914.

[3] Northumbrian monks were censured for their attachment to such poems as the *Song of Beowulf*.

[4] For the frequent references to the Beowulf Saga in late medieval sermons, cf. G. R. Owst, *Literature and Pulpit in Medieval England*, p. 111 (Cambridge, 1933).

utterly forgotten. Far removed from reality, however, were these medieval versions of classical history, fantastic variations on themes already distorted in late Roman times. Virgil the wonder-working magician, Alexander the hero of a cycle of Oriental stories, dream-like as those in the *Arabian Nights*, are but dim reflections of their actual selves. The men of these centuries, indeed, saw as through a glass, darkly, the distant figures and events of the ancient world, remote from their own conditions as medieval Europe is from the present day. Rome itself, to the awestruck pilgrim, held no longer the memory of a busy and prosperous capital. It was a holy city of shrines and martyrdom, but a city also of haunted ruins, of strange legends and happenings of a marvellous past, a city where Popes exorcized plague-dealing snakes, or bound dragons by solemn incantations in caves under the Capitol.

Yet, though a vivid picture of antiquity may have been even more unattainable for the medieval than for the modern mind, the civilization of the Roman Empire still moulded the laws, the institutions and the forms of thought which governed human life in the Middle Ages, and which were destined finally to prevail in Europe. The sculptors and architects of Italy and southern France gave inspiration to their medieval successors. All human wisdom was acknowledged to reside in the ancient authors, and the literature of the Augustan age held with a powerful fascina- tion even the half-unwilling reader. The Church retained the fabric of Roman organization, and the ideal of Imperial unity, with its hopes for a common European culture, though shattered at the death of Charlemagne, held ultimate promise of revival, for it had reared a fortress in France and the surrounding countries against which the storm-waves of Viking, Magyar, and Saracen were to dash their forces in vain, a fortress which guarded within its monastery and castle walls the treasures, spiritual and material, snatched so precariously from the wreckage of the ancient world.

APPENDIX A

The Imperial Machine in the Fourth Century A.D.

I. THE EMPEROR

In theory, still elected by senate and army. Actually, the succession principle was largely dynastic, since the reigning Emperor could indirectly appoint his successor, by naming him Augustus.

II. THE SENATE

Either sons of senators, who had held the praetorship, an office whose main duty now was to pay for the games or public works; or else members of the three orders (*illustres, spectabiles, clarissimi*), which they had entered either in virtue of their offices or as a reward on retirement. A few became senators by special grace of the Emperor (*adlectio*).

III. THE COUNCIL

The *Consistorium* was a development from Hadrian's *Consilium*. It now had permanent members (*Comites Consistoriani*), including the chief officials, was in attendance on the Emperor, and met constantly to advise on frontier policy and legislative and administrative problems. It also tried cases of treason.

IV. IMPERIAL OFFICIALS

The most important of the officers attending on the Emperor were:

(*a*) The Master of Offices (*Magister Officiorum*), who controlled a number of miscellaneous departments, dealing with appeals, petitions, embassies, ceremonies, the State Post, the State factories of arms. He also commanded the 'Scholarian' bodyguards (see below), and the *agentes in rebus* or secret agents sent on delicate missions, and especially used to report on misconduct of officials in the provinces.

(*b*) The Quaestor of the Sacred Palace (*Quaestor Sacri Palatii*). The supreme legal minister, who drafted laws and Imperial rescripts.

(*c*) The Count of the Sacred Largesse (*Comes Sacrarum Largitionum*). Finance Minister, controlling Treasury officials, mint, customs, and all financial machinery of the provinces. The revenue of the Emperor's estates was managed by the *Comes Rerum Privatarum*, who probably, after paying his subordinates, handed over the balance to the Count of the Sacred Largesse, as did the Praetorian Prefects, who each possessed a treasury (*fiscus*).

(*d*) In practice, an equally important official was the Grand Chamberlain (*Praepositus Sacri Cubiculi*), usually a eunuch, and often with great personal, though extra-constitutional, influence over the Emperor, who controlled the palace staff, and the affairs of the Imperial residences.

V. THE ARMY

The supreme command was in the hands of Masters of Soldiers (*magistri militum*). In the East there were five Masters of Horse and Foot (*magistri equitum peditumque*), of whom two were stationed in Constantinople, in attendance on the Emperor (*in praesenti*), each commanding half of the Palatine guards. The remaining three controlled respectively the troops of The East, Thrace, and Illyricum. All five were co-ordinate. In the West there were two Masters *in praesenti*, stationed in Italy, one of infantry and one of cavalry. The Master of Infantry was much the more important, and towards the end of the fourth century became supreme commander of all military forces in the West under the title of the Master of Both Services (*magister utriusque militiae*). Western policy was largely dictated by him, the Emperor becoming frequently a mere puppet. The Eastern system of co-ordinate commanders prevented such developments as a rule.

The troops may roughly be divided into:

(*a*) *Comitatenses* (i.e. the mobile field army which formed the Imperial retinue, or *comitatus*). The main striking force; usually accompanied by large bodies of barbarian troops (*foederati*).

(*b*) *Limitanei* or *ripenses*. Stationary frontier troops, commanded by *duces*, who were subordinate to the *magistri*. Inferior in quality to the mobile forces.

(*c*) *Palatini, scholarii*, &c. Various regiments of household troops, some mainly ornamental, others of considerable military value. Some were under the independent command of the *Magister Officiorum*.

VI. PROVINCIAL GOVERNMENT

For purposes of *civil* administration, the Empire fell into four great sections, or prefectures (two in the West, and two in the East), governed by four Praetorian Prefects.

(*a*) *The Prefecture of the Gauls* included, as well as Gaul, Britain and Spain and the north-west corner of Africa.

(b) *The Prefecture of Italy* included, as well as Italy, Switzerland and the provinces between Alps and Danube, and also the coast-lands of North Africa.

(c) *The Prefecture of Illyricum* covered the Balkan peninsula, with the exception of Thrace.

(d) *The Prefecture of the Orient* comprised Thrace and Egypt, and all the Asiatic territory that belonged to the Empire.

Each prefecture was subdivided into dioceses (seventeen in all) ruled by vicars, and each diocese was again split up into provinces, whose governors bore various titles (*consulares, correctores, praesides*). In Africa, Asia, and Achaea the old Republican title of *proconsul* survived.

The four Prefects controlled (subject to the Emperor) the appointment of provincial governors, the administration of both governors and vicars, the food and pay of the armies in their prefectures; they were supreme judges of appeal, and could issue praetorian edicts on matters of detail. The Praetorian Prefects of the East and of Italy were the two highest officials in the Empire. The vicars and provincial governors possessed judicial and administrative powers and supervised tax-collection. None of these officials had any military functions. The separation of civil and military authority was one of the chief reforms of the Diocletian-Constantine period.

VII. THE CAPITALS

Rome and Constantinople were at this time the centres of duplicate, parallel governments, administering the Western and Eastern parts of the Roman Empire. The two capital cities and their environs were outside the jurisdiction of the Praetorian Prefects, and subject only to the Prefect of the City (*Praefectus Urbi*), who was head of the Senate and chief criminal judge, and controlled, directly or indirectly, the police (*vigiles*), the aqueducts, the markets, the corn-supply, and the trade corporations (*collegia*).

VIII. TAXATION

(a) *Annona.* The principal tax, paid in kind (occasionally in money) by the whole Empire. The total amount to be raised was declared anew each year, by a proclamation of the Emperor (*indictio*). This amount was then divided by the Praetorian Prefects. The land was surveyed and assessed in terms of productive value, and the units (*juga*) consequently varied in size according to the fertility and character of the soil. One *jugum* was, theoretically, the portion of land sufficient to support one peasant (*caput*) and his family.

(*b*) *Periodic Taxes.* On the accession of a new emperor and on each fifth anniversary of it, huge sums were required for donations to the troops. These were raised by:

    (i) *Aurum oblaticium,* an obligatory 'offering' from the senators.

    (ii) *Aurum coronarium,* a similar offering from the magistrates (*decuriones*) of every town, originally made in the form of gold crowns.

    (iii) *Lustralis collatio* ('five-yearly contribution'), a tax on trading profits.

(*c*) *Collatio glebalis,* paid by the senatorial class; a graded property-tax, popularly known as the *follis,* because it was paid in bags (*follis,* a bag of small coins).

(*d*) *Indirect Taxes, &c.* Custom duties, mines, State factories, and the profits of the huge Imperial estates provided further revenue.

APPENDIX B

(p. 8) (i) 'Money Economy and Natural Economy.'

The problem of the transition from the 'money' economy of the first two centuries A.D. to the 'natural' economy of the early Middle Ages has recently been studied by G. Mickwitz (*Geld und Wirtschaft im römischen Reich des 4 Jahrh. n. Chr.*, Helsingfors, 1933). It seems probable that even in the fourth century A.D. private, as opposed to State, finance had never relinquished its currency basis. Thus the inflation of the late third century won no fresh fields for 'natural' economy, but merely rendered it rather more prevalent in the spheres which it had previously occupied. Even in the Italy of Theoderic, little change is observable in the system of public finance; the Ostrogothic kingdom is still far from the economic condition of the early medieval States of Western Europe (cf. H. Geiss, *Geld- und naturalwirtschaftliche Erscheinungsformen im staatlichen Aufbau Italiens während der Gotenzeit*, Stuttgart, 1931).

How far the exchange system in the West, during the centuries which followed the establishment of the barbarian kingdoms, was based on money is an intricate question. Barter and the use of a currency medium had always co-existed, and A. Dopsch (*Natural- und Geldwirtschaft*, Vienna, 1930, p. 110) rightly condemns the view that the Germans destroyed the 'money' economy of late Roman times, substituting for it a 'natural' economy more suited to their primitive needs. Money, in fact, continued in general use throughout Merovingian and Carolingian times (especially in Southern France and Italy, and for payments of fines and taxes); but the disorganization of government and trade which followed the break-down of the Roman Empire in the West led gradually to the formation of local self-sufficient communities, among whom the predominant method of exchange was probably direct barter, and the reward for services rendered was not monetary.

(p. 190) (ii) 'The Iconoclast Argument.'

The Iconoclasts' answer to the doctrinal accusations of their opponents was based equally on orthodox Christology. The Divine, it was agreed on both sides, could not without blasphemy be represented in pictures. Christ had two natures—human and divine. A claim to represent only the human nature was contrary to the dogma of the indivisibility of the two natures, and a lapse into the so-called Nestorian heresy. To claim, however, that *both* natures of Christ could be represented in a picture amounted to a denial of the distinctness of the two natures, and thus to agreement with the opposite, Monophysite, heresy. It was also a form of blasphemy, in that it signified a wish to represent the Divine. Thus any representation of Christ was impossible, for it contravened the fundamental articles of the Christian faith. Cf. G. Ostrogorsky, 'Rom und Byzanz im Kampfe um die Bilderverehrung', *Seminarium Kondakovianum*, vi (Prague, 1933), p. 62.

(p. 248) (iii) 'The Threefold Division of Medieval Society.'

The three social classes are well seen in the personal reflections which King Alfred the Great incorporated in his version of Boethius' *De Consolatione*. 'A king's raw material and instruments of rule are a well-peopled land, and he must have men of prayer, men of war, and men of work.' The approaching dissolution of this form of society, at the other end of the Middle Ages, is curiously shown by a passage from a sermon *exemplum*, preserved in a fourteenth-century English manuscript (G. R. Owst, *Literature and Pulpit in Medieval England*, Cambridge, 1933, p. 553). 'God made the clergy, knights, and labourers, but the Devil made the burghers and usurers.' The preacher, disquieted by the changing order which he vaguely discerns, represents the tripartite division of society as a divine dispensation, while the growth of trade and commerce, heralding the close of the medieval period, is looked on with apprehension and dislike.

(p. 260) (iv) 'Reason versus Dogma.'

Subsequent developments are discussed by A. J. Macdonald, *Authority and Reason in the Early Middle Ages* (Oxford, 1933). The logical system taught by Boethius, which laid the foundation of the Scholastic system, was abused in the centuries which followed, but a few keen minds, such as Berengar and John Scotus, were capable of employing it with advantage in the rational exposition of Scripture. Reason or common sense, Berengar held, must decide whether an interpretation of a scriptural passage is to be literal or tropical, or a combination of both. Hence, in the phrase *hoc est corpus meum* the words are to be interpreted literally of the bread, and typically or metaphorically of the body of Christ. Such views were inacceptable to the authorities, and the works of both men were anathematized by the medieval church. The Papacy discovered in its claim to decide doctrinal issues a powerful weapon in its struggle with the Empire, and its successful intervention in the Berengarian dispute marks a stage in the establishment of this claim. The definition of eucharistic doctrine by Innocent III at the Fourth Lateran Council in 1215 completed the victory, and pointed the way to Trent and to the

Vatican Council of 1870. 'While it set up an authority in matters of belief independently of patristic or later tradition, it set the seal of approval on the principle of tradition and thereby excluded reason from the field of dogma' (op. cit., p. 112).

(p. 261) (v) 'Ireland and the Preservation of Classical Learning.'

The Celtic aspect of the Northumbrian revival of letters has recently attracted attention (cf. L. Gougaud, *Christianity in Celtic Lands*, London, 1932, pp. l–lv). The Irish monasteries, situated in a land always outside the Empire, and thus free from Graeco-Roman cults, had less reason than others to fear the pagan associations of classical literature. In their wide reading and genuine assimilation of the ancient authors, as in their love of certain apocryphal literature condemned at Rome, in their native organization and independent outlook, the Irish Christians formed a distinct school of thought, and presented a danger to the centralized Papal authority which was only eliminated by their defeat at the Council of Whitby in 664; but not before they had, with the help of Theodore and Hadrian—neither of whom belonged to the school of Gregory— passed on much of the heritage of ancient learning; which would otherwise have perished, to Anglo-Saxon scholars, and through them to Carolingian France. Long before this time the Celtic influence had spread over Europe as far as Würzburg, Salzburg, and Bobbio, so that the predominant part in the preservation of classical culture in the West during this period may justly be ascribed to the unorthodox Celtic Church.

(p. 115) (vi) 'The Three Chapters.'

The 'Three Chapters' were originally three clauses in an edict published by Justinian in 543, in which, with a view to conciliating the Monophysites, he condemned certain writings of three fifth-century divines whom they accused of Nestorian tendencies. The name 'three chapters' was soon transferred from these clauses to the writings themselves, and is here used in the latter sense. The Council of Chalcedon (451), in which Leo the Great had played a principal part, while the Monophysites had suffered defeat, had reinstated the theologians in question, and thus a central point of contention between Alexandria and the Western Catholics was involved. Failing to obtain a result by forcible abduction of the Pope, Justinian in 553 convoked the Second Council of Constantinople, which formally gave effect to his wishes by condemning the 'Three Chapters'. Its decisions were violently resisted in the West, but even there it was eventually recognized as an Oecumenical Council, equally valid with the previous four, by the time of Gregory the Great.

EMPERORS AND POPES

678 Agatho
682 Leo II
683(?) Benedict II
685 John V
685(?) Conon
687 Sergius I
687 (Paschal, antipope)
687 (Theodore, antipope)
701 John VI
705 John VII
708 Sisinnius

708 Constantine
715 Gregory II
731 Gregory III
741 Zacharias
752 Stephen II
757 Paul I
767 (Constantine, antipope)
768 Stephen III
772 Hadrian I
795 Leo III

CHRONOLOGICAL TABLE

POLITICAL. THE WEST	POLITICAL. THE EAST	RELIGIOUS	CULTURAL
		312. 'Edict of Milan' 325. Council of Nicaea 328–73. Athanasius Bp. of Alexandria	c. 330. d. Iamblichus 340. d. Eusebius
357–8. Julian's campaigns on Rhine	330. Foundation of Constantinople		
	376. Passage of Danube by Goths 378. Battle of Adrianople	374–97. Ambrose Bp. of Milan	379. d. Basil of Caesarea
	395. d. Theodosius the Great	381. Council of Constantinople	388. d. Ulfilas c. 395. d. Ausonius
399. Battle of the Frigidus	400. Revolt of Gainas	398. Chrysostom Bp. of Constantinople	c. 400. d. Ammianus Marcellinus c. 406. d. Prudentius
406. Burgundian Kingdom on Rhine founded 406–7. Vandals invade Gaul 408. Execution of Stilicho 409. Vandals, Alans, and Sueves in Spain 410. Capture of Rome by Alaric 412. Visigoths in Gaul	413. Land walls of Constantinople built		c. 408. d. Claudian

CHRONOLOGICAL TABLE—(cont.)

POLITICAL. THE WEST	POLITICAL. THE EAST	RELIGIOUS	CULTURAL
416-18. Visigoths in Spain			419. d. Jerome
c. 420-40. Anglo-Saxons invade Britain			
428. Accession of Gaiseric	428-633. Persian rule in Armenia	428. Nestorius Bp. of Constantinople	
429. Vandals in Africa		429. Mission of Germanus to Britain	430. d. Augustine
436. End of First Burgundian Kingdom	433. Accession of Attila	431. Council of Ephesus	
439. Vandals take Carthage			438. *Codex Theodosianus*
		444. d. Cyril of Alexandria	
		449. *Latrocinium* at Ephesus	
451. Battle of Mauriac Plain	450. d. Theodosius II	451. Council of Chalcedon	
454. Assassination of Aëtius			
455. Sack of Rome by Gaiseric			
468. Accession of Euric		461. d. Leo the Great	
472. d. Ricimer			
476. Deposition of Romulus Augustulus			
481-511. Reign of Clovis		481. Schism between Rome and Constantinople	
		482. Zeno issues *Henoticon*	c. 483. d. Sidonius Apollinaris
486. Clovis defeats Syagrius			
488. Ostrogoths set out for Italy			

493–526. Reign of Theoderic in Italy	491. Accession of Anastasius I	496. Baptism of Clovis	506. Issue of the *Breviarium Alarici*
496. Clovis conquers Alamans			
c. 500. Lombards between Theiss and Danube			
507. Battle of Vouglé. Clovis conquers Aquitaine	518. Accession of Justin	518. End of Schism between Rome and Constantinople	523. Execution of Boethius
508. Ostrogoths take Provence			529. Closing of the Schools of Athens
	527. Accession of Justinian		529. Monte Cassino founded
531. Franks destroy Thuringian kingdom	531–79. Reign of Chosroes		533. Issue of the Digest
532–4. Franks conquer Burgundy	533. Belisarius conquers Africa		537. St. Sophia built
	536–7. Belisarius at Rome		
	540. Persians capture Antioch. c. 550. Avars and Bulgars on Lower Danube	c. 550. d. Benedict of Nursia	
552. Franks subdue Bavaria	552. Narses reconquers Italy	553. Council of Constantinople	
	554. Pragmatic Sanction		
	565. d. Justinian 566–7. Lombards and Avars destroy Gepid kingdom		c. 562. d. Procopius c. 565. Columba founds Iona

CHRONOLOGICAL TABLE—(cont.)

POLITICAL. THE WEST	POLITICAL. THE EAST	RELIGIOUS	CULTURAL
567. Partition of France into Austrasia, Neustria, Burgundy			
568. Lombards in North Italy			c. 584. d. Cassiodorus
575–613. Regency of Brunhilda			
584–90. Authari King of Lombards			
585. End of Sueve kingdom in N. Spain		c. 570. Birth of Mahomet	
		586. Reccared, Visigoth ruler of Spain, becomes Catholic	
590–616. Agilulf King of Lombards		590. Gregory the Great becomes Pope	
		597. Augustine's landing	594. d. Gregory of Tours
		603. Lombards become Catholic	597. d. Columba
		604. d. Gregory the Great	
	610. Accession of Heraclius		
613. Union of Austrasia and Burgundy			613. Foundation of St. Gall
	614. Persians take Damascus and Jerusalem		615. d. Columban, founder of Bobbio and Luxeuil
	619. Persians invade Egypt		
		622. The Hegira	
		622–80. Monothelite Controversy	
	626. Avar-Persian siege of Constantinople		

629–39. Reign of Dagobert	628. Heraclius finally defeats Persians	627. Conversion of Northumbria	
	633–93. Byzantine rule in Armenia	632. d. Mahomet	
	634. Omar Caliph		
	634. Arabs invade Palestine		
	636. Battle of Yarmuk	636. Issue of the *Ekthesis*	636. d. Isidore of Seville
	637. Battle of Kadesiya		
	639–41. Arabs conquer Mesopotamia		
	642. Fall of Alexandria		
643–56. Grimoald Mayor in Austrasia	642–3. Arabs conquer Persia		
	647. Arabs conquer Tripoli	648. Issue of the *Type*	
	649. Arabs conquer Cyprus		
	661–750. Umayyad Caliphs at Damascus	664. Synod of Whitby	
	664. Arabs invade Punjab	669–90. Theodore Bp. of Canterbury	
	673. Arabs attack Constantinople	678. Conversion of Frisia begins	
c. 680. Peace between Lombards and Byzantines		680. Council of Constantinople	
683. Murder of Ebroin		c. 686. Conversion of Sussex	
687. Battle of Tertry		c. 690–739. Willibrord in Netherlands	690. d. Benedict Biscop

CHRONOLOGICAL TABLE—(cont.)

POLITICAL. THE WEST	POLITICAL. THE EAST	RELIGIOUS	CULTURAL
		692. Trullan Council	
	693–862. Arab rule in Armenia		c. 700. *Beowulf*
709–10. Pipin's Alamannic campaigns			709. d. Aldhelm
			c. 710. The Great Mosque, Damascus
712–44. Liutprand King of Lombards			
713–34. Arabs conquer all Spain, except Asturias			
714. d. Pipin			
717–41. Charles Martel Mayor	717. Accession of Leo III ('the Isaurian')	715–31. Gregory II	
	717–18. Siege of Constantinople		
720–59. Arabs in Narbonne			724. Abbey of Reichenau founded
	725. Leo III begins iconoclast campaign		
		731–41. Gregory III	
732. Battle of Poitiers (Tours)		733. S. Italy, Sicily, Illyria, and Crete taken from Roman jurisdiction	735. d. Bede
735. Charles Martel subdues Aquitaine and south Burgundy.		739. Gregory III seeks help from Charles Martel	
	740. d. Leo III		740. Publication of the *Ecloga*

743–51. Childeric III, last Merovingian ruler	750. Fall of Umayyads	752–7. Stephen II	753. d. John of Damascus
748–88. Tassilo, last independent Duke of Bavaria		754. d. Boniface, founder of the German Church	
751. Lombards take Ravenna	756–65. Bulgarian campaigns	757–67. Paul I	
753. Stephen II crosses Alps			
754. Pipin crowned by Pope			
756. Abdalrahman Emir of Spain	763. Baghdad becomes capital city		763. Abbey of Lorsch founded
756. d. Aistulf		764–71. Persecution of image-worshippers	
757–74. Desiderius King of Lombards			
757–96. Offa of Mercia			
760–88. Pipin subdues Aquitaine			
768. Accession of Charles and Carloman			
771. d. Carloman	780–90. Regency of Empress Irene		
772–804. Saxon Wars	786–809. Harun-al-Rashid	787. Irene restores images	
774. Fall of Lombard Kingdom			
778. Roncesvalles		790. *Libri Carolini*	
787. Charles subdues Benevento			793. Danes sack Lindisfarne
788. Establishment of Idrisite Kingdom in Morocco		794. Diet of Frankfurt	
791–6. Charlemagne's Avar campaigns			

CHRONOLOGICAL TABLE—(cont.)

POLITICAL. THE WEST	POLITICAL. THE EAST	RELIGIOUS	CULTURAL
797. Saxon Capitulary c. 800. Tunisia becomes independent 800. Coronation of Charlemagne	797. Murder of Constantine VI	795–816. Leo III	
	802–11. Nicephorus I Emperor		c. 801. d. Paul the Deacon
	809. Bulgarian invasions		804. d. Alcuin
813. Louis (the Pious) crowned at Aix 814. d. Charlemagne	814. d. Krum, Bulgarian ruler	815. Iconoclastic synod of Constantinople	821. d. Theodulf of Orleans
		826. d. Theodore of Studium	

BIBLIOGRAPHY

For fuller information concerning the sources and secondary authorities on this period, the reader should consult volumes i–iv of the *Cambridge Medieval History* (Cambridge, 1911–23), and (for more recent studies) the *Annual Bulletin of Historical Literature*, published for the Historical Association by G. Bell and Sons, and the current bibliographies of the *Byzantinische Zeitschrift, Historische Zeitschrift, Revue d'histoire ecclésiastique*, &c. Only a brief selection can be given here of works which may be found useful in filling in the outline which this book presents.

GENERAL

Bardenhewer, O. *Gesch. der altkirchlichen Literatur*, vols. iv–v. Freiburg, 1924–32.

Boissonade, P. *Le Travail dans l'Europe chrétienne au moyen âge (Ve–XVe siècles)*. Paris, 1921. (Tr. E. Power, *Life and Work in Medieval Europe, 5th–15th centuries*. London, 1927.)

Bury, J. B. *History of the Later Roman Empire from the death of Theodosius to the death of Justinian*. 2 vols. London, 1923.

—— *The Constitution of the Later Roman Empire*. Cambridge, 1910.

Cambridge Medieval History, The, vols. i–iv. Cambridge, 1911–23.

Caspar, E. *Geschichte des Papsttums*, vols. i, ii. Tübingen, 1930–4.

Dawson, C. *The Making of Europe*. London, 1932.

Diehl, C., and Marçais, G. *Le Monde oriental de 395 à 1081*. (Vol. iii of medieval section in Glotz's *Histoire Générale*.) Paris, 1936.

Dopsch, A. *Wirtschaftliche und soziale Grundlagen der europäischen Kulturentwicklung aus der Zeit von Caesar bis auf Karl den Grossen*. 2 vols. Vienna, 1920.

Duchesne, L. *Histoire ancienne de l'Église*. 3 vols., ed. 5. Paris, 1911. (Tr. C. Jenkins, *Early History of the Christian Church*. 3 vols. 1909–24.)

Finlay, G. *History of Greece*. 7 vols. Oxford, 1877.

Fliche, A. *La Chrétienté médiévale, 395–1254* (vol. vii, pt. 2 of Cavaignac's *Histoire du monde*). Paris, 1929.

——, and Martin, V. (edd.). *Histoire de l'Église depuis les origines jusqu'à nos jours*. Paris, 1934– .

Gibbon, E. *The Decline and Fall of the Roman Empire*, ed. Bury. London, 1909.

Gregorovius, F. *Gesch. der Stadt Rom im Mittelalter*. 2 vols. Dresden, 1936.

Halphen, L. *Les Barbares* (vol. v of series 'Peuples et Civilisations', ed. Halphen and Sagnac). Paris, 1926.

Harnack, A. *Dogmengeschichte*, ed. 5. Tübingen, 1914. (Tr. N. Buchanan, *History of Dogma*. 7 vols. London, 1894–9.)

Hartmann, L. M. *Gesch. Italiens im Mittelalter*, vols. i–iv. (Gotha, 1897–1915.)

Hauttmann, M. *Die Kunst des frühen Mittelalters* (vol. vi of the 'Propyläen-Kunstgeschichte'). Berlin, 1929.

Hefele, C. J. *Conciliengeschichte*, vols. i–iii, ed. 2. Freiburg, 1873–90. (Best in French, *Histoire des Conciles*, tr. H. Leclercq, ed. 2. Paris, 1914–.)

Heyd, W. *Histoire du commerce du Levant au moyen âge*. 2 vols. Leipzig, 1885–6. Reimpression, Leipzig, 1923.

Hodgkin, T. *Italy and her Invaders*. 8 vols. Oxford, 1892–9.

Kötschke, R. *Allgemeine Wirtschaftsgeschichte des Mittelalters*. Jena, 1924.

LABRIOLLE, P. de. *Histoire de la littérature latine chrétienne.* Paris, ₁20 (tr.

W. Herbert, *History and Literature of Christianity from Tertullian to Boethius.* London, 1924).

LOT, F. *La Fin du monde antique et les débuts du moyen âge* (to A.D. 753) (vol. xxxi of series 'L'Évolution de l'Humanité'). Paris, 1927. (Tr. P. and M. Leon, *The End of the Ancient World and the Beginnings of the Middle Ages.* London, 1931.)

LOT, F., PFISTER, C., and GANSHOF, F. L. *Les Destinées de l'Empire en Occident de 395 à 888* (vol. i, medieval section, Glotz's *Hist. Générale*). Paris, 1936.

MANITIUS, M. *Geschichte der lateinischen Literatur des Mittelalters,* Part I. Munich, 1911.

PUECH, A. *Histoire de la littérature grecque chrétienne.* 3 vols. Paris, 1928–30.

ROSTOVTZEFF, M. *Iranians and Greeks in South Russia.* Oxford, 1922.

SCHAUBE, A. *Handelsgeschichte der romanischen Völker des Mittelmeergebiets bis zum Ende der Kreuzzüge.* Munich, 1906.

SCHULTZE, V. *Geschichte des Untergangs des griechisch-römischen Heidentums.* 2 vols. Jena, 1887.

WORKS OF REFERENCE

CABROL, F., and LECLERCQ, H. *Dictionnaire de l'archéologie chrétienne et de liturgie.* Paris, 1907–.)

Encyclopaedia Britannica, ed. 11. Cambridge, 1911.

GERCKE, A., and NORDEN, E. *Einleitung in die Altertumswissenschaft,* ed. 2. Leipzig-Berlin, 1914 (ed. 3, in progress).

HOOPS, J. *Reallexikon der germanischen Altertumskunde.* Strasburg, 1911–19.

LÜBKER, F. *Reallexikon des klassischen Altertums,* ed. 8. Leipzig, 1914.

SANDYS, J. *A History of Classical Scholarship from the 6th century B.C. to the end of the Middle Ages.* Cambridge, 1903.

WISSOWA, G., and KROLL, W. *Pauly's Realencyclopädie der classischen Altertumswissenschaft.* Stuttgart, 1894–.

ATLASES

Useful small atlases are: F. W. Putzger, *Historischer Schul-Atlas* (Leipzig, many editions), and W. R. Shepherd, *Historical Atlas,* ed. 7 (London, 1930). The following may also be consulted:

DROYSEN, G. *Allgemeiner historischer Handatlas.* Bielefeld, 1886.

LONGNON, A. *Atlas historique de la France.* 3 vols. Paris, 1885–9.

POOLE, R. L. (ed.). *Historical Atlas of Modern Europe.* Oxford, 1902.

SCHRADER, F. *Atlas de géographie historique.* Paris, new ed., 1907.

PART I. ROMANS AND BARBARIANS

ABBOTT, F. F., and JOHNSON, A. C. *Municipal Administration in the Roman Empire.* Princeton, 1926.

ALBERTINI, E. *L'Empire romain (to A.D. 450)* (vol. iv of series 'Peuples et Civilisations'). Paris, 1929.

BAYNES, N. H. *Constantine the Great and the Christian Church.* London, 1931.

BIDEZ, J. *La Vie de l'empereur Julien.* Paris, 1930.

BOISSIER, G. *La Fin du paganisme.* 2 vols. Paris, 1891.

BURY, J. B. *The Invasion of Europe by the Barbarians.* London, 1928.

CHAPOT, V. *Le Monde romain* (vol. xxii of series 'L'Évolution de l'Humanité').
Paris, 1927. (Tr. E. A. Parker, *The Roman World*. London, 1928.)
CHARLESWORTH, M. P. *Trade Routes and Commerce of the Roman Empire*, ed. 2.
Cambridge, 1926.
COLLINGWOOD, R. G. *Roman Britain*. Oxford, 1932.
——, and MYRES, J. N. L. *Roman Britain and the English Settlements*. Oxford,
1936.
CUMONT, F. *Les Religions orientales dans le paganisme romain*, ed. 4. Paris, 1929.
DILL, S. *Roman Society in the last century of the Western Empire*. London, 1898.
GAUTHIER, E. F. *Genséric, roi des Vandales*. Paris, 1932.
GEFFCKEN, J. *Ausgang des griechisch-römischen Heidentums*. Heidelberg, 1920.
nischen Themenfassung. Berlin, 1920.
HIRTH, F. *China and the Roman Orient*. Munich, 1885.
HUDSON, G. F. *Europe and China*. London, 1931.
JULLIAN, C. *Histoire de la Gaule*, vols. vii–viii. Paris, 1926.
—— *De la Gaule à la France: nos origines historiques*. Paris, 1922.
LABRIOLLE, P. DE. *La Réaction païenne*. Paris, 1934.
MOMMSEN, T. *The Provinces of the Roman Empire, from Caesar to Diocletian*.
Eng. tr., London, 1909.
NOCK, A. D. *Conversion*. Oxford, 1933.
PUECH, A. *S. Jean Chrysostome et les mœurs de son temps*. Paris, 1891.
REID, J. S. *The Municipalities of the Roman Empire*. Cambridge, 1913.
RODENWALDT, G. *Die Kunst der Antike (Hellas und Rom)* (vol. iii of the
'Propyläen-Kunstgeschichte'). Berlin, 1927.
ROSTOVTZEFF, M. *The Social and Economic History of the Roman Empire*, ed. 2.
Oxford, 1926.
SCHMIDT, L. *Geschichte der deutschen Stämme*, vols. i–ii. Berlin, 1910–18 (new
and enlarged ed. of vol. i, 1934).
SEECK, O. *Geschichte des Untergangs der antiken Welt*. 6 vols., ed. 3. Berlin,
1910–21.
STEIN, E. *Geschichte des spätrömischen Reiches*, vol. i. Vienna, 1928.
STEVENS, C. E. *Sidonius Apollinaris and his Age*. Oxford, 1933.
STRONG, E. *La scultura romana*. Florence, 1923.
STUART JONES, H. *The Roman Empire, 29 B.C.–A.D. 476*. 3rd impression.
London, 1916.
TOUTAIN, J. *L'Économie antique*. Paris, 1927. (Tr. M. R. Dobie, *The Econo-
mic Life of the Ancient World*. London, 1930.)
WARMINGTON, E. H. *The Commerce between the Roman Empire and India*. Cam-
bridge, 1928.

PART II. THE TRIUMPH OF JUSTINIAN

BAYNES, N. H. *The Byzantine Empire*. London, 1925 (with critical biblio-
graphy).
BRÉHIER, L. *L'Art byzantin* (in series 'Les Patries de l'Art'). Paris, 1924.
CHAPOT, V. *La Frontière de l'Euphrate*. Paris, 1907.
DALTON, O. M. *Byzantine Art and Archaeology*. London, 1911.
—— *East Christian Art*. Oxford, 1925.
DIEHL, C. *Justinien et la civilisation byzantine au 6ᵉ siècle*. Paris, 1901.
—— *L'Afrique byzantine (533–709)*. Paris, 1896.

DIEHL, *Manuel d'art byzantin.* 2 vols., ed. 2. Paris, 1925–6.
DUCHESNE, L. *Églises séparées*, ed. 2. Paris, 1905.
DUCHESNE, L. *L'Église au 6ᵉ siècle.* Paris, 1925.
GASQUET, A. *L'Empire byzantin et la monarchie franque.* Paris, 1888.
GELZER, H. *Sketch of Byzantine history in* Krumbacher, q.v.
GLÜCK, H. *Die christliche Kunst des Ostens* (vol. viii in series 'Die Kunst des Ostens'). Berlin, 1923.
HOLMES, W. G. *The Age of Justinian and Theodora.* 2 vols. London, 1905–7.
KRUMBACHER, K. *Geschichte der byzantinischen Literatur (527–1453)*, ed. 2. Leipzig, 1897.
LABOURT, J. *Le Christianisme dans l'empire perse.* Paris, 1904.
LETHABY, W., and SWAINSON, H. *The Church of Sancta Sophia.* London, 1894.
MILLINGEN, A. VAN. *Byzantine Constantinople.* London, 1889.
PARGOIRE, J. *L'Église byzantine de 527 à 847.* Paris, 1905.
PEIRCE, H., and TYLER, R. *L'Art byzantin*, vols. i, ii. Paris, 1932–4.
RAMBAUD, A. *Études sur l'histoire byzantine.* Paris, 1902.
RICE, D. TALBOT. *Byzantine Art.* Oxford, 1935.
RUNCIMAN, S. *Byzantine Civilisation.* London, 1933.
STRZYGOWSKI, J. *Orient oder Rom?* Leipzig, 1901.
—— *Origin of Christian Church Art.* Oxford, 1923.
VASILIEV, A. A. *Histoire de l'empire byzantin.* 2 vols. Paris, 1932.
WULFF, O. *Altchristliche und byzantinische Kunst.* Berlin, 1914.

PART III. THE ONSLAUGHT OF ISLAM

ANDRAE, T. *Mohammed, sein Leben und Glaube.* Göttingen, 1932.
ARNOLD, T. W. *The Preaching of Islam*, ed. 2. London, 1913.
—— *Painting in Islam.* Oxford, 1928.
BECKER, C. H. *Islamstudien.* 2 vols. Leipzig, 1924–32.
—— *Christianity and Islam.* New York, 1909.
BRIGGS, M. S. *Muhammedan Architecture in Egypt and Palestine.* Oxford, 1924.
CAETANI, L. *Annali dell'Islam,* 10 vols. Milan, 1905–26.
CARRA DE VAUX. *Les Penseurs d'Islam.* 5 vols. Paris, 1921–5.
CRESWELL, K. A. C. *Early Muslim Architecture.* Part I. Umayyads. Oxford, 1932.
DIEZ, E. *Die Kunst der islamischen Völker.* Berlin, 1915.
GIBB, H. A. R. *Arabic Literature.* London, 1926.
GLÜCK, H., and DIEZ, E. *Die Kunst des Islams* (vol. v of the 'Propyläen-Kunstgeschichte'). Berlin, 1925.
HOUTSMA, T., BASSET, R., and ARNOLD, T. W. *Encyclopaedia of Islam.* Leyden, 1913–.
LAMMENS, H. *L'Islam, croyances et institutions* (with bibliography). Beyrouth, 1926. (Tr. E. Denison Ross, *Islam: beliefs and institutions.* London, 1929.)
—— *L'Arabie occidentale avant l'Hégire.* Beyrouth, 1928.
Legacy of Islam, The, ed. A. GUILLAUME and T. W. ARNOLD. Oxford, 1931.
MACDONALD, D. B. *Development of Muslim Theology, Jurisprudence and Constitutional Theory.* London, 1915.
MARGOLIOUTH, D. G. *Mohammed and the Rise of Islam* ('Heroes of the Nations Series'). London, 1905.

MARTIN, H. *L'Art musulman.* Paris, 1926.
MIGEON, G., and SALADIN, H. *Manuel d'art musulman.* 3 vols. Paris, 1927.

PART IV. THE AGE OF CHARLEMAGNE

ÅBERG, N. F. *The Anglo-Saxons in England during the Early Centuries after the Invasion.* Uppsala, 1926.
BRÉHIER, L. *La Querelle des images.* Paris, 1904.
BROWN, G. BALDWIN. *The Arts in Early England.* 5 vols. London, 1903–21.
BRYCE, J. *The Holy Roman Empire,* ed. 8. London, 1892.
CARLYLE, R. W. and A. J. *A History of Medieval Political Theory in the West.* 5 vols. London, 1903–28.
CHAMBERS, R. W. *England before the Norman Conquest.* London, 1926.
—— *Beowulf.* Cambridge, 1911.
CLAPHAM, A. W. *English Romanesque Architecture before the Conquest.* Oxford, 1930.
CRAWFORD, O. G. S., and KEILLER, A. *Wessex from the Air.* Oxford, 1928.
CRAWFORD, S. J. *Anglo-Saxon Influence on Western Christendom, 600–800.* Oxford, 1933.
DILL, S. *Roman Society in Gaul in the Merovingian Age.* London, 1926.
DUCHESNE, L. *Les Premiers Temps de l'État pontifical,* ed. 3. Paris, 1914.
GOUGAUD, L. *Les Chrétientés celtiques,* ed. 2. Paris, 1911. (Best in English revised ed., M. Joynt, *Christianity in Celtic Lands.* London, 1932.)
HALPHEN, L. *Études critiques sur l'histoire de Charlemagne.* Paris, 1921.
HAUCK, A. *Kirchengeschichte Deutschlands,* vol. i, ed. 4. Leipzig, 1904.
HELDMANN, K. *Das Kaisertum Karls des Grossen.* Weimar, 1928.
GREGORY OF TOURS, *History of the Franks.* tr. O. M. Dalton (with full introduction). 2 vols. Oxford, 1927.
HINKS, R. *Carolingian Art.* London, 1935.
HODGKIN, R. H. *A History of the Anglo-Saxons.* 2 vols. Oxford, 1935.
KLEINCLAUSZ, A. *L'Empire carolingien.* Paris, 1934.
LAISTNER, M. L. W. *Thought and Letters in Western Europe, A.D. 500–900.* London, 1931.
LAVISSE, E. *Histoire de France,* vol. ii. Paris, 1903.
LEEDS, E. THURLOW. *The Archaeology of the Anglo-Saxon Settlements.* Oxford, 1913.
MARTIN, J. *A History of the Iconoclastic Controversy.* S.P.C.K. London, n.d.
McILWAIN, C. H. *The Growth of Political Thought in Europe.* London, 1932.
NIEDERLE, L. *Manuel de l'antiquité slave,* vol. i. Paris, 1923.
NORDEN, E. *Die antike Kunstprosa.* 2 vols. Leipzig, 1898.
OMAN, C. *England before the Norman Conquest.* London, 1910.
RABY, F. J. E. *A History of Christian-Latin Poetry.* Oxford, 1927.
—— *A History of Secular Latin Poetry in the Middle Ages.* 2 vols. Oxford, 1934.
ROGER, M. *L'Enseignement des lettres classiques d'Ausone à Alcuin.* Paris, 1905.
RUNCIMAN, S. *A History of the First Bulgarian Empire.* London, 1930.
SCHNEIDER, F. *Rom und Romgedanke im Mittelalter.* Munich, 1926.
VINOGRADOFF, P. *Roman Law in Medieval Europe,* ed. 2. Oxford, 1929.
—— *The Growth of the Manor,* ed. 3. London, 1920.

INDEX